Immigrant Families

978-0-7456-7016-4

Immigrant Families

*Cecilia Menjívar, Leisy J. Abrego,
and Leah C. Schmalzbauer*

polity

First published in 2016 by Polity Press

Polity Press
65 Bridge Street
Cambridge CB2 1UR, UK

Polity Press
350 Main Street
Malden, MA 02148, USA

ISBN-13: 978-0-7456-7015-7
ISBN-13: 978-0-7456-7016-4(pb)

A catalogue record for this book is available from the British Library.

Library of Congress Cataloging-in-Publication Data

Menjivar, Cecilia.
  Immigrant families / Cecilia Menjívar, Leisy J. Abrego, Leah C. Schmalzbauer.
    pages cm
  ISBN 978-0-7456-7015-7 (hardback) -- ISBN 978-0-7456-7016-4 (paperback) 1. Immigrant families--United States--Social conditions. 2. United States--Emigration and immigration--Social aspects. 3. Immigrant families--Law and legislation--United States. 4. Emigration and immigration law--United States. 5. United States--Emigration and immigration--Government policy. I. Abrego, Leisy J. II. Title.
  JV6475.M46 2016
  305.9'069120973--dc23
                                                                                      2015022102

Typeset in 11 on 13 pt Sabon by
Servis Filmsetting Ltd, Stockport, Cheshire
Printed and bound in Great Britain by CPI Group (UK) Ltd, Croydon, UK

For further information on Polity, visit our website:
politybooks.com

Contents

Acknowledgments

We would like to thank the many people and entities that made the writing of this book possible. We were fortunate to receive persistent and enthusiastic support from our editor at Polity, Jonathan Skerrett. Manuela Tecusan was a thorough and patient copyeditor. We would also like to gratefully acknowledge the research assistance of Alexander Agadjanian, Daniel R. Alvord, Jacqueline Caraves, Andrea Gómez Cervantes, William McDonald, and Nayely Velez-Cruz.

Cecilia Menjívar would like to thank the Cowden Distinguished Professorship at Arizona State University and the Foundation Distinguished Professorship at the University of Kansas for important resources and institutional support. Leisy Abrego would like to thank Carlos Colorado for his assistance and to recognize the institutional support received from the Hellman Fellows Fund and the Center for American Politics and Public Policy at UCLA. Leah Schmalzbauer would like to thank the Department of Anthropology and Sociology and the Department of American Studies at Amherst College for their support throughout this project.

* * *

We dedicate this book to all the families we have met during our respective studies in immigrant communities over the years. We have been inspired by their courage and have aimed to capture

Acknowledgments

their humanity and the complexity of their lives in the pages that
follow.

We also dedicate this book to our own families, as they play
important roles in the work we do:

To Victor and Sasha, to my siblings Ana and Oscar, and to
my nieces and nephews—Cecilia

To Carlos, Mateo, and Diego, and to my siblings Claudia,
Tatiana, and Natalie—Leisy

To Steve, Micah, and Zola, to my sister Anna, and to my
nieces and nephew—Leah

1

Introduction

Immigrant families, like those without a recent immigrant past, are varied, multifaceted, and dynamic. They often encompass modalities beyond the nuclear model and include a wide range of blood and fictive kin. They are comprised of chosen members, stepparents and stepsiblings, same-sex parents, and members with various legal statuses and migrant histories. Indeed, individuals' definitions of family and the boundaries around these characterizations are, in general, expanding and becoming more malleable (Powell, Bolzendahl, Geist, and Carr Steelman 2010).

Adding a layer of complexity to this heterogeneity, immigrant families often span national borders, as not all family members are able to migrate together and some never do. Some members may return to the country of origin; in other cases an adolescent or adult daughter or son may migrate first and then send for the parents or, if that is not possible, may remain separated across borders indefinitely. Families may be reconstituted units or newly formed ones; in the process of reunification; or already reunited and facing the challenges of new lives together. Indeed, migratory movements almost always entail the separation of families, as members live in at least two different contexts for varying lengths of time. During the period of separation a parent may establish a new union or the immigrant parents may have new children—actions that significantly alter the composition of the family. In many ways, therefore, these depictions defy conventions about what we think a family is and where it is located physically.[1]

Introduction

Like all families, immigrant families are malleable and embody change; they are shaped by external forces that they must negotiate. Unlike their non-immigrant counterparts, however, immigrant families are made permissible or are barred through immigration laws in general and through family reunification laws in particular.[2] These laws and continuously changing policies determine the composition of immigrant families through their definition of family (Hawthorne 2007), dictating who is allowed to come into the country, how long members stay apart, and which family relations take priority for immigration purposes (Lee 2013). Thus, for immigrant families, immigration laws and policies are fundamental in shaping their contour, location, and structure.

Immigrant families and kinship ties can certainly facilitate migration in some cases. Newcomers may find that settlement is easier when they are able to obtain an initial place to stay and a first job through a relative. Indeed, immigrant families can provide a range of resources for relatives in need (Boyd 1989; Foner 2009; Kibria 1993; Massey, Alarcon, Durand, and González 1987). However, immigrant families should not be assumed to always be a source of refuge, comfort, or support. In a world of inequalities, when many face restrictive laws and racially based discriminatory reception, families cannot always step in to help relatives ease into their new home (Menjívar 2000). Just like their non-migrant counterparts, immigrant families are complex. They have ups and downs, tensions, and fissures often rooted in inequalities along gender, generational, and other contextual inequalities. These inequalities shape what happens within immigrant families.

Immigration to the United States takes place in the context of families. The United States' policies, unlike those of other nations of immigration such as Canada, Australia, or Germany, encourage the largest sector of migration through the family (Kofman 2004). Therefore, studying the experiences of immigrant families provides access to most processes related to immigration, from decision-making to relationships to other institutions in society, to racialization, and to long-term experiences of settlement (Rumbaut 1997). In the process of entering and settling, immigrant families, through their interactions with communities,

2

institutions, bureaucracies, and civil society, contribute to shaping the United States' social landscape. Consequently, examining immigrant families can help us understand key migratory processes as well as broader societal engines of change. Immigrant families provide what Robert Merton called a "strategic research site": "an area where processes of more general import are manifested with unusual clarity" (Merton, cited in Portes 1995: 2). Thus, a focus on immigrant families can reveal knowledge about the "standard North American family" (SNAF) (Smith 1993) by providing insights into the "ideological code" that shapes how we think about families and about living arrangements more broadly.

Background to Family Migration

Public discourses about immigration and immigrant families have a tendency to compare and contrast people's integration experiences by race, national origin, and across different historical periods. In particular, they celebrate what is perceived as the quick ascendancy of Asian-origin immigrants while simultaneously deploring that immigrants from Latin America do not immediately experience mobility or the economic gains achieved by their European counterparts in the past. To explore these matters and examine how contemporary immigrant families face the manner and the context in which they are received in the United States, we turn to the twin factors that frame our general examination of families in this book: the structure of immigration law and current economic conditions.

Immigration Law and the Legal Framework

Family migration is the most important mechanism for authorized immigration to the United States today.[3] Immigrants have been coming as members of families since the founding of the nation. Many early immigrants in the nineteenth century, for instance, migrated in the context of the family, even if they arrived one by one and it took months or years to be reunited with family members (Thomas and Znaniecki 1996). This process is often referred to as "chain" migration (MacDonald and MacDonald 1964). Even the so-called "birds of passage"—those individuals who migrated alone in search of work—participated in migration with the idea of improving the lives of their family members: their intention had been to earn enough money to send their families and then to return to the origin country (Piore 1979).

These aspects of family migration—"chain" migration and the migration of "birds of passage"—have not changed over the years. What has changed, however, is the legal framework within which family members have been admitted to the United States. As Gratton, Gutmann, and Skop (2007) observe on the basis of their examination of ninety years of census data, the most important factor affecting family structure in different historical periods of US-bound migration is immigration policy. Their results, which are based on data for Mexican, Irish, Swedish, Italian, and Polish immigration flows, point to structural factors shaped by immigration policies rather than by the race or ethnicity of the immigrants themselves; these would be the sorts of factors that are central to shaping the evolution of immigrant family forms.

Since the 1960s, US immigration policies have prioritized families for the granting of legal status. By 2011 about two thirds of the 1 million immigrants who became legal permanent residents during that year were family-sponsored (US Department of Homeland Security 2011). As recently as November 2014, President Obama further reinforced the centrality of the category of family as deserving of lawful presence in the country when he issued an executive action to provide relief from deportation only to undocumented parents of US citizens or lawful permanent resident (LPR) children.

In the late nineteenth and early twentieth centuries, immigration law centered more explicitly on the racial composition of flows, on the basis of attempts to limit the migration of certain national origin and racial groups. Regularly informed by racist and nativist immigration politics, the history of US immigration laws also includes "periodic waves of harsh exclusions and deportation campaigns," which targeted different groups of people deemed to be undesirable (Johnson 2007: 48) regardless of labor and population needs. As one of the most egregious examples of this, the Chinese Exclusion Act of 1882 barred all labor migration from China to the United States. Asians were excluded, discriminated against, and barred from bringing their spouses (Glenn 2002). Upheld in different formats until the 1940s, this law prevented Chinese immigrants already in the country from thriving as a community (Takaki 1989). Developments from the 1950s onward, however, gave preeminence to family migration or family reunification and have structured a different type of "chain migration," which is less explicitly based on race. In contrast to the chain migrations of previous eras that were organized through direct family connections and social networks, post-1965 chain migration is formally organized by law. Indeed, "each new immigrant becomes a potential immigrant sponsor" (Jasso and Rosenzweig 1990: 213).

The McCarran–Walter Act of 1952 amended the Immigration and Nationality Act (INA) to revamp the immigration system, abolishing racial restrictions (but leaving the quotas intact) and creating a path for the visa preference system established with the 1965 INA, which is largely still in place today. While the 1952 Act limited the total number of annual visas to one sixth of the United States' continental population, it exempted spouses and children of US citizens, further setting the stage for a major move to favor family relations in the admission of immigrants.[4] Reflecting major shifts in society in the 1960s, the 1965 INA, also known as the Hart-Celler Act, continued with the overhaul of the immigration visa structure.

The Hart-Celler Act abolished national origin quotas in place since 1924,[5] sought to rid the system of its racist bias, firmly established a system of family preference visas that prioritized "family reunification," and radically altered the demographic composition of post-1965 flows. Migration shifted from predominantly European flows to immigration from Africa, Asia, the Middle East, and Latin America. For instance, while migration from Europe made up two thirds of the total flow in the 1930s, it constituted one third of all immigration in the 1960s and slightly over 10 percent in the 1980s. Immigration from Asia and Latin America shows the reverse trend. Whereas authorized immigration from Latin America totaled nearly 500,000 in the decade of the 1950s, it reached 4.2 million during the 1990s, making up 44 percent of the entire flow (Massey and Pren 2012).[6]

Subsequent amendments to the INA, such as the 1990 Immigration Act, instituted major changes while maintaining the main categories of the visa system—that is, family reunification, employment-based, and refugee migration—as well as narrow conceptions of family. These categories are largely defined by policy and political expediency; they are created by the receiving state and are used to determine the admissibility of immigrants at entry (Schrover and Moloney 2013).[7] Thus, these classifications are not static; rather, they evolve according to the geopolitical climate (see also Menjívar 2000). And, as we will discuss in Chapter 2, the very definition of what constitutes a family has varied from time to time, in the process informing what family relations "count" for immigration purposes.[8]

Examining family migration from the vantage point of immigration law therefore allows us to discern how categories of admission are redrawn in the public arena of immigration debates. Simultaneously, in the lived experiences of immigrants, divisions across these categories of admission—as recipients of family petitions or employment visas—are porous. Immigrants arriving through employment-based visas, for example, have family members who can join them. Refugees, too, come in as part of families and also enter the labor force and sometimes become entrepreneurs. To be sure, immigrants entering through family reunification are also likely to join the labor force.[9]

The 1990 Act created new entry visas, including diversity visas for immigrants from countries less represented in migratory flows. It authorized temporary protected status to individuals migrating from specially designated countries, it added new visas to employment-based categories, and it removed AIDS from the list of illnesses that make an immigrant ineligible for entry. Further reflecting changing general societal attitudes, the 1990 Act also removed homosexuality as grounds for exclusion from immigration (Luibhéid 2002).

The replacement of national origin quotas with family- and employment-based categories of admission that were enacted with the amendments of 1952 and 1965 altered the demographic composition and geographic origin of immigration to the United States. At the same time there were significant events in the developing world that propelled thousands to emigrate. Political upheavals, revolutions, and civil wars, as well as the implementation of structural adjustment programs that further weakened the economies of countries around the world, all precipitated emigration (see Coe 2013). Thus, in examining current migratory flows and especially the migration of families in stages, it is important to consider both the US legal framework at the particular historical time when immigrants arrive and the conditions in the countries of origin that spark migratory flows. Equally important are the social networks that migrants create in the course of migrating over the years, which facilitate connecting the motivation to migrate with a destination point (Massey and Pren 2012; Menjívar 2000).

US immigration law has had effects on the composition and flows of immigrant families even when the laws did not specifically concern family reunification. For instance, from the passing of the Chinese Exclusion Act of 1882 through World War II, "US immigration policies treated Asian male workers primarily as temporary, individual units of labor rather than as members of family groups" (Espiritu 2008: 11). This meant that there were few women immigrants from Asia; and in effect Asian immigrants were legally barred from forming families in the United States. Similarly, immigrants from Mexico who qualified for legalization through the Immigration Reform and Control Act (IRCA) of 1986 were mostly men, because men were more likely to be able to document formal employment (Zavella 2011). The same gendered pattern occurred among Guatemalan immigrants in Houston (Hagan 1994). The formal employment requirement for legalization thus often tilts the proportion of legalized immigrants in favor of men, a gender imbalance in legalization processes observed in various immigration categories (Salcido and Menjívar 2012).

7

Noteworthy, legislative changes have given preference to family ties and to job skills deemed necessary for the US economy in determining who can immigrate legally, while also promoting an image of a particular family form: the heteronormative nuclear family, which is ideologically assumed to best fit into US society. The ideological bases on which the family reunification visas and the requirements for family-based migration have been created have in turn shaped the contours of legally recognized immigrant families, often excluding a variety of family formations among contemporary immigrants. Laws have rarely recognized queer (Acosta 2013), extended, and other non-traditional families as acceptable; the latter are therefore blocked from the possibility of migration as a family unit. Existing ideology poses challenges for potential migrants whose families do not fit this model, who cannot tap into nuclear family ties to immigrate, or who do not have relatives already in the United States to petition for them.

The inability to physically reside with loved ones can be difficult for families (Abrego 2014; Chin 1999). Immigrants in these situations, however, have responded to legal constraints in a variety of ways. They have resorted to alternative paths to continue to sustain family ties—an attitude that reflects their agency. As anthropologist Cati Coe (2013: 5) observes in her examination of how Ghanaian immigrants manage parent–child separations, migrants use their "repertoires" to make sense, experience, and respond to the challenges of immigration. Such "repertoires" are composed of "a multiplicity of cultural resources and frameworks, a body or collection of practices, knowledge, and beliefs that allow people to imagine what is possible, expect certain things, and value certain goals." The "repertoires" that Coe conceptualizes on the basis of the Ghanaian case also exist among other immigrant groups, as they adapt and respond to the long-term, often indefinite, family separations that are quite common in today's migration context.

Immigrants create multiple avenues that allow them to maintain active ties with loved ones across borders. In the absence of legal pathways to family unity, many have turned to unauthorized migration (Cruz 2010). Gridlock in immigration reform efforts and extensive backlogs in the immigration bureaucracy have led to a swelling of unauthorized migration, as families tire of waiting for the ever-distant possibility of authorized reunification (Carr and Tienda 2013; Massey, Durand, and Malone 2002; Zavella 2011). Thus, while family reunification has been a cornerstone of US immigration policy, family reunification for the more numerous groups today tends to be delayed for long periods of time due to backlogs in processing or limited visas (Abrego 2014; Enchautegui and Menjívar 2015; Zavella 2011).

Certain definitions and requirements in legal immigration provisions are designed to reconfigure immigrant families. Citing Hawthorne (2007: 619), Zavella argues that the provision of the 1986 IRCA stating that the "family group shall include the spouse, unmarried minor children under 18 years of age who are not members of some other household, and parents who reside regularly in the household of the family group" established a narrow view of the family (Zavella 2012: 1). Zavella notes:

> This provision codifies a heterosexual nuclear family and excludes other types of family structures that are prevalent in the United States and Latin America—such as single parents, the elderly, multigenerational, extended, those headed by minors, or same-sex families—as well as children born "out of wedlock" or who have informal foster relationships with parents (in loco parentis) such as grandchildren cared for by their grandmothers when the parents migrate (Zavella 2012: 1).

Undeniably, such codification and legal recognition of only certain types of families has consequences for the settlement process and general well-being of immigrant families, as many are excluded. This book will explore how, in some cases, this leads to the long-term separation of families across borders or to the complicated experiences of mixed-status families by exacerbating inequalities within families. (See Tables 1.2 and 1.4 for contemporary compositions of immigrant families and households.)

Introduction

The Economy, Economic Restructuring, and Immigrant Families

Together with the immigration laws in place at the time of arrival, economic trends and concomitant labor market dynamics have significant bearing on immigrant families. The economy is essential in determining how family migration is organized and how family members fare. Many migrate to the United States in search of a better future for themselves and their families, often on the basis of perception of access to better employment opportunities. Changes in the availability and quality of jobs, shrinking budgets for social services, economic and wage decline, and decreases in purchasing power dramatically affect where and how immigrants are able to enter the labor force, whether and how they provide for their families, and the paths to mobility they will follow. Thus, economic trends, broader structural shifts, and labor market opportunities impact immigrant families in multiple and profound ways.

In the late 1800s and early 1900s, for example, when Southern, Central, and Eastern (SCE) European immigrant families arrived and settled in the United States, they had access to jobs in growing manufacturing sectors that allowed even poorly educated workers to move up the socioeconomic ladder (Lieberson 1980; Steinberg 2001). And, when employment waned, public and private programs were established to provide relief (Fox 2012). However, not all immigrant groups had access to the same resources that helped financially stabilize and more fully integrate SCE European immigrants. Many of these disparities are seen across racial groups today (Fox 2012).

Following general trends for the US population, the economic decline of the past several decades also impacts immigrants. As the United States shifted from manufacturing to a service-based economy, the unionized, more secure jobs that were available in the post-World War II era disappeared after the economic drop (or reversal) of the mid-1970s. The economic transformation that dramatically expanded the service sector shaped the dynamics of the labor market for new immigrants (Hamilton and Chinchilla

Introduction

2001). New jobs are mostly concentrated in the low end of the service sector, particularly for immigrants who arrive with little formal education. Moreover, in the contemporary immigration regime (see Chapter 2), even immigrants with high levels of education are unable to secure jobs or wages commensurate with their professional capacities if they are undocumented or have otherwise unstable legal statuses. Thus, there is a high concentration of immigrants in low-paid service sector jobs that do not provide benefits or enough hours for full-time employment (Abrego and Gleeson 2014). This situation leads to economic insecurity, as many immigrant families try to make ends meet in the United States as well as in the countries of origin, where relatives receive remittances (Abrego 2014; Schmalzbauer 2005).

To be sure, not all contemporary immigrants to the United States enter the low-end jobs of the service sector; it is rather the case that "contemporary immigration features a bewildering variety of origins, return patterns, and modes of adaptation" (Portes and Rumbaut 2006: 13). Indeed, as Portes and Rumbaut note, today's immigrants are also professional and highly skilled workers, engineers, scientists, physicians, entrepreneurs, and skilled mechanics and laborers who show a bimodal distribution in that large numbers have low levels of education and work-related skills but there are also large numbers who are highly skilled and educated.[10] For example, 76 percent of Indian immigrants in the United States have a bachelor's or a higher degree, and South Korean and Chinese immigrants are closely behind them, with 53.9 percent and 49.6 percent, respectively. At the other end of the spectrum, only 5.6 percent of Mexicans and approximately 7.4 percent of Salvadorans and Guatemalans have a bachelor's or a higher degree (see Table 1.1). Many immigrants fall in between this bimodal picture. The trend across generations seems encouraging, as members of the second generation generally have higher levels of educational attainment than their parents (Kasinitz, Mollenkopf, Waters, and Holdaway 2008). And immigrants who arrive as refugees often cover a wide range of educational backgrounds and work experience as well.

Although educational level at the time of arrival is a key

11

Table 1.1 Demographic Profile of the Largest Immigrant Groups from Asia and Latin America

Country	Population size	Gender (% male)	Median age (years)	Education			% in labor force
				High school	BA degree	Graduate/ professional degree	
Asia							
China	2,292,233	44.0	45.0	15.8	21.7	27.9	61.3
India	1,967,998	52.5	37.9	7.5	33.7	42.3	71.3
Philippines	1,868,316	40.3	48.1	15.0	40.6	8.7	69.9
Vietnam	1,258,979	46.9	45.7	22.3	16.5	6.4	68.9
South Korea	613,838	43.5	42.7	18.6	34.5	19.4	59.7
Latin America							
Mexico	11,563,374	52.9	39.0	23.6	4.1	1.5	69.1
El Salvador	1,271,859	51.1	39.6	24.9	5.8	1.6	77.1
Cuba	1,113,901	49.3	51.4	33.0	13.6	6.9	58.9
Dominican Republic	957,376	44.0	43.5	26.0	10.1	3.4	66.7
Guatemala	858,530	59.2	34.9	22.2	5.5	1.8	77.8

Source: American Community Survey 2012.

determinant of how well families will fare, it does not alone determine immigrants' position in the labor force. For instance, immigrants with high levels of education and work experience who are sponsored by a family member or by an employer are able to secure higher paying jobs, often in high-technology fields or in the healthcare sector. On the other hand, many immigrants have opened up their own businesses. Whether because their qualifications were not valued in traditional fields or because they faced institutional racism in traditional jobs, they used their human capital to create economic opportunities for themselves and for their relatives, their co-ethnics, and others beyond the immediate immigrant community (Valdez 2011). In fact this has been a common experience for some immigrant groups (Min and Bozorgmehr 2000), including South Koreans (Kim 2008), and Iranians (Dallalfar 1994).

Although most immigrant groups develop ethnic businesses that cater to the specific tastes and lifestyles of their co-ethnics, there are immigrants with higher rates of entrepreneurial activity. These groups have high concentrations of immigrants who bring business experience, have access to resources to finance their ventures, and can draw on their co-ethnics for needed labor (Portes and Rumbaut 2006). Such groups have created what scholars call ethnic enclaves. Notable examples are Cubans in Miami and Koreans in New York and Los Angeles (Portes and Rumbaut 2006). Other immigrant business owners work outside enclaves and run establishments to cater to a non-ethnic clientele, including inner-city residents. Although some immigrant-owned businesses constitute large enterprises, most tend to be small restaurants and shops. These small enterprises are likely to use family labor, often unpaid (Espiritu 1999).

The Great Recession of 2008–2010 exacerbated trends already under way since the mid-1970s, affecting all workers, including immigrants. Those who worked in housing and construction suffered most acutely. Latino/a immigrants in particular lost union jobs at higher rates than native-born workers with equivalent qualifications (Catron 2013). Coupled with increased immigration enforcement, immigrant workers' vulnerability intensified during the Great Recession (Menjívar and Enchautegui 2015; Schmalzbauer 2011). But immigrants also experienced greater employment gains than native-born workers during the recovery, even if the quality of jobs declined (Enchautegui 2012). These macroeconomic dislocations create poverty, unemployment, and underemployment for immigrant families, blocking their ability to survive and thrive (Schmalzbauer 2014).

These effects, furthermore, are not contained solely within US borders. For many immigrants, wages stretch internationally, in the form of remittances designed to sustain non-migrant family members in the origin country, sometimes in transit countries, and, given dispersion patterns in the United States, in other US destinations as well. Immigrants' remittances dropped notably in 2008, when the economic downturn hit. Since then, however, they have increased, slowly but steadily, and have now surpassed 2007 levels (Orozco 2012).

Main Demographic Characteristics of Immigrant Families

In this section we situate the demographic patterns of immigrant families in a broader structural context and consider the influence of cultural dynamics on demographic patterns in the home and host countries. We depict the demographic profile of the largest US immigrant groups from Asia and Latin America, the main sending regions in the world today, paying special attention to family-related indicators (for a detailed overview, see Glick 2010).

The five largest groups of immigrants from Asia originate in China, India, the Philippines, Vietnam, and South Korea; the largest groups from Latin America come from Mexico, El Salvador, Cuba, the Dominican Republic, and Guatemala, and they present a range of sex ratios within and between regions (see Table 1.1). It should be noted that some of these groups are also the fastest growing ones from each region. For instance, it is estimated that the size of the Central American immigrant population has multiplied several times from 1960, when it was 48,900, to 2011, when it reached over 3 million (Stoney and Batalova 2013). And Asians as a pan-ethnic group are the fastest growing racial group in the United States (Okamoto 2014).

The age distribution of Latin American immigrants varies significantly by national origin, reflecting the age distribution of the origin country but also variations in the migratory flow over time. Cubans have the highest median age of all Latin American immigrant groups, namely 51.4 years; they are followed by Dominicans, who have a median age of 43.5. Immigrants from El Salvador, Mexico, and Guatemala are on the whole younger, having median ages of 39.6, 39 and 34.9 respectively. Among Asians, the median age of Filipino/a immigrants is the highest at 48.1, being followed by that of Vietnamese at 45.7, of Chinese at 45, of South Koreans at 42.7, and of Indians at 37.9 (see Table 1.1).

In general, intermarriage is on the rise (Wang 2012): marriages involving an immigrant comprised 16.9 percent of marriages between 2008 and 2012 (Lichter, Qian, and Tumin 2015). Researchers note that intermarriage where one partner is a US-born non-Hispanic white is positively associated with integration (Glick 2010; Landale and Oropesa 2007). Further strengthening the assimilation argument, immigrants who marry outside of their ethnic group are more likely to stay in the United States and not return to the origin country (Moran-Taylor and Menjívar 2005). And yet the picture is more complicated, as research reveals that "ethnic replenishment" (Jiménez 2010)—that is, a sustained migration from a country of origin—can entrench marriage segregation; this suggests that segmented (and not classical) assimilation is also at play in certain contexts (Lichter, Brown, Qian, and Carmalt 2007; Vasquez 2015). Intermarriage also shapes immigrant identities (Perlmann and Waters 2007). While Asians have historically had higher rates of intermarriage with non-Hispanic whites than have other immigrant groups, Asians born abroad intermarry at lower rates than third- and fourth-generation Asians in the United States (Qian, Blair, and Ruf 2001), and Asian women are more likely to marry whites than are Asian men to marry whites (Qian and Lichter 2001). Thus we can assume that, as immigration

Introduction

Table 1.2 Marital Status of the Largest Immigrant Groups from Asia and Latin America

Country	Marriage (%)	Never married (%)	Divorced (%)	Separated (%)
Asia				
China	64.3	24.1	5.4	1.0
India	77.8	16.2	2.1	0.6
Philippines	62.5	20.8	7.1	2.2
Vietnam	63.7	22.1	7.4	1.7
South Korea	64.0	24.1	6.0	1.2
Latin America				
Mexico	58.1	28.3	6.0	4.2
El Salvador	49.4	35.9	7.6	4.5
Cuba	49.6	21.4	15.3	4.2
Dominican Republic	42.9	31.3	13.6	7.6
Guatemala	47.6	40.1	5.8	4.1

Source: American Community Survey 2012.

patterns become more varied across origin groups, so too will immigrant marriage patterns.

Analyses of US census data (see Table 1.2) show that Mexicans have the highest marriage rates among Latinos/as, at 58.1 percent, and Dominicans the lowest, at 42.9 percent. Cubans, Salvadorans, and Guatemalans fall in the middle, with marriage rates of 49.6 percent, 49.4 percent, and 47.6 percent respectively. Marriage rates among Asian immigrants are markedly higher. Of the Indian immigrants aged 15 or older, 77.8 percent are married; Chinese immigrants follow, with 64.3 percent, then South Korean immigrants with 64 percent, Vietnamese with 63.7 percent, and Filipinos/as with 62.5 percent.

There are debates about how much fertility is impacted by the factor of time spent in the United States (Glick 2010). While some research shows that fertility rates in marriages between native-born whites and Latinos/as converge as the time spent by Latinos/

16

Introduction

as in the United States increases (Parrado and Morgan 2008), other research, with Mexicans, suggests that fertility may decline at first, only to rise again in later generations (Bean, Lee, Batalova, and Leach 2004). It is clear that, while marriage rates are higher among Asians than among Latinos/as, the story is reversed in terms of fertility. According to 2012 data from the American Community Survey, Latinos/as also have higher rates of children outside of marriage: 49.1 percent of Dominicans, 46.9 percent of Cubans, and 33 percent of Mexicans fit into this category. On the other hand, the highest percentage of out-of-marriage births among Asians is among Filipinos/as, who register 17.7 percent, while only 1.3 percent of Indians have children outside of marriage, and, according to the American Community Survey (ACS), 14.9 percent of Vietnamese births have been outside of a marriage. This percentage is followed by 7.5 percent among South Koreans and 6.4 percent among Chinese (see Table 1.3).

Marital dissolution is sometimes interpreted to be a marker of immigrant integration, especially for immigrants from countries

Table 1.3 Fertility Rates among the Largest Immigrant Groups from Asia and Latin America*

Country	Fertility out of marriage (%)	Fertility of women aged 15–50
Asia		
China	6.4	5.0
India	1.3	7.9
Philippines	17.7	5.78
Vietnam	14.9	6.26
South Korea	7.5	5.4
Latin America		
Mexico	33.0	7.76
El Salvador	38.2	7.0
Cuba	46.9	4.5
Dominican Republic	49.1	5.6
Guatemala	37.8	9.6

* Ratio of live births in an area to the population of that area, per 1,000 population per year.
Source: American Community Survey 2012.

17

Introduction

where divorce is uncommon. Bean, Berg, and van Hook (1996) found that the longer Mexicans reside in the United States the more likely they are to divorce. Divorce rates among Latinos/ as and Asians deviate little. According to the ACS, Cubans have the highest divorce rate among both groups, at 15.3 percent (and 4.2 percent of couples are separated). They are followed, among Latinos/as, by Dominicans, who have a divorce rate of 13.6 percent (but a higher separation rate than Cubans, at 7.6 percent). Among Salvadorans, 12.1 percent are divorced or separated—a figure followed by 10.2 percent for Mexicans and 9.9 percent for Guatemalans. The highest combined rate of divorce and separa- tion among Asians is found among Filipinos/as, at 9.3 percent, who are followed closely by Vietnamese, at 9.1 percent. South Koreans come next, with a combined rate of 7.2 percent of couples that are divorced or separated, and then come the Chinese, with 6.4 percent. Indians have by far the lowest rates: 2.1 percent of couples are divorced and 0.6 percent separated (see Table 1.2).

Important to this demographic story are the many family part- nerships that are divided by borders and thus spend time apart. Hence we resist the assumption that a geographically bound nuclear family is the norm. Indeed there are many immigrants who negotiate partnerships, married or not, across borders. In other cases, which involve lengthy separations and uncertain reunifica- tions, unions sometimes dissolve and new families are formed both in the home countries and in the United States. Geography, cultural practices, and legal status may complicate marriage, separation, and divorce, as immigrants must also negotiate partnerships in dif- ferent national contexts (see Dreby 2015; Foner 2009).

Immigrants live in a variety of family forms. For example, 57.4 percent of Mexican families are headed by a married couple, whereas this proportion is 50.3 percent for Salvadorans, 48.8 percent for Cubans, 47.6 percent for Guatemalans, and 34.6 percent for Dominicans. Relatedly, among Latinos/as, Dominicans have the highest percentage of female-headed households with no husband present, at 34.7 percent, and Cubans the lowest, at 15.2 percent. Among Latinos/as, Mexicans have the largest household size, at 4.27 percent, and Cubans the lowest, at 2.99 percent (see Table 1.4).

18

Table 1.4 Household Composition among the Largest Immigrant Groups from Asia and Latin America

Country	Household head, married	Female-headed household, no husband present	Homeownership (percentage of owner-occupied housing units)	Household size
Asia				
China	59.1	9.4	61.0	2.91
India	77.1	3.1	53.6	3.10
Philippines	59.7	16.1	61.3	3.50
Vietnam	63.6	13.7	66.8	3.62
South Korea	59.1	8.2	47.4	2.74
Latin America				
Mexico	57.4	18.5	44.9	4.27
El Salvador	50.3	22.1	41.2	4.09
Cuba	48.8	15.2	55.3	2.99
Dominican Republic	34.6	34.7	24.2	3.38
Guatemala	47.6	19.6	28.4	4.17

Source: American Community Survey 2012.

According to the ACS, Asians have higher percentages of married, couple-headed families than do Latinos/as. Indians have the highest rate of married, couple-headed households, at 77.1 percent. They are followed by the Vietnamese, at 63.6 percent, by Filipinos/as, at 59.7 percent, and by South Koreans and Chinese, both at 59.1 percent. Asians also have lower rates of female-headed households with no husbands present. Indians have the lowest rate of female-headed households, at 3.1 percent, and Filipinos/as the highest, at 16.1 percent. The remaining Asian groups are the Vietnamese at 13.7 percent of female-headed households, the Chinese at 9.4 percent, and South Koreans at 8.2 percent. Household size among Asians ranges from a high of 3.62 for the Vietnamese to a low of 2.74 for the South Koreans (see Table 1.4).

Extended households are common among recent immigrants;

the latter are also likely to live in multigenerational households (Qian 2014). Once immigrants start to experience upward socio-economic mobility, they tend to move out and establish their own households. The economic context for this decision is critical, as research suggests that, if economic conditions worsen, immigrants are likely to return to extended households (van Hook and Glick 2007).

Important to the demographic story of non-family households is the recognition that cohabitation without marriage is common across the life course in many Latin American countries, a practice that may impact household formation in the United States (Castro Martín 2002). In contrast, cohabitation is much less prevalent in Asian countries, and so it should not be surprising that Asians have the lowest rates of cohabitation among all immigrant groups (Brown, van Hook, and Glick 2008).

Homeownership has long been lauded as symbolic of incorporation and mobility in the United States; it is often held up as indicative of one's having achieved the "American dream," with important implications for families. According to Census figures, immigrants have diverging patterns of homeownership. Notably, Asian immigrants have higher rates of homeownership than do Latinos/as. Among Asians, Vietnamese have the highest rate of owner-occupied housing, at 66.8 percent; they are followed by Filipinos/as at 61.3 percent, by Chinese at 61 percent, by Indians at 53.6 percent, and by South Koreans at 47.4 percent. Cubans have the highest homeownership rates among Latinos/as, at 55.3 percent; they are followed by Mexicans at 44.9 percent, by Salvadorans at 41.2 percent, by Guatemalans at 28.4 percent, and, lastly, by Dominicans at 24.2 percent (see Table 1.3).

Much immigration into the United States is motivated by immigrants' search for higher wages and socioeconomic mobility, which in turn is met with a persistent demand for immigrant labor in key US economic sectors (Sassen 1990). Thus, it is not surprising that labor force participation rates are high among all immigrant groups in the United States. Guatemalans have the highest participation rate, at 77.8 percent, being followed by Salvadorans at 77.1 percent, by Indians at 71.3 percent, by Filipinos/as at 69.9 percent, by Mexicans at 69.1 percent, by Vietnamese at 68.9 percent, by Dominicans at 66.7 percent, by Chinese at 61.3 percent, by South Koreans at 59.7 percent, and by Cubans at 58.9 percent (see Table 1.1).

Scholars disagree about how labor force participation translates into socioeconomic mobility. Portes and Zhou (1993) theorize that assimilation is segmented, channeling second-generation youth from disadvantaged backgrounds to low-paying jobs and downward mobility, so they do not go above the socioeconomic status of their poor parents. Yet research by Kasinitz, Mollenkopf, Waters, and Holdaway (2008) paints a more optimistic picture. Although these authors agree with Portes and Zhou that not all immigrant groups are doing equally well, noting the stark challenges faced by black Dominican men and Puerto Ricans, they argue that, in comparison to Americans as a whole, second-generation immigrants are doing well. While most of the second generation has not been launched into the elite, university-educated class, Kasinitz et al. point out that this is true of all Americans, including the white native-born. Besides, there are now more racial–ethnic minorities in the middle and upper echelons of the labor force than ever before. Waters, Tran, Kasinitz, and John Mollenkopf (2010) attribute this rise to post-civil rights policies, which have opened access to employment and education previously off limits to minorities. Alba (2009) boosts this optimism by theorizing that, as white educated baby boomers exit the work force, racial–ethnic minorities, including the second immigrant generation, are certain to enter these jobs.

The employment story is complex, as not all work is full-time or secure. For example, immigrants continue to dominate low-skill agricultural work, which is physically grueling and low-paying (Holmes 2013). Additionally, the gendered challenges of work–family balance are often invisible in the demographic portrait of labor force participation. Most notably, labor force participation rates do not include the reproductive labor that occurs on the home front, or wage work like that of domestics and nannies, which straddles the private and public sphere (Flippen 2013; Hondagneu-Sotelo 2009). For instance, in immigrant families reproductive labor may take place in the home country and productive labor in the host country (Schmalzbauer 2004; 2005), although this may be a simplistic picture. As families move, mix, and recompose themselves across borders and geographies, the boundary between work and home and private and public is further blurred and complicated (Aulette 2007).

An important goal of this book is to challenge the notion that the SNAF is or should be the norm (see also Gamson 2015; Powell et al. 2010). Indeed, immigration complicates definitions and understandings of family composition. It is increasingly common for parents to migrate and leave children behind, in the home country (see Carling, Menjívar, and Schmalzbauer 2012), or for couples to be separated for undetermined periods of time in the context of migration. While in the United States, immigrants may also re-partner, or marry and have children. This results in families containing half-siblings, stepsiblings, and sometimes partners or spouses who live in different countries although they are still engaged in a mutual relationship. Whereas the US Census does not keep statistics on this diverse range of family compilations and formations, we note it here in order to challenge any assumption of normativity of family in general and of immigrant families in particular.

Emphases of the Book

Often the decision to migrate takes place in the context of the family and is intended for the benefit of its members. These decisions and experiences are, however, determined along different social axes that shape people's lives. This book is about immigrant families as shaped by various intersecting social, structural, and legal markers. To achieve this proposed picture, we would like to emphasize three key factors that are central in assessing immigrant families' experiences and well-being.

First, we take a structural vantage point. While we give attention to immigrants' "repertoires" in Coe's (2013) conceptualization— that is, beliefs, values, attitudes and systems of meaning in the context of their families—and thus we attend to their cultural practices, we highlight the interplay between structural and individual factors as well as systems of meaning in shaping immigrant families' experiences (also see Glick 2010). Specifically, we look critically at who is included in the family, where families are allowed to live, and the structures that shape their access to societal institutions and social services. We examine how institutions shape immigrant family life and how immigrants navigate institutions, thereby exposing the wide range of variability in these intersections. In this process we reveal how the macro-level context interacts with micro-level processes of intimate family life, following C. Wright Mills' concept of the sociological imagination. This perspective moves us beyond facile notions of families as spaces of comfort and support, toward rendering the complexity of family life in changing locations and expectations. Our approach underscores patterns of inequality, stratification, and asymmetry in the structure of opportunities that deeply shape immigration and settlement.

Second, while we focus on the experiences of immigrant families in the United States, we look beyond this single national context, because immigrant families' lived experiences may play out across borders. Given the links between US-based families and loved ones abroad,[11] we incorporate these experiences throughout the book rather than in a single, isolated chapter. For a variety of reasons that span voluntary arrangements to forced circumstances, immigrant families increasingly live apart from close family members in the countries of origin (or transit). It is common for immigrants in the United States to continue to support families in the country of origin, to remain involved in their decisions, and, for all practical purposes, to actively participate in family life there. We examine these spaces, underlining the efforts and successes of immigrants to remain connected across borders as well as the underside of these separations. As we will highlight, several vectors—including gender, age, race, and national origin—shape the contours of these experiences. Moreover, such transnational links are molded by global structures of inequality that foment inequities across borders and within families divided by borders (Dreby and Adkins

2010). In these processes, immigrant families in the United States are transformed by, and also transform, their societies of origin, infusing change through economic and social remittances (Levitt 2001). We highlight these complexities and nuances throughout the book.

Third, as in general sociological examinations of the family (Aulette 2007; Cherlin 2008), we devote chapters to key dimensions of social stratification such as social class, gender, and age or generation; and we add legal status. To underline the centrality of racialization in immigration processes in the United States (see Kibria, Bowman, and O'Leary 2014), we weave an examination of race and ethnicity throughout the book, emphasizing how these social constructs are deeply intertwined with the other factors, cumulatively and simultaneously shaping immigrants' experience. As Kibria, Bowman, and O'Leary (2014: 5) observe, "the race–immigration nexus" constitutes a "fluid and intertwined bundle of linkages ... among institutions, ideologies and practices." Unlike the overtly racist immigration policies of the past, such as the Chinese Exclusion Act, the approach at this historical junction is to deem "illegal" certain activities that are common among some immigrant groups, like Latinos/as. In this light, we note how legal status today can serve as a proxy for race (see Luibhéid 2013; Møller 2014) in immigration enforcement and control at different levels of government and in various spaces in society. To the extent that immigrants are racialized through law, they and their families will face unequal and discriminatory treatment in communities and institutions in society. Our analysis also draws on other forms of stratification, including sexuality. Systems of social stratification shape what families do and when and how they do it; thus, they affect marriage and divorce patterns and household composition. Importantly, immigrant families are not monolithic spaces and we do not wish to erase differences within them. Instead we shed light on the rich diversity of family forms within and across groups of national origin—a portrait that brings visibility to family members who sometimes remain invisible under orthodox understandings of family. In effect, we offer a portrayal more attuned to the reality of immigrant families today.

Introduction

Readers will come to understand immigrant families as dynamic and malleable forms of social organization, not as static or constant constructs based on idealized notions of what immigrant families should be.

Organization of the Book

Having established our conceptual and theoretical approach to the study of immigrant families in this chapter, in Chapter 2 we explore how the legal framework of the US immigration system impacts families. We focus on both the legislative and the enforcement side of the immigration system, analyzing them separately and in relation to each other. Following our focus on how axes of stratification shape immigrant families, we turn our attention to immigrant legality as a factor influencing immigrant families' access to goods and services and structuring families from within. Chapter 3 explores how social class shapes the immigrant experience. Class determines the security that accompanies migrants as they cross physical and legal borders, the geographic and temporal separation of families, opportunities for social mobility in the host country, and the role of remittances for families who live across borders. Chapter 4 hones in on gender. We pay attention to how gender and structural-level factors interact in terms of job opportunities, geographic mobility, and immigration enforcement, as well as to how gender and ideological factors shape expectations of behavior and cultural practices. Gender maps onto the private and public spheres and shapes relations between women and men, both within and outside of immigrant households. Chapter 5 highlights how individual family members' life-course position—that is, their generation—influences relations within families as well as the family's well-being more generally. Age is important at the time of arrival and settlement, and it intersects with other social positions, like gender and legal status. In Chapter 6 we turn our attention to the relationships between immigrant families and core institutions in society, like education and health care. Whereas Chapter 2 focuses on the legal framework created by federal immigration law that immigrant families navigate, in Chapter 6 we examine how immigrants' legality intersects to influence families' relationships to social institutions and local policies and we discuss the mediating role that community organizations play. We conclude by summarizing the main arguments in the book and embark on preliminary analyses of immigration policies that unfold even as this book goes to press.

By exploring axes of stratification within the family and by presenting them as vectors that shape immigrant families' relationships with communities and institutions, our work looks closely at the private spaces of families but also examines areas where private, public, and political realms intersect and sometimes clash. We also call attention to how immigrants respond to current conditions by organizing politically and demanding justice and rights on behalf of their families. Thus, we shed light on the spaces where the private and the political aspects of immigrant family life intersect.

2

Families and Immigration Law

Immigration laws and enforcement practices are powerful enough to structure the day-to-day lives and long-term trajectories of immigrant families, as well as their internal dynamics (Menjívar 2011b). In this chapter we examine the legal framework of immigration, as it structures and reconfigures the contours of immigrant families (Antognini 2014; Demleitner 2004; Hawthorne 2007) and molds relationships between parents and children and between partners in couples. We focus on the federal level, because this is the only level of government with the authority to formally include certain immigrants and exclude others. (In Chapter 6 we address how local laws shape the well-being of immigrant families.) While the legislative side of the immigration regime serves to regulate who is admitted, the enforcement side determines who is excluded through detention and deportation. We examine both components, separating them for analytic purposes only; for, in practice, they are deeply intertwined. Someone who is processed through the enforcement side of the system (e.g., detained for immigration infractions or deported) is highly unlikely to be able to enter the country under family reunification law. And, even though the two sides of the system may work at cross-purposes, so as to include and exclude, in this chapter we show that often the consequences for immigrant families are similar.[1]

Although we focus here on immigration law that directly impacts the composition and the dynamics of families, we note that the employment-based visa system also has significant consequences for immigrant families. Access to employment-based visas affects the likelihood of family members entering the labor market as well as when and how they do it, and therefore the income they can derive from their work. This visa system also impacts immigrant families when the legal status of accompanying family members ("derivatives," in immigration law language) is tied to that of the principal visa holder, which often renders accompanying family members dependent on this person. This situation has particularly salient consequences for women who enter as derivative benefi-ciaries of their husbands' visas, as it exacerbates already unequal gender roles and expectations in families.[2]

Legal statuses, as created through immigration laws, deter-mine immigrant families' access to goods and services while also shaping their sense of belonging in US society. Today's context of enforcement and implementation of immigration law has increased the value of legal status in a way that directly affects life chances. Legal status facilitates—and lack of it hinders—access to well-paid and secure jobs, housing and homeownership, educa-tion, health care, and a host of public goods (Bean, Bachmeier, Brown, van Hook, and Leach 2014; Castañeda and Melo 2014; Gonzales 2011; Hall, Greenman, and Farkas 2010; Massey 2014; McConnell 2013; Menjívar and Kanstroom 2014; Sousa-Rodriguez forthcoming; van Hook and Balistreri 2006). Parents' legal status has been found to have effects on future generations, even when those generations are born in the United States (Bean, Brown, and Bachmeier 2015). Thus, it has been argued, legal status constitutes an axis of social stratification that is similar to other markers, for example social class, gender, and race (Gee and Ford 2011; Massey 2007, 2013; Menjívar 2010). However, a key difference between legal status and other forms of stratification is that, while it is against the law to deny services or social goods to individuals on the basis of social markers (e.g., gender, race, or religious creed), this is not the case with legal status. Indeed, it is a central feature of the law today to deny goods and services on the basis of legal status, as we will see in Chapter 6. Legal status is therefore not only a new form of stratification but, because discrimination based on it is formalized in law, it can trump the effects that other social positions have on life chances, even diminishing the potential effects of an important factor like education.

We would like to make three caveats. First, immigrant families of the past, around the beginning of last century, did not face the same complex web of legislation that immigrant families face today (Fox 2012; Steinberg 2001). As laws have changed over the years to recognize different family relationships as bases for immigration, these new legislative actions—enacted at a different historical moment—contain requirements that many immigrants today find difficult to meet (see also Pallares 2014). Second, through its laws, the state creates the various legal categories into which immigrants are classified (Menjívar and Kanstroom 2014), and these categories shift or are reaffirmed with the political winds of the time. The legal categories that the state creates channel individuals through variegated paths, so that those who are classified as legal entrants are afforded certain rights and responsibilities in a way that those who are classified as undocumented are not (see also Bean, Leach, Brown, Bachmeier, and Hipp 2011). Presence in the country alone is not a guarantee of rights (Ahmad 2011); it is the state, through its system of admissions and classifications, that ultimately grants rights and benefits to individuals (Bosniak 2007). Such legal categories permit immigrants to form or reconstitute their families or restrict them from doing so, and thereby set individuals onto various paths of socioeconomic mobility, which in turn affect immediate families, communities, and ultimately society. And, third, immigration law and enforcement do not affect all immigrant families in the same way, because immigrant groups are unequally positioned socially, racially, historically, economically, and politically in the face of technically impartial laws.

We first explore family reunification law, which affects all immigrant families, as it determines which relationships are recognized in law as the basis for family migration and reunification. These legal determinations are based on particular conceptions of what a family should be—for example, nuclear, heterosexual, and formalized through marriage (Enchautegui and Menjívar 2015; Hawthorne 2007; Pallares 2014). We also include a section on temporary statuses—such as the status guaranteed through the

Deferred Action for Childhood Arrivals (DACA) program and the temporary protected status (TPS)—and we offer a short discussion of the H-2 guest worker programs. All of these statuses, policies, and programs are part of the legislative side of the immigration system, each affecting a different subgroup of immigrant families. While temporary statuses do not lead to legal permanent residence and represent increasing gray areas in immigrant legality today (Abrego and Lakhani 2015; Bailey, Wright, Mountz, and Miyares 2002; Menjívar 2006a, 2006b), they have important immediate and long-term implications for immigrant families. We then move to a discussion of the enforcement strategies that directly and more visibly affect the composition of immigrant families, particularly Latino. Together, the two components of the immigration system fundamentally shape the constitution of immigrant families, with different degrees of intensity for different immigrant groups.

Although family reunification is meant to bring families together, given the requirements for family sponsorship, family reunification law may have the opposite effect on some immigrant groups, as it may contribute to keeping family members apart for undetermined periods of time (Enchautegui and Menjívar 2015). On the other hand, enforcement practices work to separate families—mostly through deportation, but also through detention (ibid.). Both types of separation impact all members of families during the time of separation and after reunification (Dreby 2015). Temporary statuses fall somewhere in between, as they are meant to provide temporary relief from deportation but do not constitute (nor do they lead to) permanent status. With the increased impetus to move more immigrants into temporary statuses—which has become a signature project of proposals for immigration legislation, including President Obama's November 2014 Executive Order of Deferred Action for parents of US citizens and lawful permanent residents—even legal permanent status is becoming less permanent. Indeed, legal permanent residents are now being deported (Golash-Boza 2014) and immigrants increasingly experience the uncertainty inherent in temporary forms of relief (Cebulko 2014). We include these forms of temporary status to signal their importance today and their associated consequences for families. In the final section we discuss mixed-status families, as their experiences capture the effects of both the legislative and the enforcement sides of the contemporary immigration regime.

Family Reunification Law

We start with definitional questions because these form the basis of how family reunification law is laid out, operates, and delimits the range of relations that constitute a family. Demleitner (2004) notes that family reunification law not only affects the composition of families but actually defines the family by attaching specific meaning to such concepts as "child," "family," and "spouse," which most people take for granted. In the legal arena these terms have specific meanings, which vary at different historical moments and conform to a particular view of what the "family" is. Thus, according to Hawthorne (2007), in immigration law the concept of "family" is based on an idealized notion of the nuclear heterosexual family. It leaves out family modalities that are widespread around the world but are not included in what sociologist Dorothy Smith (1993) defines as SNAF—the Standard North American Family.

Indeed, the structure of family preference visas does not always match the variety of family relations that exist among immigrants (Enchautegui and Menjívar 2015). The law creates family preference categories that do not follow cultural scripts prevalent in the societies from which immigrants arrive. This means that many immigrants are unable to legally reunite with loved ones, who are excluded from, or not prioritized in, immigration law. For instance, a second wife's relationship with her husband is recognized socially and legally in societies where polygamy is accepted, but not in the United States (Demleitner 2004). Until the overturning of the Defense of Marriage Act (DOMA) in 2013, lesbian, gay, bisexual, transgender, and queer (LGBTQ) partners were also unable to benefit from family reunification policies (Acosta 2013). Grandparents, grandchildren, aunts, uncles, and cousins

Families and Immigration Law

do not qualify for family reunification benefits either, regardless of the closeness of their relationship with immigrants. At the same time, in some cases—particularly the case of fiancés and fiancées—family reunification recognizes fluidity, thus granting status even in situations where family relations are in transition during the application process (Antognini 2014).[3]

Family Preference Categories

The three main types of formal admission to the United States are employment, family ties, and refugee status. Of these, family-based immigration is by far the most common; family is codified as the basic unit of society and therefore the law gives it priority. Accordingly, it is estimated that 65 percent of the approximately 1 million visas for legal permanent residence in 2011 were allocated to relatives of US citizens and family-sponsored immigrants (US Department of Homeland Security 2011). These visa allocations are based on what the law defines as a family relation and on its priority for petitioning purposes.

The most recognized right to family reunification is granted to heterosexual spouses, followed by minor, unmarried, and dependent children of migrant parents. "The rights of adult, married children to be united with their parents are much more limited as are the rights to unification with siblings or members of a more extended household, such as aunts or cousins" (Demleitner 2004: 277). The family reunification provisions of US immigration law have no numerical limits for visas to immediate relatives of US citizens such as spouses; parents, as long as the petitioner is not older than 21; unmarried children under the age of 21 with at least one US citizen parent; widows or widowers of US citizens, if they were married to the deceased for at least two years and within two years of applying for the visa; adopted children of US citizens, if the adoption was completed before the child turned 16; and stepchildren or stepparents as long as the formal relationship began before the eighteenth birthday of the stepchild.[4]

The number of family-based visas granted beyond what the law defines as an "immediate" relative is numerically limited. Every

32

year the US Congress approves the number of visas allocated to family preference visas and no one country can obtain more than 7 percent of the total number. Family preferences include several relationships, all of which conform to a certain ideal of what a family should be (Enchautegui and Menjívar 2015). Minor children and spouses of legal permanent residents and married children and siblings of US citizens can enter the United States, but their visas are subject to this annual numerical cap. Such visas are divided into four categories:

1 first preference goes to US citizens' unmarried sons and daughters under 21 years of age;
2 second-preference visas are designated for the spouses, children, and unmarried sons and daughters of legal permanent residents—namely spouses and unmarried children under the age of 21 receive F2A visas and adult children receive F2B visas;
3 third preference goes to married sons and daughters of US citizens, their spouses, and their children; and
4 the fourth category is reserved for siblings of US citizens, their spouses, and their children.

In addition, the law permits "derivative beneficiaries"—that is, spouses and children of the individuals petitioned through family reunification categories. There are no visa preferences for the parents, siblings, and married children of legal permanent residents. Also, if the child of a legal permanent resident turns 21 while waiting for an F2A visa, s/he may be moved to the F2B queue and face an even longer waiting period (Enchautegui and Menjívar 2015).

The numerical limits for each category and the large number of visa applications from certain "oversubscribed" countries (e.g., China, India, Mexico, and the Philippines) give rise to long visa backlogs. Each of the numerically limited family reunification categories listed above is allocated a specific number of visas every year, and usually there are more applications than available visas. For instance, the total number of visas for the second preference category (spouses or unmarried children of legal permanent residents) is 114,000, but every year there are more applications than visas and thus the waiting time is four years for an F2A visa and six years for an F2B visa.[5] For applicants from oversubscribed countries the waiting times can be longer. These waiting times amount to long-term separations between couples or between parents and their children (if the petitioned family member lives outside the United States) or to years spent in a legal limbo (if the petitioned family member is already in the United States and is readjusting his/her status) (see Jasso 2011).

Thus, definitional questions in family reunification law are critical for understanding how the law structures immigrants' families. For example, Hawthorne (2007: 815) observes that the definition of a "child" in family preference categories has important consequences because it can easily exclude someone whom a parent considers to be a child, and it ignores relations within multigenerational households that in practice are as close as those that the law defines as holding between "immediate relatives."[6] By prioritizing family bonds that conform to the ideal of a heteronormative, nuclear, formally married family, immigration law excludes family members who do not fall within these parameters.

Long Waiting Periods of Separation and Their Effects

The narrow strictures of family reunification law mean that millions of families live in extensive periods of separation. These separations exist in families that are eligible for reunification but face the long backlogs inherent in the current immigration system. They also exist in families headed by undocumented immigrants, who are ineligible to apply for reunification and cannot bring their family members safely to the United States. In both cases, indefinite family separation can be traumatizing, especially for children, and can lead to union dissolution in couples.

When children are left behind by a parent's (or parents') migration, with no clear timeframe for reunification, they may sometimes feel abandoned or unloved (Abrego 2014; Dreby 2014) and often report feelings of resentment. Children tend to center their resentment more directly on their absent mothers, whom they blame for failing to fulfill gendered expectations of direct care and nurturing (also see Carling, Menjívar, and Schmalzbauer 2012). While monetary remittances can ease this resentment, financial support does not fill the emotional gap left by an absent parent (Abrego 2014), and the scars of separation fester for years (Menjívar and Abrego 2009). To make matters worse, during separation children often struggle with behavioral and emotional problems (Dreby 2014; Schmalzbauer 2015).

For couples who are forced to live apart, extensive periods of separation can lead to union dissolution or to a sense of abandonment and insecurity about the strength of the union. Menjívar and Agadjanian (2007) observed such cases in Armenia and Guatemala. Even though spouses kept in regular communication, sometimes calling several times a week, the women's insecurity and sense of potential abandonment increased when the men would not call. Similarly, in Honduras (McKenzie and Menjívar 2011) women felt insecure about a potential break of their relationship when men did not send money or did not call as promised. Migrant men's access to the resources needed in order to initiate communication and send money increased non-migrant women's dependence and insecurity. The women's fears were not baseless, as they had heard of, and witnessed, cases in which unions dissolved—usually initiated by men, who found a new partner in the United States—in the context of long-term and uncertain separations.

Temporary Statuses with Implications for Families: TPS, DACA, and H-2 Worker Visas

Temporary forms of legality share the feature that they provide relief from deportation and offer employment authorization, with consequences for the structure of immigrant families and their prospects for future well-being. There are important differences as well. For instance, TPS and H-2A temporary worker visas for agricultural workers and H-2B temporary visas for low-skill service workers produce families that remain separated across borders for indefinite periods of time, while DACA has the potential to create differentiation within families already residing in the United States. Eligibility for DACA is also closely tied to education, while eligibility for the other two forms is not.[7]

TPS and DACA grant their recipients 18 and 24 months (respectively) of access to a work permit and protection from deportation provided that certain requirements are met. Although aimed at different populations of immigrants, they share key aspects of "liminal legality" (Menjívar 2006b). Similar forms of temporary legality are being expanded, and even considered to be viable solutions in the absence of comprehensive immigration reform.[8] However, temporary legality does not provide access to the goods and benefits that come with permanent legal status or with citizenship, either acquired by birth or through naturalization. Although TPS is law, the designated countries can change and TPS can effectively end for those countries after the 18-month designation. DACA, enacted through presidential executive order, can be terminated at any time, especially when an administration's period ends. These statuses, while beneficial, can also be harmful to the long-term stability and well-being of families by blocking their recipients from petitioning for family members and by denying them access to public goods, voting, social security benefits, or federal financial aid for college.

TPS provides relief from deportation to persons who arrived by a specific date from countries that the Department of Homeland Security designates as having conditions that temporarily prevent their nationals from returning safely; such conditions include ongoing armed conflict or environmental disaster.[9] During the designated time, individuals are conferred work authorization and stay of deportation. As of this writing, the countries designated for TPS are El Salvador, Guinea, Haiti, Honduras, Liberia, Nepal, Nicaragua, Sierra Leone, Somalia, Sudan, South Sudan, and Syria. However, the majority of TPS holders are Salvadoran (estimated to be 212,000 out of 340,310 beneficiaries), followed by Hondurans (64,000). Several of these nationality groups have held TPS for years; Somalis, Hondurans, and Nicaraguans have held TPS longer than any other group—24 years for Somalis and 16 years for Hondurans and Nicaraguans—renewing their permits every 18 months. In no case does TPS lead to permanent status. TPS holders usually do not know whether this status will be reapproved for their national origin group. Once their group is given the green light to reapply, they must get their paperwork and payments in order, so as to renew in time, if they are to keep their protection uninterrupted. Importantly, because TPS does not provide the opportunity to petition for visas for any family member (or to include any in one's TPS applications) this status has contributed to keeping families separated for indefinite periods of time (Enchautegui and Menjívar 2015) and has been one of the factors encouraging the migration of unaccompanied Central American children who seek to reunite with their parents (Sánchez Molina 2015).

Marcos, a participant in Schmalzbauer's studies, migrated from Honduras to the United States in 1999, without legal authorization, after he lost his job due to the economic devastation in the aftermath of Hurricane Mitch. He left behind his wife and three sons, all of primary school age at the time. Like many labor migrants, Marcos intended for his migration to be temporary, pending Honduras's economic recovery. Within a year of migrating to Boston, Marcos applied for and was granted TPS. The temporary permit initially eased some of the stress of living undocumented, but it also added more uncertainty to Marcos's life. Every year and a half since then, he has gone through the stressful period of waiting to see whether his TPS will be renewed, followed by the bureaucracy of the reapplication process, all the while hanging onto the hope that his temporary status would someday translate into full legal authorization. And, while Marcos has felt some security in being able to work with authorization, TPS has prevented him from traveling home to see his family.[10] The guilt of having missed his father's funeral continues to haunt him.

In the meantime the situation in Honduras has worsened, politically and economically (Frank 2014). Over the years of Marcos's separation from his family, his oldest son became adamant that he too should risk his life and migrate to Boston. Marcos initially told him not to come, to be patient, that with immigration reform

TPS would turn into something more permanent. Yet that permanency still did not come; and the endless limbo of temporary status became too much.[11] In 2009 Marcos's oldest son, who had been a top student and a scholarship-supported soccer player, left behind his university studies as well as his mother and brothers in Honduras, risked his life crossing multiple borders, and joined Marcos in Boston. He now works as a janitor. Marcos is frustrated and disheartened that there is no solution to his family's separation. If he returns to Honduras, he would have to give up his TPS and his job and would miss his long-awaited chance of benefitting from any "real" immigration reform. Yet, after 15 years of living in flux, his hopes have dwindled. As we write, his youngest sons, too, are contemplating the risk of an unauthorized border crossing, while his wife—too afraid to make the journey—is aggrieved at the prospect of being left alone in Honduras (see also McKenzie and Menjívar 2011). Marcos, who was sober for twenty years, recently took to drinking, in response to the anxiety and frustration that have permeated his and his family's lives.

President Obama enacted the DACA policy through executive action on June 15, 2012 to provide temporary relief to approximately 1.7 million young immigrants who arrived to the United States as children. As with TPS, the administration has made it clear that DACA offers only temporary protection and is not "a path to citizenship." For families, the passage of DACA has brought mixed results, which researchers are still examining (Gonzales, Terriquez, and Ruszczyk 2014; Pérez 2014). While individuals are able to obtain better paid jobs in their areas of expertise, they also have to take on more responsibilities within their families, in order to provide for members who are still undocumented and vulnerable. Moreover, not knowing whether DACA will be extended in the future, families worry about how long they would have access to protections from deportation and about the potential dangers of having shared personal information with government entities in order to qualify for this program.

In her study of Brazilian immigrant youth in Massachusetts, Kara Cebulko (2014) provides another revealing example of the parallels between DACA and TPS. She disentangles the different legal categories into which her study participants are classified and observes that the youth with DACA authorization were similar to those in liminal legality in terms of the partial rights and security that accrued from their limited legality. While noting the gains that came from DACA, the youth in her study also highlighted the limits this status placed on their socioeconomic and geographic mobility.

Furthermore, DACA is so legally tenuous that states vary widely in their interpretation and implementation of it. Some states, for example, deny a range of resources, including driver's and professional licenses, to DACA recipients, although as of this writing all states and the District of Columbia now issue driver's licenses to DACA recipients.[12] These decisions have significant ramifications for immigrant families. For instance, a young woman who pooled resources with her relatives and paid the $465 fee to obtain DACA authorization in Phoenix, Arizona (field notes, Menjívar) was able to enroll in, and complete, a course in respiratory therapy at a technical school. However, upon completion of the course in 2013, the State of Arizona Licensing Board would not recognize her DACA documents as proof of "legal presence" and thus could not give her a license to work in her field. On the one hand, this young woman was able to live without fear of deportation and to hold a job because she has work authorization. On the other hand, she could not obtain a job commensurate with her skill level and could not drive to work (in a car-centric city like Phoenix). As of this writing, Arizona will begin issuing driver's licenses to DACA recipients, but this example underscores the complexities inherent in the temporary forms of legality we see today.

The H-2A and H-2B visa programs are two of the only paths open to poor and working-class immigrants to come to the United States with a work visa. As such, they impact families directly. The H-2A and H-2B programs differ from the more widely recognized H-1B program, which grants temporary work visas to high-skilled workers. High-skilled workers on the H-1B visa are able to remain in the United States year-round, with their families, for renewable two-year stints, with the possibility of eventually obtaining residency and citizenship through their employers. The lesser known

H-2A and H-2B programs, on the other hand, create temporary transnationality and give workers no hope of permanency in the United States. H-2A and H-2B workers are granted 8–10 months of work authorization in agriculture or low-skill services, and they must rely on their employers for the annual renewal. Importantly, the majority of H-2 (A and B) workers are Mexican—but there is also a significant number of Jamaicans among them (see Hahamovitch 2011). Underscoring the class and racial biases in immigration admissions, H-2 workers cycle in and out of the United States for years on end; but they are not allowed to ever transfer their temporary status into permanent residency or citizenship.

While in the United States, H-2A and H-2B workers are in principle guaranteed basic workers' rights; but the programs have been heavily criticized for their weak oversight (see Hahamovitch 2011; Pastor and Alva 2004). Critiques of the programs typically center on the rule that workers are tied to the employer who granted their visa. For example, if work hours dwindle or workers experience mistreatment on the job, they are unable to search for work elsewhere and have little negotiating power (SPLC 2007). The impacts of this liminally legal status (Menjívar 2006b) are felt by temporary workers and by their non-migrant family members, who depend on remittances.

Perhaps most importantly in terms of family well-being, H-2A and H-2B workers are unable to bring their partners or children with them to the United States. As a result, their families must adjust to the cyclical temporariness of unity and separation. And, since wages within the program are low, families find it difficult to ever get ahead financially (Hwang and Parreñas 2010; Schmalzbauer 2015). Just like TPS recipients, H-2A and H-2B families endure indefinite periods of separation, which breed more uncertainty in their lives. In Schmalzbauer's interviews with H-2A fathers—and here it is important to note that the vast majority of H-2A workers are men (Griffith 2006)—she learned that, while men suffer from the isolation and loneliness of working in remote agricultural areas, their wives and children at home suffer from the disruption and insecurity of having their husbands and fathers cycle in and out of their lives (Schmalzbauer 2014, 2015).

Enforcement of Immigration Laws

Deportations have reached historic highs in the past six years. During the Obama administration the number of deportations has increased steadily, from 281,000 in 2006 to close to 400,000 annually since 2009; there were 419,384 deportations in 2012 and between 2009 and 2012 there were 1.6 million deportations (Gonzalez-Barrera 2014). Of the 397,000 deportations in the fiscal year 2011, 22 percent were of parents of US citizen children (Wessler 2011). Furthermore, changes to the Immigration and Nationality Act (INA) instituted through the Illegal Immigration Reform and Immigrant Responsibility Act (IIRIRA) of 1996, as well as a provision contained in the Immigration Reform and Control Act (IRCA) of 1986 (see Inda 2013), have made possible the removal of legal permanent residents as well.

Berger Cardoso and colleagues (2014) termed families separated by deportation "involuntary transnational families." These families differ from voluntary transnational families in that spouses and children in them are left behind in the destination country instead of being left behind in the country of origin, and removal of a family member is enforced by law. In their survey of male deportees to El Salvador, these researchers found that the majority of the men in these involuntary transnational families intended to remigrate (see also Hagan, Eschbach, and Rodriguez 2008). Indeed, those who were separated from their spouses and had left US citizen children in the United States showed the highest likelihood of making the trip again. This held true even for those who were deported for criminal offenses and thus faced a long incarceration (around 20 years) in case they were detained in their attempt to remigrate. This indicates a strong desire for family reunification on the part of deported fathers.

Detentions have not received as much attention in the context of family separations, but they do contribute to removing a family member and therefore to restructuring immigrant families in ways that make them similar to deportations. For instance, 440,500 individuals were held in detention in 2013, up from 200,000 in 2001 (Simanski 2014: 5), and there are on average 31,000 immigrants detained in any one day in the United States today, the average length of detention being thirty days (Menjívar and Kanstroom 2014).[13] However, close to 5,000 people were held for at least six months in 2012 and approximately 5,000 were held for one year or longer (TRAC Immigration 2013).[14] Detention, particularly when it is prolonged and indefinite, can have severe repercussions on detainees and their families.

When detainees are placed in remote detention facilities away from their families, have restricted access to telephone communication, are away from communities and networks, and are moved around detention facilities regularly (Human Rights Watch 2011)—as is the case with immigrant detainees—there can be multiple effects on their families, both in the United States and in the country of origin. The organization Physicians for Human Rights observed that individuals who are held in detention with no specified ending point and no information about their release and who experience sensory deprivation for long periods of time suffer a host of psychological harms, which persist beyond their release (Physicians for Human Rights 2011). Immigrant families immediately experience the effects of detention—for example the hardships that result when a family member is no longer able to contribute financially, including home foreclosure proceedings (Chaudry et al. 2010; Dreby 2012)—with significant long-term consequences.

In 2007 Alejandro, an undocumented father and husband from Mexico, was arrested at the construction site where he worked in rural Montana. Alejandro and his wife Nora had a new baby, and the family depended on Alejandro's wages; when he was detained they lost all economic support. The rural destination context of Montana made the family's already dire situation more challenging (Schmalzbauer 2014). For example, in Montana at that time there were few jobs available for immigrant women, so Nora's economic prospects were limited. She did not have a driver's license nor did she know how to drive, and the area in which they lived had no public transportation. As a newcomer to Montana, Nora had a network of support that was small and weak. In these circumstances, Alejandro's detention intensified her isolation and vulnerability. Furthermore, Nora did not have access to a Spanish-speaking lawyer. She decided she had no choice but to return to Mexico. But neither Nora nor her son had Mexican passports, and the closest Mexican consulate was in Boise, Idaho—an eight-hour drive away. After a few months of stress and anxiety and of having to rely on the support of the local food bank and Catholic church for survival, Nora was able to get a passport when the Boise consul visited Montana. Ultimately Nora decided to give up the dreams she had for her US citizen baby to be educated in the United States and she returned to Mexico, to join Alejandro.

Through the removal of a parent or parents, detentions and deportations add long-term uncertainty and thus can significantly reshape or even restructure immigrant families. These effects are felt in the short and long term, altering the financial, emotional, and psychological well-being of family members. Abrego (field notes, 2013) interviewed Jake, a Filipino college student in California whose undocumented father, Arvin, had returned to the Philippines to be with his ailing mother. At the time of the interview Jake had not seen Arvin in two years, because Arvin could not legally return to the United States. Jake and his brothers tried to help support their mother, who had become the family's only provider in the wake of this separation; but the situation was difficult. Jake explained that his father had to make an impossible choice between not seeing his mother alive one more time and losing indefinitely his ability to be with his wife and children. There are thousands of family members today who face similar situations.

When parents are detained or deported, children are likely to suffer anxiety, depression, and difficulties at school (Dreby 2014; Chaudry et al. 2010). Children's struggles are intensified when friends and kin hesitate to get close to them because they fear that association with a deportee's relative could heighten their own vulnerability to deportation (Dreby 2012). Additionally, children absorb the stress of the parent or caretaker who remains with them, as they witness that person's struggles to manage the legal, emotional, and financial traumas of having his/her partner placed in detention or deported (Dreby 2012; Schmalzbauer 2014).

Spouses, too, are impacted, and sometimes relationships weaken or break as a result of detention or deportation (see López 2015). In a case that Hagan, Castro, and Rodriguez (2010) depict, a Salvadoran man was deported and had no possibility of return to a future in the United States. His wife remarried and the new couple moved to another state with the deportee's children. The deportee lost track of his former wife and his children and now lives only with the illusion of becoming reunited with his children, but no one knows if or when.

To be sure, detentions and deportations do not affect in the same way all immigrants living in illegality; racial distinctions are created through the implementation of these policies. Latinos/as have become overwhelmingly targeted, which suggests an increasing reliance on legal status as a proxy for race (Møller 2014). For instance, whereas in 1992 Latinos/as were only 23 percent of offenders charged with unlawful entry, in 2012 they made up 48 percent of their total (Light, Lopez and Gonzalez-Barrera 2014).

Overwhelmingly, immigrants who are detained and deported belong to four immigrant groups: Guatemalans, Hondurans, Mexicans, and Salvadorans, with Mexicans constituting the great majority. According to Golash-Boza and Hondagneu-Sotelo (2013: 274), "between 1993 and 2011 ... there was a 10-fold increase in the number of Mexican deportees, and a 12-fold increase in the number of Central American deportees." The authors note that during this period the deportations of Asian and European immigrants increased fourfold and those of African and Caribbean immigrants only doubled.

Guatemalan, Honduran, Mexican, and Salvadoran immigrants may be at higher risk of detention and deportation because, given today's legal structures, there are high numbers of undocumented persons among them. Even so, these groups are vastly overrepresented among detainees and deportees. Of the approximately 11.4 million undocumented immigrants in the United States recorded in 2012, it is estimated that 52 percent are of Mexican origin (a decline from 56 percent in 2007) (Passel, Cohn, and Gonzalez-Barrera 2013). However, in the same year, 73 percent of all deportees were Mexican nationals, 9 percent were Guatemalan (even though they

constituted 5 percent of the undocumented population), 8 percent
were Hondurans (even though they constituted 3 percent of the
undocumented population), and 4 percent were Salvadorans (but
they made up 6 percent of the undocumented population) (US
Department of Homeland Security 2012). In contrast, that same
year, Filipinos/as made up 3 percent of the undocumented population but comprised 0.1 percent of deportees; Indians constituted
2 percent of the undocumented population, but were 0.1 percent
of deportees; and South Koreans, who were 2 percent of the
undocumented population, made up only 0.07 percent of deportees. These figures reflect the lopsided enforcement practices that
affect Latino immigrant families disproportionately and demand
attention to the racialization of these practices (Vaquera, Aranda,
and Gonzales 2014). As Douglas Massey (n.d.) observes, the
race-based enforcement system today has come to affect Latinos/
as in ways similar to those in which the criminal justice system
has impacted blacks. Consequently, the racialization of Latinos/
as through immigration law today will contribute to exacerbating
inequalities—with long-term consequences for this group.

As enforcement has expanded from the Mexico–US border to
the interior of the country (Kanstroom 2007), so too have com-
plaints of racial profiling and related discrimination, for instance
in Arizona. However, this is also the case in new rural immigrant
destinations in the Midwest and Intermountain West, whose
demographics are predominantly white European (Maldonado
2014). In these contexts, Latinos/as are conspicuously marked
both by their skin color and by their language (Licona and
Maldonado 2013; Schmalzbauer 2014). In her research in rural
Iowa, Maldonado observes the "hypervisibility" of Latinos/as
via their racialization in public spaces. She found that, due to this
hypervisibility, they tried to stay out of the public eye, avoiding
participation in community institutions and living in a constant
state of fear (Maldonado 2014). Schmalzbauer (2014) found
the same phenomenon in rural Montana, where Latinos/as com-
plained about the "impossibility of anonymity" in a place where
the public gaze is constantly focused on the difference that they
represent. In both Iowa and Montana, the conflation between

the Latino/a element and criminality meant that even authorized Latinos/as were burdened by their racialization, a situation that has become common in other states across the country (see Adler 2006; Santos and Menjívar 2013). Ironically, while Latinos/as are hypervisible in new rural destinations, they remain invisible to mainstream institutions and civic activities like electoral politics and jury selection, which persistently exclude them (Vaquera et al. 2014).

The contemporary detention and deportation regime is also highly gendered, as the overwhelming majority of detainees and deportees are men (Golash-Boza and Hondagneu-Sotelo 2013), especially Latinos. Deportations are traumatic, as men report being stripped of their dignity and their importance as providers and protectors in their families (Golash-Boza 2014). Jaime, an undocumented Mexican husband and father of a new baby, was detained and eventually deported in 2007. The language he uses to describe his deportation symbolizes how he felt his detention to be an attack on his dignity in general.

> they treat you as if you were a delinquent. When they detained me they put me through the process as if I were a criminal and one feels powerless because you have not done anything wrong. It is ridiculous that they stop us for doing nothing wrong, that we have to go to jail just for going to work. They detain us like we are criminals, like those who do drugs ... It's like they take your courage away. (Schmalzbauer 2014: 56)

The persistent threat of deportation weighs heavily on undocumented Latinos/as, as they are particularly targeted. They worry not so much for their own safety as about what a deportation would mean for the well-being of their families. Women are not spared. They are almost always left as the sole support when their partner is deported (Dreby 2015; Schmalzbauer 2014). The most immediate and often devastating burden for the female partners of male deportees is economic (Dreby 2015). As they lack the legal ability to apply for emergency relief, the entire family suffers.

Das Gupta (2014) argues that, when detentions and deportations are focused on immigrant men, traditional gender roles are

socially reproduced in immigrant families. Since gender constructions prioritize women's reproductive labor over that of men's,
there is little public outcry when men are arrested and removed
from their families, while public sympathies are immediately
ignited when mothers are removed. Yet testimonies from detained
men show that they suffer because they have been removed from
the care work they were doing for their families. This finding challenges gendered stereotypes that might covertly be at the base of
what Golash-Boza and Hondagneu-Sotelo (2013) term a "gendered removal system."

Importantly, while some might assume that undocumented
immigrants are recent arrivals, in 2012 half of the approximately
11 million undocumented immigrants had been in the United
States for at least 13 years: 62 percent had been in the country for
over one decade, and about one fifth (21 percent) had been in the
country for two decades or more (Passel, D'Vera Cohn, Krogstad,
and Gonzalez-Barrera 2014). Furthermore, over one third of
undocumented adults (38 percent) lived with their US-born children. And there are approximately 5.5 million children in the
country who have at least one undocumented parent. About 4.5
million of these children are US citizens (Passel and Cohn 2009).
Moreover, undocumented immigrant parents with US-born children have lived in the United States for a median of 15 years,
longer than the median estimate of 12 years spent in the country
by all undocumented immigrants (Passel et al. 2014). These figures
reveal that the undocumented population, particularly those who
are parents of US citizens, are a settled population, being socially
embedded in their families and communities.

Therefore deportations have severe consequences beyond the
level of individual deportees. The length of time for which deportees are barred from reentering is determined by how long they
have resided in the country without documents; their mode of
entry; the type of contact they have had with the authorities; and
the reason for deportation. Deportees who entered the country
without inspection (EWIs) are barred from reentry for three years
if they resided in the United States between 180 and 364 days and
for 10 years if they resided in the country without authorization

Families and Immigration Law

for 365 days or longer; and they get prison sentences of 20 years or they are barred for life if they have been deported previously, because deportation itself constitutes a felony and thus triggers a bar to readmission (see the Immigration and Naturalization Act of 2006, 8 USC § 1182(a)(9)). And, with the expansion of crimes for which immigrants, both undocumented and legal permanent resident, can be deported, deportations related to criminal activity have increased (Menjívar and Kanstroom 2014).

Furthermore, Section 245 (i), or the LIFE Act Provision (245i) that allowed undocumented immigrants classified as EWIs to adjust their status within the United States, expired in 2000 (it was extended until April 30, 2001). Consequently, EWIs who would have the opportunity to regularize their status (say, through a family member who can petition for them) must leave the country; but at that point the bars on reentry become activated. In practice such a person may not be able to return for 10 years or longer.[15] This can be avoided if the person files an affidavit stating that not returning to the United States will cause extreme hardship for their US citizen spouse (children are not considered for this); but the document must be filed once the person is already in the country of origin, which means that the person risks being unable to return if the affidavit is not approved. This aspect of the law contributes enormously to family separations today, as certain immigrant families (those belonging to the four national groups overly represented in detentions and deportations) can in principle remain separated indefinitely (Enchautegui and Menjívar 2015).

Notably, there are racialized consequences through the bars on readmission (see also Gomberg-Muñoz 2015), as these only apply to EWIs—in other words, those more likely to have crossed the Mexico–US border. Visa overstayers, who are more likely to be middle class (because they can obtain a visa to immigrate) and to originate in countries other than Mexico and Central America, do not face the same bars. In practice, these bars affect immigrants who must cross the border and do not have resources to come in with a visa. This racialized and classed system applies overwhelmingly to poor and working-class Mexican and Central American immigrants, sustaining the racialization process that clearly also plays out in the enforcement of detention and deportation among these groups. While nothing in the language of these immigration laws singles out Central Americans and Mexicans, the lack of access to visas and other restrictions, combined with political and economic turmoil in the region, makes them most likely to be categorized as EWIs and therefore to suffer the brunt of the criminalization of immigrants through immigration law and enforcement practices.

In this context of increased enforcement, many children, especially those from the national origins targeted, are being left without parents. For instance, in the first six months of 2011 alone more than 46,000 mothers and fathers of US citizen children were deported (Wessler 2011). In the face of deportation, families have to decide to either send the children back to the countries of origin, to avoid separation from the parents, or make arrangements for the children to remain in the United States with the remaining parent or other relatives.[16] A report on research based on cases from six locations across the United States and conducted by Chaudry et al. (2010) examined the consequences of parental arrest, detention, and deportation on the children of Mexican, Guatemalan, Salvadoran, and Haitian immigrants; it noted the serious threats that parent–child separations pose for the children's present well-being and long-term development.

In some cases children of deported parents have been transferred to Child Protective Services, and sometimes parents have lost parental rights in the process. An undocumented Guatemalan immigrant mother who was arrested during a workplace raid at a poultry processing plant in Missouri lost her parental rights to her seven-month old son (Maddali 2014). She received a mandatory two-year sentence upon pleading guilty to identity theft because she worked with a fake social security number. The judge deemed her unfit as a parent when she did not show up to the hearing because she was in immigration detention. When her parental rights were terminated, the judge granted a local couple the right to formally adopt the child. This may not be an isolated case, however, as there were approximately 5,100 children in foster care in 2011 due to the detention or deportation of their parents (Wessler 2011).

Mixed-Status Families

Given the complexities of the contemporary immigration system—both in its legislative and in its enforcement components—some family members are admitted legally into the country and others are not, and there are varying waiting times for applications to be adjudicated. Thus, it is not unusual to find members of immigrant families in different legal statuses—what Fix and Zimmerman (2001) called "mixed-legal status families."[17] A parent who arrived first in the United States may be a legal permanent resident, or perhaps already a naturalized US citizen. In turn s/he may sponsor his or her spouse who, as a result, may have obtained a temporary work permit while his or her legal permanent residence is being processed. The children may include a combination of US-born citizens and undocumented immigrants. As legal status has become increasingly consequential for immigrants' access to goods and services (see Sousa-Rodriguez forthcoming), individuals in mixed-status families may have vastly different experiences and prospects for the future (we return to this point in Chapter 6). And, according to the Pew Research Center (2013), at least 9 million individuals live in mixed-status families. These figures change, of course, as people move from one status to another, given that these legal designations are neither fixed nor intrinsic to certain immigrant families.

The Umaña family, originally from El Salvador and now residing in Phoenix, Arizona, exemplifies the potential consequences of living in mixed-status families (Menjívar 2008). Each of the five members holds a different legal status. Carlos, the father, applied for legalization through the Nicaraguan Adjustment and Central American Relief Act (NACARA), a law put in effect in 1997 that secures special dispensation for Guatemalans and Salvadorans, and is now a permanent legal resident. It took so long for him to regularize his status that his two sons turned 21 during the process, which meant that their applications were moved to a lower priority category in family reunification. Carlos was able to petition for Isabel, his wife, but she spent approximately six

years regularizing her status. Their oldest daughter, Marisa, submitted her NACARA application and was still waiting for it to be
adjudicated at the time Menjívar interviewed her in 2002. In the
case of one of the sons, Israel, the paperwork got lost twice in the
immigration offices, but after years of waiting he finally received a
social security card. The other son, Federico, married a US citizen
and received a social security card that allowed him to enroll in a
program that would train him in law enforcement. Federico is the
only member of the family who does not have a red stamp on his
social security card that reads "not valid for employment," and
this fact affords him opportunities that the others do not have.

As a result of the legal complexities that configure individuals'
legality differently, it is estimated that more than three quarters
of the children of immigrants are US citizens and one third live
in mixed-status families (Capps and Fortuny 2006; Fortuny,
Capps, Simms, and Chaudry 2009). The UndocuScholars Project
(Teranishi, Suárez-Orozco, and Suárez-Orozco 2015: 6) noted the
following situation, among college students who received DACA:

> The majority of the undocumented college students live in mixed-
> status households. A large percentage of participants (64.1 percent)
> reported that at least one member of their household had attained
> citizenship status or was born into it. The majority reported having
> at least one documented sibling (59.9 percent) or that one or both
> parents were documented (13.0 percent). More than half of the partic-
> ipants (55.9 percent) reported personally knowing someone who had
> been deported. Fifty-two of our participants (5.7 percent) reported
> that their parents had been deported and another 29 respondents (3.2
> percent) reported that a sibling had been deported.

In many mixed-status families, insecurity spreads regardless of whether all members are undocumented or not (Dreby
2012; Rodriguez and Hagan 2004; Suárez-Orozco, Yoshikawa,
Teranishi, and Suárez-Orozco 2011; Yoshikawa 2011). For
example, 20-year-old Nayeli grew up with a documented Mexican
immigrant mother and an undocumented father and had to keep
her father's undocumented status a secret in her conservative
hometown (Abrego forthcoming). When Abrego asked her what

was the hardest part of growing up in a mixed-status family, she stated:

> The silence ... when it comes to talking about it with people that I trust, it's hard just to even talk about it. It's hard for me to even admit that my father is undocumented. I've kept it a secret for so long, and I feel like it's my secret and I don't want to tell people about it. It's the way I internalize it. We do it to protect my dad. (Abrego forthcoming)

Mixed-status families also experience other consequences of immigration policies, as when gender inequalities map onto the differential legal statuses of spouses. For instance, when a husband has petitioned for his undocumented wife through a family reunification visa and a situation of domestic violence arises in the couple, the husband sometimes threatens the woman with stopping the legalization process if she reports the violence to the police (Salcido and Adelman 2004). Or, if siblings do not share the same legal status, there can be tension and resentment when US citizen children have access to more resources and opportunities than their undocumented or temporarily protected siblings.[18] Stratified access to health care on the basis of legal status (Chavez 2012; Sousa-Rodriguez forthcoming) means that parents have to provide what seems like preferential treatment for some children, owing to their legal status (Menjívar and Abrego 2009).

Conclusion

In this chapter we aimed to demonstrate how the contemporary immigration system shapes the experiences of immigrant families, their ability to reside together, and their social position, with all its consequences, and how it impacts the length of separation for families who live across borders. We have shown that, whereas family reunification law and policies are based on the ideal of keeping families together, in the contemporary context of enforcement this legislation often contributes to keeping families apart (see Enchautegui and Menjívar 2015). We have called attention to the increasing significance of temporary legal statuses, as these are expanded and affect immigrant families' composition and dynamics in various ways. And we have called attention to the consequences of the immigration regime—in its legislative and enforcement sides—as it impacts dramatically the families of immigrants from Mexico and Central America, based on classed and racialization practices.

In mixed-status families, laws that supposedly target only undocumented immigrants actually have consequences for all members. Laws force partners in unions and parents and children to live across borders over prolonged periods; multiply families' vulnerability when all members are undocumented and residing together; and complicate family relationships when only one or a few members have a tenuous status but reside with members who enjoy more rights and protections.

Whether families live apart or together, US immigration policies and contemporary enforcement practices contextualize their day-to-day lives and relationships as well as their long-term prospects. Laws and enforcement practices can limit parents' authority while adding responsibilities for parents and children. Because these laws and practices separate partners or impose burdens when families live together, parents' roles are altered and children often carry part of the burden. As a result, the immigration regime of today reconstitutes dynamics within families and alters their structure. Tenuous and liminal legal statuses, moreover, prevent immigrants from petitioning for partners and children and block access to social services for adults and children even when the latter are legally eligible, as we will discuss in Chapter 6.

Contemporary immigration laws and policies reshape immigrant families, determine their efforts to thrive, and stratify the life chances of family members. Those who qualify for legalization are more likely to access basic resources and will have an entirely different experience on the path to mobility. Those who do not qualify, on the other hand, live through prolonged periods of vulnerability (Menjívar and Abrego 2012) and face structural barriers to their incorporation. Importantly, these challenges are mediated by other axes of inequality, including social class, gender, and generation—the themes of the next three chapters.

3

Immigrant Families and Social Class

Introduction

We were always poor in Mexico, but we never suffered from hunger because my father planted crops, and we always had a little cow, a little pig, some chickens, so we didn't go hungry.... If my son were here, he would cry telling you about how poor we've been [in the US], but at least we've had shelter.... We used to sleep in a garage ... the rats were our neighbors because they would jump ... all around us. Sometimes I would not sleep, watching that they wouldn't bite my baby. I would stay up until the sleep beat me. And sometimes we would wake up and there would be dead rats under us. But that's the place we could afford because it was $150 per month.

Abrego field notes, 2014

Social class—the designation of social status and its associated financial circumstances and opportunity structures—is a central and complex factor shaping migration and settlement experiences for immigrant families. In the interview above, Hilda describes how her experience of poverty shifted before and after migration. Earlier in her narrative she had shared with Abrego that in Mexico, while their basic housing and food necessities were met, access to education was extremely limited and she wanted her children to attend high school. She and her family lived off the land, with meager wages from various types of domestic work. In the United States she continued to be poor. Her undocumented status led to a different type of poverty—one that allowed her children to graduate from public high schools, but that left them often hungry, unable to purchase food. Unlike in Mexico, in Los Angeles most of her wages were used for housing, and they could only afford unsanitary, overcrowded spaces. Both experiences of poverty were difficult, but in different ways.

Sociologists have long debated the meaning and relevance of social class (Lareau 2003; Lareau and Conley 2010). In its broadest sense, social class is a designation of social status that is generated by one's relationship to economic capital. Though economically grounded, class also has important social and cultural implications (Bourdieu 1984); it is related to identity, belonging, and family life. For immigrant families, US immigration policies make it likely that social class will overlap in patterned ways with national origin. Lingxin Hao (2010) observes that preferential treatment by US immigration policies leads to inequalities that depend on nationality, but also to inequalities among immigrants of the same ethnicity, so that immigrants who are advantaged by policies of reception end up doing better socioeconomically even than the native born. In this way families are racialized according to their class-based resources and backgrounds. In the US context of race relations, however, social class is often expressed in ways that intersect with race and, as a result, we tend to perceive differences as being based solely on race. And, although the familiar narrative of immigration is one of people arriving with nothing and working their way up the socioeconomic ladder through the generations, there is significant social class diversity among immigrants that explains diverse outcomes in the settlement processes. In this chapter we use social class as a lens through which to examine immigrant families' access to resources and opportunities, and we analyze how social class position impacts the integration process and the meanings immigrant families ascribe to diverse daily life experiences.

Social class shapes the experiences of immigrant families in myriads of ways. It affects families' reasons for migration as well as the migratory process itself (Abrego 2014; George 2005; Gu 2012; Sladkova 2010). It influences families' modes of incorporation into the United States (Menjívar 2000; Rumbaut 2005;

55

Zhou and Bankston 1998), the ways transnationalism shapes family life (Abrego 2014; Dreby 2010; Schmalzbauer 2005), the roles individuals play within their families, and the relationships between family members (Schmalzbauer 2008; Thai 2014; Vallejo 2012). The values and aspirations family members hold are also determined in large part by the economic opportunities connected to social class position (Hirsch 2003). As the experiences of, and meanings attached to, social class are malleable, being influenced by geographic position, generation, and gender among other social markers, family members may develop divergent goals, values, and expectations (Carling 2008; Schmalzbauer 2008). In this chapter we look at social class in its relationship with the roles, dynamics, strategies, and meanings that develop in contemporary immigrant families in the United States.

The chapter unfolds in four sections. We first explore how social class shapes family migration decisions, the path to immigration, and the experiences that characterize the journey. We then explore how social class informs family formation and influences parenting strategies. Third, we turn to the relationship between social class and opportunities for upward mobility within and among immigrant families. In this section we pay special attention to the intersections between family, social class, and formative institutions, namely schools and social services. Finally, we explore the unique ways in which social class is experienced among transnational families.

Social Class as a Platform for Family Migration

Social class is one of the most powerful factors that determine why, how, and when people migrate. Most often, the very poor do not have the resources necessary for migration. It is therefore those who have some resources, who can pull together the money to fund authorized or unauthorized travel, who are the more common migrants. Among members of the middle class, those who view migration as one of various forms of investment designed to increase their wealth are likely to migrate, as are people whose middle-class status is slowly eroding in their home countries. Migration and settlement experiences vary greatly depending on the level of families' financial and other class-based resources.

The social class position that migrants occupy in their homeland shapes their motives and modes of migration in important ways. Over the past few decades, international trade policies, structural adjustment programs, and persistent economic crises in poor countries have disrupted traditional modes of subsistence and weakened the social safety net of poor and working-class families in some regions of the world (Benería 2003; Sassen 1998). In response, many families that have experienced declining quality of life have turned to international migration as a survival and mobility strategy (Abrego 2014; Boehm 2012; Dreby 2010; Schmalzbauer 2004). The same global economic forces motivating the migration of the poor and of working-class people have simultaneously increased migration flows of high-skilled and high-wage workers into global cities around the world (Sassen 2008). In this class-bifurcated global economy, lower- and working-class workers migrate for survival, to maintain their lifestyle, to obtain resources that their countries' governments do not provide, for mobility, and for family reunification, whereas high-skilled workers tend to migrate to enhance their careers and increase their wealth (Chao 2013; Gu 2012). Thus reasons for migration reflect individuals' assessment of where they are and where they would like to be with regard to socioeconomic standing. This kind of assessment produces a motivation for migration that Stark and Taylor (1989) call "relative deprivation."

Furthermore, social class position in the home country often determines the mechanisms by which individuals and families migrate. For instance, wealthy migrants from around the world can acquire investor visas and can qualify for legal permanent residency status.[1] International students and high-skilled workers from middle- or upper-class backgrounds typically go to the United States with visa in hand (George 2005; Gu 2012). Middle-class immigrants can sometimes avail themselves of visas through employment or family reunification. The working class and the poor, on the other hand, are more likely to travel without visas, thus becoming part of the undocumented population—if they are able to successfully complete the journey (Abrego 2014; Boehm 2012; Dreby 2010; Menjívar 2000).

Although some class diversity is evident among migrants from all over the world, in recent decades there has been a concentration of middle-class and upper-middle-class migrants from a handful of Asian countries. At the other end of the spectrum, most of the poorer migrants come from the countries closest to the United States—Mexico, Guatemala, Honduras, and El Salvador. This class-based bifurcation is reproduced through immigration policies and enforcement practices that cumulatively benefit groups seemingly along racial lines. The disparities, though initially based on class inequalities, become intertwined with legal and racial inequalities that can essentialize entire racial groups of immigrants.

International migration is an expensive affair no matter the process by which it happens. Therefore, perhaps counterintuitively, people from the poorest countries or the poorest sectors within countries are the least likely to migrate (Massey et al. 1993). When those with fewer resources do attempt to cross international borders, they do so without basic financial, legal, or social support. Among Honduran migrants, for example, lack of resources makes it difficult to succeed in reaching the United States (Sladkova 2010). Also, migrants with limited resources are more likely to experience abuse and trauma during their journey (Abrego 2014; Martínez 2013; Sladkova 2010). For these reasons, the socioeconomic standing of potential migrants affects their likelihood of obtaining a visa; hence they resort to undertaking a financially and physically costly journey without a visa. This means that they must travel by land or by sea, as in the case of migrants arriving in the United States from Asia or the Caribbean, and usually under extremely perilous conditions. Travel by land from Central America could cost $6,000 or more in 2013, and travel by sea from Asia can cost $10,000 or more. Such high costs explain the stratification of transportation. Sladkova (2010) found that Hondurans who traveled by land but had relatively more resources were able to pay a smuggler (and "good" smugglers charged more). Those who had less money (or almost no resources at all) were forced to undertake the treacherous journey on their own, riding "the Beast," as the infamous freight train has come to be known. This is one of the most dangerous forms of transportation that migrants take in the world today.

Migrants are able to finance these journeys with loans from relatives in the United States or from lenders in the countries of origin who specialize in doing business with migrants (see McKenzie and Menjívar 2011; Menjívar 2000; Stoll 2013). Migrants are expected to repay these loans soon after arrival, especially when they have put a home or a plot of land in the home country as collateral for the loan (Abrego 2014; McKenzie and Menjívar 2011; Stoll 2013). This situation contributes to straining a family's socioeconomic conditions, an effect that can reverberate for years, as these migrants' incomes upon arrival tend to be low but must be stretched to cover loans acquired to pay for the trip, send remittances, and survive in the new context.

Since social class often determines the level of formality and security with which migrants are able to travel, it can influence whether families move as a unit or in a "chain migration" over time, and whether and for how long they will live divided by borders. Because unauthorized migration is expensive and dangerous, poor and working-class families often have to decide which family member will attempt the journey—a decision most commonly determined by the criterion of who has the greatest wage-earning potential in the United States (Schmalzbauer 2005). In such cases the family becomes separated for the sake of securing income for its own survival. Among poor Salvadoran immigrant families, for example, parents had to make the decision of whether to stay in El Salvador with their children and struggle daily with survival or to leave children behind and go in search of better wages (Abrego 2014). Deciding in favor of the latter meant traveling without legal authorization and without the guarantee of return.

Poor families have few paths to formalize their emigration. Guest worker programs are one of these few options. The H-2A and H-2B visa programs, as detailed in Chapter 2, permit a limited number of low-skilled agricultural and service workers to migrate to the United States with temporary authorization. It is typically men who migrate on H-2A or H-2B visas, while women and children must stay behind, as demanded by visa regulations. It is important to note that increasingly women are being recruited for H-2B visas, especially for work in seafood processing (Griffith 2006). Family reproductive and productive work is therefore rigidly divided by borders (Hwang and Parreñas 2010; Schmalzbauer 2015). Given the low wages that predominate in work available to H-2A and H-2B visa holders, few temporary workers are able to arrange for their unauthorized family members to accompany them; and upward mobility eludes most. As a Mexican H-2A guestworker told Schmalzbauer during her field research,

> with the H-2A visa we have the security of a job ... In Mexico there is no work. So we say, ok, we'll go to the United States for eight months, and this is how we will maintain our families. But listen ... this is not a good job ... But we are eating and that counts for something. (Schmalzbauer 2015: 217)

Thus, temporary visa programs are class-specific. Social class inequalities are especially evident when comparing the affordances of H-2A and H-2B visas with those of H-1B visas (see Chapter 2 for details): H-1B families are overtly advantaged over H-2A and H-2B families (Hwang and Parreñas 2010). As the comparison between the demographics of H-2A and H-2B, and H-1B visa-holding families shows, the country of origin often maps onto the social class composition of immigrant families (see Haller, Portes, and Lynch 2011). The majority of low-wage, guest worker, and undocumented labor migrants in the United States come from Latin America and the Caribbean (Passel and Cohn 2009). In contrast, the majority of high-skilled immigrant workers come from China and India. Indeed, 61 percent of Asian immigrants to the United States have bachelor's degrees—twice more than non-Asian migrants (Pew Research Center 2012). This demographic profile indicates a highly selective migration from Asia (i.e., only a select few—the educated—can engage in this financially costly migration), as is the case with migratory flows from sources that are geographically farther from the destination. On the basis of their study of Chinese and Vietnamese immigrants, sociologists Jennifer Lee and Min Zhou (2014a) refer to this phenomenon among Asian immigrants as "hyper-selectivity." This selectivity at origin translates into cumulative advantages in immigrant integration and socioeconomic mobility in the United States.[2]

One of the consequences of US immigration policies that stratify the migration experiences of groups of different national origins is that race and class often interact in ways that generate the racialization of people mostly on the basis of their class position and resources (see Ochoa 2013). This means that, while Mexican and Central American immigrants are more likely to be undocumented and to come from poor and working-class backgrounds, their inability to move up to middle-class standing within a single generation is interpreted as being inherent in their racial and cultural background (ibid.). Similarly, by comparison to Latino/a immigrants, middle-class Asian immigrants display an ability to maintain middle-class status and to increase their wealth, which is often interpreted as evidence of their cultural values (Lee and Zhou 2014a, 2014b; Louie 2004). The prevalent patterns, when viewed through a lens of US race relations, may suggest that there is something inherent in the cultures of groups of different national origins that guides their members to financial success or stagnation. But, as Vivian Louie (2004) reveals in her examination of Chinese cases, class and race matter a great deal in shaping the messages that parents give their children regarding education. It is actually social class-specific resources, cultural capital, and "hyper-selectivity" that explain the high performance of Asian immigrants in the US educational system (Lee and Zhou 2014a; Zhou and Lee 2014). Here we highlight some of the reasons behind the incorrect assumption that it is mostly cultural values that shape the prospects of immigrants in the United States.

When race and national origin are mapped onto class, differences in median economic resources for each group are overlooked, which makes it easy to gloss over the vast class distinctions within and among ethnic groups (see Fukui and Menjívar 2015). These differences also shape how and why families migrate. For example, while there may be a temptation to categorize all Asian immigrant families as being positioned favorably socioeconomically, social class is actually an important indicator of their migration paths and of the length of time for which they are separated. Gu (2012) found that social class played a major role in shaping motives for migration among Taiwanese migrants. Lower-class Taiwanese migrated for family reunification, while middle-class Taiwanese were mostly motivated to pursue higher education. Most middle-class Taiwanese migrants were graduate students when they first moved to the United States. After successfully completing their education, many settled in the United States, in order to take advantage of professional opportunities. The middle-class status of educated Taiwanese allowed them the flexibility of considering return to Taiwan as an option, and they settled in the United States as a strategy for advancement, not as a survival strategy. The opposite, however, was true among poor and working-class Taiwanese immigrants, who saw settlement as essential to their well-being and that of their families. For lower-class Taiwanese families, return was rarely an option to be considered.

Sheba George (2005) studied the class and gender patterns of migrant families that come from Kerala, India to the United States. Supported by visas to become registered nurses, women were the first to migrate. In these predominantly middle-class families, separation lasted for a few years. Once the family had accumulated sufficient savings, the father and children joined the mother in the United States. As George's study reveals, in those families that had uniquely high levels of wealth and education, the gender pattern of migration was flipped: it was typically the father who migrated first, and the rest of the family joined him soon afterward. These examples show the very many ways in which immigrant families' social class can intersect with their nationality and their gender to create multiple and divergent migration and settlement experiences.

In some cases immigration policies and the legal status conferred on immigrants can mediate and lessen the potential consequences of social class differences (see Bean, Leach, Brown, Bachmeier, and Hipp 2011). Such is the case for the Vietnamese refugee families studied in Nazli Kibria's (1993) research. Kibria found that the differentials in modes and strategies of migration were evened out by the refugee context of migration. Many Vietnamese families, rich and poor alike, fled Vietnam and lived in separation, often with some members residing in refugee camps while they reconstituted their families through reunification in the United States. US social-service agencies often facilitated family migration, as many families had lost their livelihoods in the war and in the collectivization campaigns that followed. Importantly, despite the hardships of refugee life, refugee families of all class backgrounds were guaranteed legal passage and assistance for resettlement. Perhaps Cubans, who receive legal permanent residence one year after arrival and a generous package of assistance for their resettlement through the Cuban Adjustment Act, provide the best example of how immigration policy can shape life chances.

Social class interacts with legal status, as undocumented family members often find that their social class background does not result in advantages (Bean et al. 2011). Even college-educated immigrants may be blocked from professional jobs commensurate with their experience (Abrego 2014). Throughout the course of her studies in various Central American communities, Menjívar (2000) has encountered former professionals working in low-paid jobs in restaurants or in home services. In these cases entire families are affected, because parents are unable to work in their fields of training and cannot earn higher wages to provide a better life for their families. However, the advantages that come with higher education are not entirely lost, as the parents' human capital allows them to help children navigate school requirements and to shape children's goals for higher education (Lee and Zhou 2014a, 2014b; Ochoa 2013; Zhou and Lee 2014).

Social Class, Parenting, and Divisions of Labor within Immigrant Families

Citlalli Valero Calderon, a 35-year-old upper-class Mexican, migrated with her family from their posh neighborhood in Mexico

City to the upper-middle-class suburbs of Dallas, to flee insecurity in their country. Although they have maintained most of their social class advantages after migration, they can no longer afford to pay for live-in domestic workers, who had made their lives as parents so easy in Mexico. "Life without the nanny is not very sexy," she complains, as her children run and scream wildly at the mall (Corchado 2014). Similarly, immigrant families experience a postmigration downward mobility that, in turn, shapes their family dynamics.

Since social class and its associated financial resources may fluctuate for families before migration, shortly after migration, and in the long-term process of incorporation, these changes are likely to influence parenting responsibilities and approaches. Social class influences how family members participate in the US job market, which adult family member has the highest earning power, and how many hours family members must work outside of the home to make ends meet—all of which influence the roles and approaches they adopt as parents.

Among working-class Latino families in urban and suburban southern California, Vasquez (2011) observed a "survival mode of parenting." Parents channeled most of their energy and time into securing economic provision for their children. Their poverty required them to work long hours outside the home, sacrificing time and energy they would otherwise devote to their children. In these families, the demand for female labor and income challenged gender expectations from mothers, who were considered solely as cultural educators.

Intersections of social class and the geographic context in which immigrants live impact the time parents distribute between work and family as well as the gender divides in migrant households. In her study of working-class Mexican families in rural Montana, Schmalzbauer (2014) found that, because there were few employment opportunities for low-skill migrant women, mothers spent most of their time at home, focusing their energy on parenting. Migrant fathers, on the other hand, worked long hours outside the home, which intensified the rigidity of the gender division of labor within the home. Ironically, in this case the phenomenon of "intensive mothering," which sociologist Sharon Hays (1996) associates with middle-class native-born US women, became the default experience of poor and working-class rural migrant women. In this case, however, intensive mothering was resource-strapped, not done by choice, and was accompanied by struggles associated with social isolation.

In middle- and upper-class immigrant families, there may be more flexibility in parenting and less conformity to gender roles. George (2005) found that, when Indian women migrated to the United States to work as nurses, their husbands often took over childcare responsibilities at home. When the family was reunited, men continued bearing a significant part of child care upon their arrival in the United States. This, however, should not be interpreted as a radical gender transformation. George found instead that men engaged in child care because, as accompanying spouses, they did not have legal authorization to work outside the home. As many of the nurses' husbands were employed in white-collar work in India, they experienced downward mobility after migration. In the upper-class Indian families in George's study, the men were able to find high-paying jobs in the United States and their wives stayed home with the children. In this example, social class strongly influences the gender division of labor within families.

Some middle-class families migrate specifically in order for one member to pursue graduate degrees and specializations. In such cases families may experience a change in their social class standing while the parents are full-time students. In graduate housing, for example, families may find themselves living in smaller quarters and with more limited economic resources than they had prior to migration (Chao 2013). These examples are noteworthy because they reveal the significance of social class and of its associated forms of capital in mediating the financial (and often temporary) limitations that middle-class immigrant families face upon arrival in the new country. In a study of Chinese immigrant families in a Southeastern city, Chao (2013) finds that graduate students' parents, though they experienced a temporary financial decline, were still able to use their class habitus and cultural capital to help their children fit in and thrive in school. One

Chinese immigrant mother speaks about Ping, her 14-year-old daughter, as follows:

> I took Ping to visit her school campus before classes started. I tutored her English and treasured our dinner table talks. I ordered her textbooks for home use and paid for her summer trip to France. We also went to church on Sundays. I didn't mean to impose Christianity on her. Just let her get more familiar with the ways Americans live. She didn't want to go at the first, but she went for enjoying church choral music. We went to the university gym, bookstores, libraries, grocery stores, museums, etc. I also let her be responsible for mail check. I think these activities might help her with subconscious reading practices and cultural understanding. (Chao 2013: 66)

As a highly educated middle-class immigrant, this mother understood the kinds of activities that would facilitate her daughter's integration and further development as a member of the middle class—even during a period in their lives when their financial resources were limited. Only able to afford to live in an apartment, she intentionally exposed her daughter to the practices and spaces of the middle class (see also Louie 2004; Zhou and Lee 2014).

Navigating the various transitions that come with migration, immigrant parents from advantaged social class backgrounds can draw on their financial and cultural capital to help smooth their children's settlement. In the previous example, the immigrant mother's middle-class background in Beijing meant that she had already mastered the English language before arriving in the United States. Such is typically not the case for many immigrants, especially those who arrive from working-class backgrounds. In her study of the translating practices of children in Latino immigrant families in Illinois and California, education scholar Marjorie Faulstich Orellana (2009) finds that many poor and working-class immigrant families rely heavily on children's English speaking skills to navigate both public and private matters. Immigrant parents with limited levels of education in their home countries are not likely to speak English upon migration. Developmentally, children will learn the new language much more quickly than their parents and will therefore serve as key participants in the families' day-to-day lives (see Chapter 5 for more on these children's roles). While children in such families lack the financial resources of middle-class families, by helping their families they stand to gain important social and educational skills, which in turn help them integrate in society (Katz 2014; Orellana 2009).

For workers with limited agency to choose their job or industry, feelings of dislocation may occur. Given the strong draw of low-skill immigrant labor into sectors of the economy that provide services for US professionals, immigrant families may find themselves straddling two social class worlds: their place of residence and their place of employment. Poor and working-class immigrant women in particular experience a strong pull into the care industry, where they work as nannies and housecleaners, often in the homes of middle-class and wealthy white families (Ehrenreich and Hochschild 2002; Hondagneu-Sotelo 2009).

Social Class and Mobility across the Life Course

International migration is often undertaken in a search for more opportunities and a better life for one's family. Social class shapes migrants' aspirations and potential for upward mobility. Social class standing at entry impacts the jobs and the resources that migrants can access in the host country, their financial obligations to family in the home and host country, as well as the way in which they are perceived by social brokers in schools and social services. Social class is therefore pivotal in shaping lives and family well-being from the very beginning of the migration process.

Contemporary immigrant families, like all families in the United States, confront a stratified economic opportunity structure. Deindustrialization, a weakened social welfare system, and the recent crash of the housing market have greatly harmed many US families, but particularly the working class and the poor (Massey 2014). Since the family is an institution through which advantage and disadvantage are transmitted generationally, the children of poor and working-class parents confront notable barriers to upward mobility early on in the life cycle. Poverty negatively influences child development outcomes (Brooks-Gunn and Duncan 1997; Yoshikawa 2011) and presents barriers to future economic self-sufficiency (Carlson and England 2011). On the other hand, immigrant families from advantaged pre-migration backgrounds are likely to carry on and transmit some of those benefits in human and economic capital to their children (Chao 2013; Lee and Zhou 2014a). Immigrant families' experiences of economic stratification deserve special attention, as they are molded in relation to other barriers—such as legal status, English language proficiency, racial profiling, and anti-immigrant policies (Bean et al. 2011).

When focused rather narrowly on levels of educational and occupational attainment, sociological research on immigrant assimilation is largely based on what we can consider to be post-migration class mobility. Indeed, for many years, sociologists conflated assimilation with upward mobility: the full assimilation of immigrants required those of "immigrant stock" to be indistinguishable from native-born middle-class whites in their schooling levels and earnings (Gordon 1964). More recently, sociologists have complicated the conceptualization of assimilation, suggesting that we understand the processes not as unidirectional but as segmented—a variegated path that can lead to downward or upward mobility. Segmented assimilation scholars (Portes and Zhou 1993; Portes and Rumbaut 2001) theorize that the neighborhoods in which immigrant families settle, immigration policies in the context of reception, the schools that the children attend, and the strength of the ethnic communities in which the families are situated determine the direction of immigrants' mobility (Portes and Zhou 1993).

According to Alejandro Portes and his associates, immigrants who do well are often those who are able, due to certain advantages, to move into white middle-class neighborhoods. Another successful path is that of immigrants embedded in strong ethnic enclaves that have the human and economic capital to encourage education and mechanisms of incorporation into the broader US society while simultaneously nurturing co-ethnic ties. Furthermore, these scholars argue, immigrants who settle in poor, native-born minority areas are more likely to experience downward mobility, as they assimilate into poverty, live in contexts of discrimination and racism, and adopt the negative outlooks and entrenched struggles that accompany these communities. Privilege spawns privilege, as wealthier migrants high in human capital come in with resources, tend to enjoy a positive context of reception, and integrate into more affluent enclaves.

On the other hand, poor and working-class migrants, especially undocumented ones, are likely to arrive with low levels of human capital and to face a negative context of reception, which impacts their incorporation and limits their mobility (Rumbaut 2005; Zhou and Bankston 1998). The advantages (and disadvantages) of class position are therefore cumulative and reverberate by shaping immigrants' long-term paths of incorporation.

Education scholar Vivian Louie (2012) complicates the relationship between social class and immigrant assimilation, arguing that it is not only the character of the immigrant community or the proximity of poor, minority neighborhoods that shapes the potential for upward mobility among immigrant families, but the interaction among families, institutions, and non-family support. By examining the patterns of middle-class college-educated Latinos/as in the northeastern United States, Louie finds that upward mobility can depend on numerous factors. Her research reveals the need to consider the relationship between immigrant families and the job market, schools, social services, and supportive non-ethnic individuals. Each of these can play an important role in determining why certain immigrant families or their individual members experience upward mobility, while others do not—regardless of the families' initial social class.

As noted in Chapter 2, another key factor in determining the possibilities for upward mobility is legal status (see also Bean et al. 2011; Bean, Bachmeier, Brown, van Hook, and Leach 2014). Sociologist Jody Vallejo (2012) interviewed middle-class Mexican Americans in southern California, many of whom had benefited from their own parents' middle-class advantage. Among those whose parents had little formal schooling, however, the ability to attain legal permanent residence through past immigration policies permitted families to establish businesses. Entrepreneurship then proved to be an important pathway to middle-class status, including residential integration into neighborhoods and school districts that facilitated the children's access to higher education.

Vallejo's study (2012) also reveals middle-class experiences that are unique to adult Mexican Americans whose parents continued to be poor or working class, as social class background impacts the obligations and practices of giving within families. Those who were upwardly mobile but came from poor families had multiple requests for money and support from poor family and kin.[3] Given their educational and linguistic capital (and their extended family's lack of these same resources), they were positioned to give exceptional amounts of time as "language and cultural brokers" (Vallejo 2012: 176). All this "giving back," Vallejo argues, made this generation of upwardly mobile middle-class Mexicans vulnerable. The monthly sums they supplied to parents, the extra time they spent translating and helping siblings, and their conforming to the expectation that they provide for the extended family in times of crisis translated into fewer resources for investment and wealth accumulation for themselves and their own immediate families. On the other hand, Mexican Americans whose parents were also middle class resembled white middle-class members of society, who are less likely to give money or other resources to family and kin. Thus, their lack of giving was rooted *not* in a deficit of family obligation but in the advantage of not having family in need.

Family need and position vis-à-vis resources are at the heart of forms of giving among immigrant families that impinge on mobility. Poor immigrants from countries where the economy is weak are under unique pressure to remit money and gifts to family and kin (Abrego 2014; Dreby 2010; Menjívar 2000). This obligation often means that migrants are unable to save money in the host country (McKenzie and Menjívar 2011; Schmalzbauer 2005). Thus, being poor before migration, coming from a country with a weak economy, and having limited employment opportunities in the host country, combined with obligations toward a family characterized by poverty, are factors that restrict upward mobility. Whereas family obligation is built in part on cultural and especially on gender expectations (Abrego 2014), such expectations cannot be separated from the economic context in which they are constructed (González-López 2005; Hirsch 2003; Menjívar 2000).

Notably, culture is often confused with social class in public discourses that seek to explain why some immigrant families do well while others struggle (Hsin and Xie 2014). In her research on upwardly mobile Dominican and Colombian immigrant youth, Louie (2012) found that Latino/a children are often celebrated as having more ambition than African Americans because they are immigrants, but less ambition than their Asian immigrant peers, who are often held up as "model minorities."[4] These contrasts, she notes, are constructed without interrogation of the social structural context that frames individual aspirations and the potential success of children from different ethnic and racial groups.

Despite substantial evidence that it is structure more often than culture that shapes behaviors and attitudes (see also Lee and Zhou 2014a), the two are often conflated. Ochoa (2013) found that stereotypes that construct Asians as smart and ambitious and Latinos/as as lazy and uninterested in school impact how Asian and Latino/a youth and their families are treated by teachers and administrators as well as the opportunities presented to them. In the Southern California high school where Ochoa conducted her study, poor and working-class blacks and Latinos/as were commonly tracked into non-college prep courses. They also reported experiencing overt racism from teachers. Gender intersected with race and class in shaping the stereotyping they endured. Latino and black boys were much more likely than black and Latina girls to be labeled "troublemakers." Additionally, Ochoa found that Latino/a students were often depicted by teachers and staff as "culturally deficient" (248). Asian American students, on the other hand, were praised as good students, even when their schoolwork did not always justify such characterization.

The Latino/a students at the high school in Ochoa's study tended to come from poor families, in which the children's parents had not attended college. This meant that they did not have access to the material resources or the social and cultural capital necessary to navigate a path to college. Most Asian American students, on the other hand, came from middle-class homes and had college-educated parents who were able to provide tutoring support and to make demands of teachers and administrators so as to ensure that their children strived for college. Meanwhile, staff and faculty understood school performance as a cultural phenomenon rather than as the product of social class and structures—a view that benefited Asian American students and harmed Latino/a students.

Upwardly mobile Chinese youth also benefit from their parents' participation in strong Chinese communities where information is shared about how to maneuver the educational system (Louie 2011). Moreover, their middle-class transnational networks offer economic support for upward mobility strategies. Parents in a Chinese community in Flushing, New York, intentionally invest in what they understand to be the development of their children's cultural capital (Lu 2013). Established by middle-class Chinese immigrants, the music schools in the area focus on teaching Chinese American children to play European classical music, which requires skills that these parents deem necessary for their children's future in the most selective colleges and universities (see also Lee and Zhou 2014a; Zhou and Lee 2014). In those spaces parents develop social networks that help them navigate the educational system.[5] Notably, the working-class Chinese immigrant families who participate in these ethnic spaces also benefit from the social networks at the music schools. Thus, although the success of Asian immigrants is commonly characterized as having cultural origins, it is rooted in the "hyper-selectivity" of these immigrants (Lee and Zhou 2014a, 2014b). As Lee and Zhou (2014b: 20) observe on the basis of their comparative study of Asian and Latino/a immigrants in Southern California, there "is not something essential about Chinese or Asian culture that promotes exceptional educational outcomes"; rather, Chinese or Asian immigrants thrive due to their hyper-selectivity, as they bring with them class-specific practices and cultural institutions.

Commonly legal status intersects with class, further subordinating poor immigrant families and limiting their mobility. It is believed that, because families from advantaged backgrounds are better able to migrate with legal authorization, their prospects for family well-being and mobility in the host country will be enhanced. However, this is not always the case. Blocked entry to living-wage jobs, coupled with increased deportations, has been especially damaging to immigrant families of Latinos/as who, according to Massey (2014: 1750), "have joined African Americans in the underclass at the bottom of the socio-economic hierarchy." Massey further argues that, because of the family context in which illegality is experienced, Latinos/as have become "the most vulnerable and exploitable population in the USA today" (1750).

The potential for mobility among undocumented workers and their families is limited not only by low wages and the lack of economic and legal protections, but also by the fear of deportation, which can discourage them from seeking services for which they are eligible (Menjívar and Abrego 2012; Schmalzbauer 2014). Children of documented parents (or refugees) have greater opportunity for upward socioeconomic mobility, as they have access to better schools, social protections, and public benefits (Bean et al. 2011; Bean et al. 2014; Vallejo 2012; Yoshikawa 2011). On the other hand, children of undocumented parents, even when born in the United States, have to cope with numerous limitations in access to basic social services and opportunities, because their parents are afraid of contacting agencies in order to request services to which their children are entitled (Yoshikawa 2011).

Conley and Glauber (2008: 197) remind us that "family is a pivotal player in the assignment of social status and works not in a vacuum but in reaction to the resources within and the constraints and opportunities without." This becomes especially salient for mixed-status families in which resources for siblings with different legal statuses are stratified within and beyond the family (see also Conley 2004). Abrego and Menjívar (2011) highlight the challenges that confront parents when one child has access to health care via the entitlements of citizenship and another child does not. Societal constraints on class mobility may intensify inequality among mixed-status siblings—as for instance when children with different legal statuses move into adulthood and one has access to college while the other does not (Abrego 2006; Gonzales 2011; see also Conley 2004).

The last example is especially poignant when we consider research showing that the barriers to mobility among poor immigrant families are significant, especially for undocumented members (Hagan 1994; Menjivar 2000; Schmalzbauer 2014); mobility arises in families when children have access to higher education (Vallejo 2012). In this vein, Jiménez (2010), whose research focuses on Mexican American families, argues that we must look beyond two generations to fully capture mobility trends. In their longitudinal study of Mexican Americans, which carries into multiple generations, Telles and Ortiz (2008) concluded that the racialized experiences of those who did not achieve upward mobility in the first or second generation were likely to keep them in the same poor and working-class positions that their ancestors had.

Along these lines, Louie (2011) found that those immigrant children who experienced upward mobility shared with their parents the optimistic view that they could become successful in school and life. Therefore they had close relationships with their parents and enjoyed strong parental supervision—all of which inspired them to want to please their parents. While on the face of it we might attribute success to what parents do, social class influenced how parents felt when interacting with their children's school. Poorer parents were more likely to have language barriers and to feel culturally excluded from formal education. Therefore they had to work extra hard to overcome these types of marginalization, which also shaped their relationships with their children.

Social class also determines where immigrant families live, which in turn influences socioeconomic mobility and the ease or difficulty with which it is achieved. In her qualitative study of Dominican and Colombian upwardly mobile youth, Louie (2011) found that, whereas most of the families were working class, Dominicans tended to live in racially segregated neighborhoods where housing and schooling were low quality and crime was rampant. Colombians, on the other hand, tended to settle in predominantly white, middle-class areas where crime levels were low and the schools strong, which made their journey toward upward mobility smoother than the Dominicans'. Likewise, in another comparative study of immigrant parents in New York, Yoshikawa

(2011) found striking contrasts between Dominicans, comprised of a high proportion of blacks, and Mexican immigrants. Even though the Dominicans had a lower percentage of undocumented immigrants than their Mexican counterparts, both groups had similarly low socioeconomic status. These intra-Latino/a comparisons bring out key insights about how social class, legal status, and race intersect.

Families Divided by Class and Borders

Just as social class is an indicator of whether a migrant will journey with authorized or unauthorized status, it is also an indicator of whether families are able to move together or whether they must live separated for indefinite periods of time. For those families that are divided by migration, social class likely determines whether, when, and under what circumstances they are able to reunite, as well as the process of and risk entailed by reunification.

As mentioned in our introduction, most immigrant families experience a period of separation across national borders. During separation, family members in the United States send money home in the form of remittances designated to support those who stay behind. But remittances do not only represent material betterment; they often acquire emotional meaning for those involved (Abrego 2014; McKay 2007; McKenzie and Menjívar 2011). However, the coupling of monetary remittances with the shifts in meaning and expectations that come with migration can spark divisions within transnational families, especially those separated for extended, if not interminable, lengths of time (Carling 2008; Menjívar 2012; Schmalzbauer 2008). Class divisions within families are similarly influenced by the intersection of their members' geographic position, gender, and generation (Thai 2014).

Transnational families are commonly characterized by structural inequalities that are shaped in part by each member's geographic location (Dreby 2006; Parreñas 2005; Pessar and Mahler 2003). Within such families, the distance between members—coupled with geographically based divergence in ordinary, everyday experiences—can accentuate differences in one's access to resources, mobility, and decision-making (Landolt and Da 2005; McKenzie and Menjívar 2011). Those in working-class families who remain in the home country, for example, sometimes become dependent on the remittances their family member(s) send, while family members in the United States are burdened with the responsibility of maintaining remittance flows from a position of low-wage and insecure employment (Abrego 2014; Dreby 2010; Menjívar 2000; Pribilsky 2007).

In his ethnographic exploration of low-wage transnational Vietnamese families, Hung Thai (2014) shows the implications of this divergence for resource access, as well as the meanings that individual family members attach to class identities. For example, when migrants from transnational families travel between their home and the host country, they can shift social class positions as they change geographic locations. Social class is malleable and dynamic, and its complexity is exacerbated by migrants' ability to translate incomes from low-wage labor in the United States into high-income living when they return, in this case, to Vietnam. This situation is found among other immigrant groups as well (see Mahler 1998). Transnational Filipinas, for example, experience disruptions in their social class identities when, as immigrants, they take jobs as domestics, even though most of them have post-secondary education from the Philippines (Parreñas 2001).

The story of social class in a transnational context is more complicated still when we explore how economic and social remittances can alter the consumption practices and expectations of non-migrant family members, leading to a shift in class identity (Schmalzbauer 2005, 2008; Thai 2014). Non-migrant Haitian children who received remittances from their parents, for example, were much more optimistic about school and their future than children who did not receive remittances (Glick Schiller and Fouron 2001). Similarly, Honduran children in receipt of remittances from parents developed middle-class aspirations that were shaped by the schooling and consumer practices that these remittances afforded them (Schmalzbauer 2008). These children tended to know very little about the working or living conditions of their parents in the United States, most of whom were undocumented and struggling financially. In this respect, a class divide had developed within such families—a divide that was intensified by misunderstandings among family members about the realities of each other's daily life (Menjívar and Abrego 2009).

In addition to complicating the meanings and experiences of social class within family, class position shapes how immigrants are able to stay connected to loved ones in their home countries. George (2005) found that middle-class Indian immigrants traveled often to India to attend weddings, funerals, and other important family events. Working-class immigrants, on the other hand, were prohibited by their lack of resources from maintaining the same level of involvement in their extended families' lives.

However, for many poor and working-class immigrant families, it is the intersection of legal status and social class that prevents transnational visits. In her ethnography of Mexican immigrant families, Schmalzbauer (2014) showed that many immigrants had to miss funerals, weddings, quinceañeras (special parties for a girl's fifteenth birthday), and graduations because of a mix of low income and undocumented status. As a result, families were afflicted with a suffering that was rooted in the structural violence of poverty and in the legal violence of family rupture (see Menjívar and Abrego 2012). Victoria, whose father and brother died in the same year in Mexico, told Schmalzbauer this:

> I may be a good mother, but I have failed as a daughter. I can't believe that I could not be there with my father when he died, and that I cannot be there now to support my mother through her own grief. We come to get ahead for our children, but in doing so we have to fail in our responsibilities as daughters, siblings and family members. The pain I feel is almost unbearable. (Schmalzbauer, field notes 2014)

Often the sacrifice that poor and working-class immigrants must make when they leave family behind is accompanied by emotional pain—on the part of both the parent and child. Poor Central American immigrant mothers who were working as domestics in California to support their children back home felt like they were "here but there," their heartache intensified by the charge of caring for someone else's children when they could not afford to care directly for their own (Hondagneu-Sotelo and Avila 1997; see also Menjívar 2000). Their social class position and the associated financial barriers prevented them from doing otherwise. In these cases, despite achievements related to better schooling and upward socioeconomic mobility, the lengthy separations present significant challenges when parents and children eventually reunite (Menjívar 2006a).

Conclusion

Social class is a fundamental social marker for all facets of life, and this is no different for immigrant families. The economic, social, and cultural resources shaped by a family's social class standing determine the reasons and modes of migration, whether families migrate together or live divided by borders, the actual nature of the journey, and where and how immigrants integrate into the United States. The process of migration, however, can lead to unique shifts in social class for families. Some of these shifts—particularly for middle-class families who experience downward mobility upon migration—may be temporary, as families get settled. Other shifts—from poor to middle class—may be gradual, taking place across one or more generations. In all of these cases, social class intersects with legal status, race, and other key social markers to shape individual families' experiences along the social class spectrum.

4

Gender and Immigrant Families

Gender refers to the system of social rules and expectations that informs individual behavior and to the structural opportunities and barriers that shape how males and females live. It is a central constitutive element in all human life (Lorber 1994), and a complex aspect of family life (Ferree 1990). Immigrant family life is no exception. Gender may take on complex expressions within immigrant families, as it may be constructed and lived across national borders. Gender ideologies, structures, and practices operate simultaneously to shape women's and men's opportunities in labor markets and in other social institutions that, in turn, shape family experiences (Abrego 2014; Abrego and Menjívar 2011; Alcalde 2010; Hagan 1994; Hondagneu-Sotelo 2003; Lutz 2010; Mahler and Pessar 2001; Salcido and Menjívar 2012; Schmalzbauer 2011). This chapter explores how gender plays out in the lives of immigrant families at different points in the migration and settlement process.

Locating Gender in Immigrant Families

While gender can refer to social psychological processes within the family, it is also a multilevel and dynamic force that shapes family life from the outside (Ferree 2010). Gender may be used to understand "socially created meanings, relationships, and identities organized around reproductive differences" (Glenn 2002: 7), to locate relationships of power external and internal to families (Ferree 2010), or to describe the ways gender is performed through social relations and interactions (West and Zimmerman 1987).

Since gender is fluid and produced through ongoing, interactional, representational, and structural processes, the behaviors considered acceptable for girls and boys, women and men, at any given moment in history can seem natural and normal (Lorber 1994; Menjívar 2011a). The role of gender, particularly as it creates and maintains inequalities, is often difficult to locate and explicate. Gendered inequalities, moreover, cut across multiple institutions (schools, employment, criminal justice, etc.) while intersecting with social categories (race, sexuality, class, etc.). Thus, gendered expectations of behavior shape individual family members' relationships with institutions as well as individuals' experiences of institutional inequalities (Ferree 2010; González de la Rocha 1994).

Gender relations and expectations of behavior within immigrant families are significantly altered in the process of migration, as the new context calls for new behaviors and practices, and new lifestyles and demands lead immigrants to undertake new roles within their families (Cantú 2009; González-López 2005). Individuals may be pushed to redefine their roles within families, since they adapt to different contexts and changing responsibilities (Boehm 2012; Hirsch 2003; Hondagneu-Sotelo 1994, 2003; Kim 2006; Pessar 2005; Schmalzbauer 2011; Smith 2006; Stephen 2007). And, while some immigrants may strive to uphold orthodox gender practices, such as a strict division of labor in the home, in spite of outside pressures that demand otherwise, gendered practices do change and women challenge and negotiate relations that afford them greater freedom and equality (Kibria 1990; Mahler and Pessar 2006).

However, changes in gender relations do not always occur in the direction of equality. Sometimes patriarchal structures are reaffirmed in the context of economic dependency, as Kibria (1990, 1993) observed among Vietnamese families in Philadelphia. Some immigrant women have gained independence and some immigrant men have taken on more chores at home (Hondagneu-Sotelo

1994; Levitt 2001; Mahler 1999). Yet such gendered negotiations are fraught with tension (Contreras and Griffith 2012; Parreñas 2005; Pessar 2005)—particularly in the context of gendered labor market opportunities and experiences (Parrado and Flippen 2005). Thus, Menjívar (1999) concluded that, even though Salvadoran immigrant women in San Francisco contributed economically to the family as much as (and sometimes more than) men, the gender division of labor in the home did not change because women did not want to challenge men's perceived authority. As this chapter will show, recent scholarship reveals that intersections of legal status, social class, ethnicity, and geographical location can undermine potential gains in gender equality in the home and generate nuanced experiences of gender relations in immigrant families.

Our goal is to integrate a gender analysis of immigrant families at the structural level, while highlighting how gender ideals inform immigrant women's and men's individual and collective agency within families. Immigrant families do not exist in a vacuum. Gendered ideals shape one's expectations about one's own and others' behavior so thoroughly and consistently that people often assume persistent patterns to be unchangeable. Within families, this can create deep-seated inequalities—including the uneven burden of child care for women and the greater decision-making power for men—that are difficult to erase, especially when families negotiate relationships across national contexts. The ways family members make decisions, share resources, develop common goals, and work together or against one another to achieve goals are informed by broader social understandings of what the proper behaviors, the acceptable desires, and the conventional spaces are—for males and females. Therefore everything—the reasons for migration, the decision-making process, the journey, and the settlement of migrant families and individual family members—is shaped by gender (Hondagneu-Sotelo 1994).

Along with having an immigrant background, individual family members are situated in multiple social locations, which shape their gender experiences (Zavella 1991). Indeed, as Crenshaw (1991) observes in her foundational study of intersectional theory, immigrant family members are influenced by what can be understood as interlocking systems of oppression based on gender, race, class, legal status, sexual orientation, nation of origin, language ability, culture, ethnicity, and abilities (see also Collins 1998). Given that members of immigrant families have multiple and diverging social locations, their individual experiences may at times put them at odds with each other socially, culturally, and politically (see Chapter 5 for a more detailed discussion of this topic).

In our research we have found certain patterns that bring these interlocking systems of oppression into relief (Menjívar and Abrego 2009; Schmalzbauer 2008). For instance, even though poverty and undocumented status harm immediate and long-term patterns of integration (as discussed in Chapter 3), gender positions women and men dissimilarly as they confront similarly weak opportunity structures. As Paula, a Salvadoran woman in San Francisco, insightfully explained to Menjívar (2000: 157),

> Since I was very little ... I have always known that women and men do different things, they are supposed to do different things ... so it's not just one thing, it's many. Look, Ceci, we all know that what men do, women don't, and what women do, men don't. Men and women were born to do different things.... Just look at an old man and an old woman; they are different, don't you think? A Salvadoran man and a Salvadoran woman are different ... Even undocumented women and undocumented men are different *(laughs)* ... So of course our lives here [as immigrants] are going to be very different, even though we're all in the same situation.

In this chapter we seek to capture Paula's perceptive assessment as it is manifested in the context of immigrant families, and to expose how gender inflects various aspects of family life and intersects with other power hierarchies. Our discussion to follow is organized into six sections. First we examine the intersections of gender with micro and macro forces at the place of origin—intersections that shape the motivation and decision to migrate. The subsequent three sections investigate how gender organizes settlement and integration, focusing on the interface of gender, families, and the state; the gendered division of labor in the market and in the home; and the way gendered social networks play a role in the process of incorporation, both for families and for communities. We end with a section on gender relations across borders and one on care networks.

Gendered Expectations and the Migration Process

Gender centrally informs the entire migration process. The decision to migrate is often made in the context of a household, on the basis of family goals or in response to family ruptures (Pessar 1999) where gender expectations weigh significantly. Immigrant women and men, in their roles as partners, mothers and fathers, or daughters and sons, migrate in response to different social expectations, pressures, and opportunities. While family practices are ever changing, ideals about behaviors in marital unions or about motherhood and fatherhood are often naturalized and defined in sharply contrasting ways. In much of Latin America, for example, motherhood is venerated as the ideal form of womanhood (Chant and Craske 2003; Hume 2004; Menjívar 2011a; Padilla 2012), while fatherhood is presented as only one of several acceptable forms of masculinity (Hume 2004; Madrigal and Tejeda 2009). Similarly, families often have different expectations from daughters than they do from sons. Specifically, orthodox gender scripts suggest that daughters are expected to care for their parents in old age, while sons are typically relieved of this responsibility (Schmalzbauer 2013). Families also put vastly different limits around sons' and around daughters' sexualities (González-López 2004, 2005), a pattern observed across groups and cultures (see Espiritu 2007; Pyke and Johnson 2003). These gender distinctions in values and expectations shape men's and women's migration experiences, potentially setting fathers and sons up to be celebrated, while mothers and daughters are stigmatized (Espiritu 2008).

Immigrant mothers are expected to sacrifice themselves in the name of their families (Chant and Craske 2003; Menjívar 2011a). These sacrifices can mean different things in diverse contexts. While middle- and upper-class mothers are often charged with being the main caregivers for their families, poor and working-class mothers must also participate in the public sphere—through employment in the labor market, political action, or migration—to support their children (Alcalde 2010; Chant 1992; Menjívar 2011a). Fatherhood, on the other hand, regardless of social class standing, is closely tied to authority, protection, and guidance of the family through participation in the public sphere (Arriagada 2002). For fathers, therefore, migration and family separation are acceptable acts that allow them to fulfill their role as breadwinners and thus do not attract disappointment and the disapproval of relatives or society in the same way as a mother's migration might do (see Parreñas 2005).

Consequently, while for fathers migration may extend their options to provide for their families, mothers are sometimes stigmatized when they migrate—and for the very same reason for which fathers are praised (Abrego 2014; Parreñas 2005; Pratt 2012). Only in areas where there is a long-standing tradition that frames the migration of mothers as normal, as in the case of Afro-Trinidadian (Ho 1993) and Cape Verdean migrants (Åkesson, Carling, and Drotbohm 2012), are women migrants spared negative judgments. For this reason women often avoid migration until this becomes the only means for them to improve their situation (Abrego 2014; Hamal Gurung and Purkayastha 2013; Hondagneu-Sotelo and Avila 1997). Even then the decision is difficult, particularly if they leave children behind. Research has identified an increased risk for depression among Latina mothers who are separated from their children in the context of migration (Miranda, Siddique, Der-Martirosian, and Belin 2005). In spite of these challenges, women have been migrating at similar rates to those of men, with important variations by country of origin (see Chapter 1). In many cases women have migrated at even higher rates than men, which has led to what Donato and Gabaccia (2015) refer to as the "feminization of migration."

Kinship systems in the countries of origin influence women's migration patterns. Massey, Fischer, and Capoferro (2006) examined US-bound migratory configurations from several Latin American countries and concluded that, in patriarchal societies, the key determinants of women's migration are the migrant status of the husband or partner, the existence of relatives in the United States, and the availability of documents (a visa) to enter the country. In contrast, these factors do not weigh as heavily in the migration of women from matrifocal societies, where women's own migratory experiences are more important.

Once individuals opt for migration, gender expectations can determine the elements of order and timing. For example, in some cases men lead the way in the chain migration process because they are assumed to be the family members best suited to work for pay and to lay the groundwork for the future migration of their family (Hondagneu-Sotelo 1994). In other cases women lead the way. This trend is exemplified by the Salvadoran women who migrated to Washington, DC in the 1970s without consulting their fathers or partners, thus pioneering this type of chain migration (Repak 1995). Similarly, responding to the demand for nurses in the United States, many South Indian women led the way in their families' migrations in the 1990s (George 2005). Also responding to labor demands in wealthier countries, Jamaican women leave husbands and families behind and go to work in service sector jobs in the United States and Canada. They (and their husbands) adjust to transnational marriages over time by resorting to cultural understandings of formal unions in Jamaica (Douglas-Harrison 2014; Foner 1995).

Gendered migration decisions typically reflect broader structural forces and social practices. For example, a single mother may engage in rural-to-urban migration in her country in order to work in factories. Such factories are created through the increased movement of US capital and offshore investment, which contribute to the feminization of wage labor in developing countries (Sassen-Koob 1984). In these factories women produce goods for export to the countries wherefrom capital originates (and where women eventually migrate) (Sassen 1988). At the receiving end, as in the United States, the availability of jobs for women in domestic work, cleaning, and garment industries makes their migration more likely (Toro-Morn 2013). The growth of the immigrant-dominated care industry in the United States, and in the Global North more generally, has intensified the pull of immigrant women across national borders (Ehrenreich and Hochshild 2002). Gender also intersects with race, as is evident in hiring practices in different industries: Asian immigrant women are racially stereotyped as particularly docile and fitting for jobs in the manufacturing technology sector (Hossfeld 1994) or in beauty-oriented jobs, such as in nail salons (Kang 2010), while in the southwest Latina immigrants are perceived as maternal, caring, and skilled for domestic labor (Hondagneu-Sotelo 2009). Given the shifting gender context of the US economy and the decreasing economic opportunities of the Global South, more women are now migrating in order to seek work than for family reunification (Ehrenreich and Hochschild 2002).[1] This change in the demographics and economics of migration has significant implications for immigrant families, especially when gender expectations conflict with economic realities.

Sexuality is another factor that may shape the migration decision-making process. Lionel Cantú's (2009) research in Los Angeles with Mexican immigrant men who have sex with men (MSM) shows the complex ways in which sexuality plays into migration. The men Cantú interviewed cited their sexuality as the primary motive for migration. Specifically, they spoke about resorting to migration as a means of distancing themselves from "traditional" Mexican familism, which considers homosexuality taboo. Cantú found that, even in cases where sexuality was central to migration, the political economy of migrants' lives was also important. Thus, gay stigma and discrimination often meant that in Mexico it was impossible both to be "out" and to get a job. The United States represented not only a space more accepting of non-hetero lifestyles and identities, but a place where one's sexuality would not be a barrier to economic mobility. Similar patterns hold for sexually non-conforming Latina immigrants (Acosta 2013). In the postmigration context, Gloria González-López (2004) observes, views about sexuality—particularly young women's—do not change much, as immigrant fathers continue to be vigilant about preserving their daughter's virginity (see also Espiritu 2001 for similarities among Filipino/a immigrants).

Gender, Family and the State

Historically, gendered ideals and power relations have been subsumed in immigration law and other social institutions. Laws and policies, in turn, have shaped the formation and long-term settlement experiences of immigrant families—even barring the formation of Chinese families at one point (Glenn 2002). As early as 1855, for example, Congress declared that a foreign-born woman who married a US citizen man automatically became a US citizen. Meanwhile, a US citizen woman who married a foreign man lost her citizenship (Lee 2013). This gender inequity was further cemented in the Expatriation Act of 1907, which not only stripped women of citizenship when they married non-US citizens but also rendered them stateless until their husbands died, the marriage dissolved, or their husbands were naturalized (Lee 2013: 68). In the National Origins Act of 1924, the law further protected the rights of male US citizens to family unity, allowing them to bring in their wives and children. Female US citizens, in contrast, were not granted this right until 1952, in the McCarran-Walter Act (Lee 2013: 67). Immigrant women, moreover, had to conform to rigid constructions of femininity in order to be admitted into the country. Not only did they have to be heterosexual; they had to be "morally astute," as prescribed by the reigning social norms of the day. Prostitutes in particular were deemed immoral and thus ineligible for family unification (Lee 2013; Luibhéid 1998, 2002, 2008).

In the contemporary world the state remains a powerful actor in shaping the gender and family experiences of migration (see Chapter 2). Rhacel Parreñas (2001), for example, shows how the Filipino government, because of its dependency on remittances, has created a program to facilitate the emigration of its citizens, primarily Filipina women. The Philippines thus sustains a difficult paradox, as it encourages female migration while continuing to perpetuate gender ideals that migrating mothers in particular can never fulfill.

Perhaps the area in which the state most visibly impacts immigrant family life is the determination of who is authorized to enter (see Chapter 2): through such decisions the state reshapes the structure of immigrant families by creating immigrant "illegality."[2] The social exclusion associated with migrant illegality can mean different things for women and men, mothers and fathers, blocking their attempts to fulfill gendered expectations (Abrego 2009; Hagan 1994; Hondagneu-Sotelo 1994; Menjívar 2000). Legal instability prevents undocumented immigrants from providing financially for their families, as an insecure legal status influences access to the job market and determines wages and employment security (Massey and Gelatt 2010; Takei, Sáenz, and Li 2009). The gendered consequences can generate anxiety and fear when men know that an arrest or deportation would put their family's well-being in jeopardy (Schmalzbauer 2014), as men are overwhelmingly more likely to be detained and deported (Das Gupta 2014). But the intersection of gender and legal status, particularly in the context of mothering, also has profound effects on women, as legal status affects their caregiving practices, their access to services for themselves and their children, and their perceptions of the self (Sousa-Rodriguez forthcoming).

Undocumented men's jobs often place these men in public places where they become easy targets for detection; however, they must earn an income to support their families—in the United States or in the country of origin. Martín, a Salvadoran day laborer, explained: "We put ourselves at risk [when we seek work on the street] because there is no other choice. As a man, you have to work and you have to wait for the consequences" (Abrego 2013: 151). Entering the male-dominated day-laborer market is one of the few possibilities Martín has to earn money and fulfill social expectations as a husband and father; but participation in day labor also makes him vulnerable to detection. Migrant male vulnerability is especially evident in the numerous counties and cities that have enacted laws and ordinances in order to prohibit or restrict workers from looking for day-labor work (Valenzuela 2002). In public debates leading to ordinances, day laborers, who are overwhelmingly immigrant Latino men, have been heavily associated with illegality and criminality, buttressing the race–illegality link for Latinos/as.

The focus of immigration law enforcement on Latino men (Das Gupta 2014; Golash-Boza and Hondagneu-Sotelo 2013) has gendered costs for heterosexual immigrant families. Women are left bearing the responsibility for their family's sustenance when their male partners are deported (Dreby 2012, 2015). This burden may be especially high in destinations where women do not have access to living-wage jobs, strong networks, or social supports, such as in the new destinations that have emerged within the past two decades. In sum, when men are deported, women pick up the pieces (Schmalzbauer 2014).

Gendered forms of illegality within the family are further complicated by immigrant generation. In her work with undocumented 1.5-generation immigrants, Abrego (2011, 2013) identifies youth-specific experiences of gendered illegality. Undocumented young women shared with Abrego that they sometimes feel self-conscious about their looks when people learn about their legal status (Abrego 2013). In contrast, undocumented young men seemed more concerned with illegality as a barrier to developing romantic relationships and a social life. Unable to get jobs that pay well enough to afford going on dates or other social outings, undocumented young men feel excluded from the social scene of their peers, which often leads to feelings of shame.

Gendered Work:
In the Labor Market and in the Home

The labor market intersects with gendered work and gendered divisions of labor in the home. Gendered work affects family relations and dynamics in multiple ways (Menjívar 1999; Min 1998; Parreñas 2001). While some immigrant women participate in the paid labor force for the first time only after migration (Kibria 1993; Menjívar 1999; Pessar 2005; Tienda and Booth 1991), many others arrive in the labor market with substantial experience from their home countries. Earning an income outside the home is nothing new for them (Menjívar 1999). However, with migration, the entanglements of economic participation and gender relations can enhance women's autonomy in certain contexts *and* increase both tensions within the household and women's complicity in maintaining patriarchal control. Work outside the home in the context of migration thus has the potential to reaffirm *and* at the same time transform gender relations (Menjívar 1999). However, the advantages (or disadvantages) that come from women's paid employment do not stem from purely economic gains in the form of wages but from the gendered meanings that immigrants attach to economic activities.

In general the participation of immigrants in the US labor market follows distinct gendered patterns, even as we consider important caveats informed by the intersection of other social positions, such as race and legal status. For instance, Latina immigrant women who arrive with low levels of education are largely concentrated in menial, poorly paid jobs, in the often exploitative low-wage service sector (Abrego 2014; Hondagneu-Sotelo 2009; Menjívar 1999; Sánchez Molina 2015). However, the same is true of Latina women who arrive with higher educational levels but are undocumented (Menjívar 2000). And, given other vectors of inequality, women from other backgrounds face similar job prospects. For instance, Nepali women find employment as nannies with wealthier Indian families in Boston and New York (Hamal Gurung and Purkayastha 2013), and Pakistani, Bangladeshi, and other South Asian women engage in low-wage work within the ethnic labor market, doing retail and providing child care (Banerjee 2013). In grocery, jewelry, and other small businesses, women find themselves in often exploitative employment with male co-ethnics whose job expectations blur the lines between public and private work. Chinese immigrant women in New York also have a long history of similar types of poorly remunerated work in male co-ethnic-owned shops and restaurants (Bao 2001). Along these lines, unpaid family labor is not uncommon among immigrant women; Sanchez's (2015) work among Mexican sharecroppers in strawberry farms in California sheds light on the gendered system of unpaid family labor.

Even as they move outside of ethnic enclaves, immigrant women face low pay and demanding jobs in sectors like hotel housekeeping (Chin 2013) and garment work (Abrego 2014). While immigrant men also start out from a disadvantaged position in the labor market, immigrant women across immigrant and occupational groups systematically earn less and are hired into less prestigious jobs than their male counterparts with similar levels of education (Waldinger and Gilbertson 1994).

The geography of immigrant destinations shapes gendered economic opportunity structures (Schmalzbauer 2014). For example, in large cities immigrant women are likely to have access to entry-level jobs in the care industry as well as in restaurant kitchens and hotels. Immigrant men in the same localities may also find work in kitchens or as commercial cleaners, but are less likely to find work in private homes (Abrego 2014; Flores-González, Guevarra, Toro-Morn, and Chang 2013; Schmalzbauer 2005). In rural destinations, specifically in the agricultural sector, the majority of workers are male. Yet women do work in agriculture, and their labor extends beyond the actual tasks of harvesting. In her research on sharecropping families working in strawberry fields in California, Sanchez (2002) observes that women's labor creates new forms of discipline and work ethic, which in turn meet the need for specific physical demands in this sector.

In new rural immigrant destinations in the US South and Midwest, the restructured food-processing industry draws both women and men into some of the most dangerous yet stable immigrant jobs (Marrow 2011; Striffler 2005). Steve Striffler (2005), in his ethnography of a chicken-processing plant in the rural South, found that, even though immigrant women and men were both recruited to work in processing, women, especially older ones, tended to have the lowest paying and the most tedious and repetitive line jobs, while men worked with heavy equipment. Such work was deemed to be of higher status than the line jobs; thus, even within the same job site, gender and race informed who did what job and how each job was valued. In new destinations in the rural Mountain West, Mexican immigrant families tend to be drawn by construction or agricultural work, both of which are socially constructed as male in that context. In this region, therefore, it is common for women to stay home. The few jobs that do exist there for immigrant women tend to be low-wage service jobs that do not pay anywhere near the equivalent jobs in construction or skilled agricultural work. Immigrant women's economic dependency on men in that context is therefore high (Schmalzbauer 2014).

The organization of mothering provides an important window into how immigrant women enter paid employment while they balance expectations of motherhood in a context of shifting resources. In a study of middle-class educated Korean immigrant women, Seungsook Moon examines the factors that affect mothering practices and finds that mothering arrangements—for example, "shared mothering based on transnational, transgenerational, and nuclear family networks; isolated and privatized mothering; and mothering after retreat from employment" (Moon 2003: 841)—depend on the labor market prospects of educated women, the family's financial resources, and gender ideologies. Each mothering practice configures differently conjugal relations as well as the power to negotiate them.

The Great Recession that took place in the late 2000s shifted gendered economic opportunities within many immigrant families. This crisis highlighted how structural barriers and socioeconomic inequalities can prevent poor and working-class immigrant parents from fulfilling their social expectations. The crisis prompted changes in gender norms in some families, as some immigrant men, who previously forbade their wives to work, became more comfortable with the idea of their wives taking jobs outside of the home. This was especially true in heterosexual families dependent on male wages in the construction industry, which was hit particularly hard by the recession (see Hout, Levanon, and Cumberworth 2011). Schmalzbauer (2011, 2014) found that, in the rural Mountain West, Mexican immigrant men lost their jobs in high numbers during the recession, which put pressure on their female partners to go to work. These women found work primarily in private homes, as cleaners, in fast-food kitchens, or in small motels.

In every situation that Schmalzbauer encountered in which a Mexican immigrant woman entered the labor force in Montana, the wages were too low to support a family, even if the woman were working full time. Menjívar encountered similar patterns of Central American women's earnings in San Francisco (Menjívar 2000), in Los Angeles (Menjívar 1999) and in Phoenix (Menjívar 2012): in all these places women often worked at several jobs—cleaning, babysitting, and selling food or cosmetics, for instance—in order to stitch together enough income to approximate what they would earn from a full-time job. Significantly, Menjívar (1999) found that, in reconstituted immigrant families in which partners have their own children and their own obligations of support, incomes go in different directions and usually stretch across borders. This can lead partners to maintain separate finances, so that they may support their respective families back home while contributing to the new family they have formed in the United States: essentially these immigrants have "three families to support" (Menjívar 1999: 613). In such cases, despite immigrant women's significant labor market activities, the gender division of labor and the gender-role expectations in the home remain almost unchanged (Menjívar 1999, 2000).

Schmalzbauer (2014) similarly found that, despite major economic shifts, gender expectations changed little in most families she studied. Immigrant men who worked in construction would rather be unemployed or underemployed than take on what they deemed to be "women's work." This sectoral difference is further supported by Menjívar (1999), who found that such perspectives are informed by immigrants' experiences in their home countries. Menjívar (1999) compared the views that immigrant Guatemalan Ladinos and Mayans have about women's work, both outside and inside the home. She notes that Ladinos, who originated in contexts with more orthodox expectations regarding gender behavior, experienced significant change when their partners entered the US labor force and, as a result, they themselves had to pick up more chores in the home. However, this was not the case for Mayan men. The Mayans came from relatively more egalitarian social structures and were accustomed from early ages to seeing their female partners earn an income in the labor market and to doing chores in the home. These men's assessments of their present experiences were therefore vastly different than other immigrant men's.

In the context of economic instability, women are additionally burdened by social surveillance. Gossip and interactions with others can serve to police women into fulfilling their expected roles as self-sacrificing providers, regardless of the scarcity around them (Dreby 2010; Hagan 1994; Menjívar 2000, 2011a). The geographic context of immigrant women's lives may intensify or diminish the presence and impacts of social surveillance. Mexican women migrants in Atlanta, for example, were able to escape the oppression of gossip and social surveillance, which had characterized their lives in rural Mexico, simply because of the anonymity created by urbanity (Hirsch 2003). Similarly, gender non-conforming immigrant Latinas were able to live more freely with same-sex partners after migration (Acosta 2013). Economically disadvantaged immigrant fathers may also be targets of gendered forms of gossip. And yet gossip does not necessarily undermine their masculinity and self-worth (Dreby 2009; Menjívar 2011a). When immigrant men are structurally blocked from economically based sources of masculine identity, they can negotiate and maintain their masculinity through other means, including by repressing their emotions, by demonstrating physical strength, by drinking alcohol, or by signaling freedom and sexual prowess (Madrigal and Tejeda 2009; Pribilsky 2004; Smith 2006).

The economic shifts brought about by migration and economic crises can realign the household division of labor and shift the economic contributions of men and women, situations that can prompt tensions and heightened anxieties within immigrant families (see Banerjee 2013; Kibria 1993; Min 1998; Segura 1994). These situations can lead to domestic violence, as men develop a sense of loss of control in the home and then try to reassert themselves through physical or psychological abuse (Menjívar and Salcido 2002). In their study of heterosexual South Asian immigrant women in Boston, Raj and Silverman (2002, 2003) observed that immigrant women are disproportionately affected by intimate partner violence due to immigration-specific factors like language barriers, isolation, economic dependency, loss of social supports, the heightened vulnerability of women that comes from migration itself, legal status, and anti-immigrant sentiment (Dasgupta 2005;

Menjívar and Salcido 2002; Raj and Silverman 2002, 2003). Margaret Abraham (2000), also examining South Asian women in situations of domestic violence, argues that their experiences should be examined in relation to structural and cultural factors that exacerbate women's vulnerabilities in the context of migration. Such vulnerabilities are intensified among undocumented women, who sometimes depend on their husbands not only economically, but also for "papers," for instance when men petition legal permanent visas for their partners.[3] In these cases, the abuse includes regular threats about stopping the legalization process and having the women deported (Salcido and Adelman 2004).

It is not surprising, then, that women who transgress gender boundaries by migrating internationally and entering the labor force still seek to conform to gender norms in other ways (Abrego 2014).[4] Kibria (1993), for example, found that Vietnamese women in the United States worked hard to maintain patriarchal norms in the home even while they challenged traditional gender norms by engaging in wage labor outside of the home. Menjívar (1999) found that Guatemalan women performed "balancing acts" in the home by doing all the household chores while at the same time they worked full-time outside the home (sometimes earning more than their partners) so as to reassure their husbands' male authority in the home. Schmalzbauer (2014) similarly found that, when the most recent economic crisis pushed Mexican migrant women into the workforce while their husbands stayed at home, women embraced their "double shift" (see also Hochschild 2001) with a smile, so to speak, so as to protect their partners' sense of masculinity.

Gendered Social Networks in Families and Communities

A significant body of work has pointed to important differences in the networks that immigrant women and men build in their places of destination and to the consequences that such gendered networks have for families and for community building. In a

Gender and Immigrant Families

study of Lao refugees, Muir (1988) observed that men tended to create networks in a patron–client fashion, whereas women's networks tended to be more horizontal and cooperative. In Cuban and Chinese enclaves women derive fewer economic advantages from co-ethnic networks than do men, mostly because women have different access to goods and benefits and the goods they can exchange are different from those of men (Portes and Jensen 1989; Zhou 1992). Among Salvadoran immigrants, women exchanged goods in kind and men tended to help each other with loans of money and material goods, but these exchanges were deeply informed by gender ideologies and cultural practices that regulate the behaviors of women and men (Menjívar 2000). Notably, social networks in general have been established as critical to immigrant women's and men's well-being and to that of their families (Baluja 2003; Bui 2003; Hagan 1994, 1998; Massey, Alarcon, Durand, and González 1987; Menjívar 2002b).

Important intersections must be noted when discussing gendered social networks. For instance, social class, race, sexual orientation, and position within enclave economies highlight the differential benefits that social networks have for women and men. But social networks can deteriorate and lose their usefulness during an economic downturn (Chin 2013; Menjívar 2000). Women's hiring networks, which are based almost entirely on their positions in low-wage work in the Chinese ethnic enclave, were no longer useful because their contacts in the enclave were too financially strapped to hire employees. Chinese immigrant men, on the other hand, had more extensive social networks outside the enclave, and these helped them to quickly access service sector jobs in other neighborhoods (Chin 2013).

Social networks also intersect with legal status in nuanced and strikingly consequential ways. Undocumented women may feel especially vulnerable to sexual advances or community control when they try to build networks with immigrant men in order to access the more financially valuable goods that men control—an exercise often considered gender-inappropriate (Hagan 1994, 1998; Menjívar 2000). Depending on the context, gender norms may lead to network formation that benefits or disadvantages women by

96

either making them privy to or excluding them from information critical to their families' well-being (Salcido and Menjívar 2012). In the 1980s Maya Guatemalan women in Houston, for example, were excluded from the predominantly male networks that shared information about legalization under the Immigration Reform and Control Act (IRCA) of 1986 (Hagan 1994). On the other hand, in the early 1990s Salvadoran immigrant women in San Francisco were able to network through community organizations so as to access community resources necessary to themselves and their families (Menjívar 2000). For instance, Yolanda, an undocumented Mexican woman and a stay-at-home mother in Los Angeles, echoes the sentiments of several immigrant women with whom Abrego (2013) spoke when she explained how daily life challenges are different for men and for women because of how gender shapes networks and access to them:

> I think that for us as women, perhaps it is easier because it's rare that they [ICE] will come to look for you at home. So I can be there with my family, taking care of them. The hard part is that we don't know where to find help anymore. Like if one of my children is sick or has some kind of problem, I don't know where to go, aside from my family. So it limits who you can seek out for help. (Abrego 2013: 151)

Thus, new law enforcement practices have shaped the social network dynamics in the destinations where migrants settle, leading to specific gendered expressions. For example, unauthorized Mexican women in Montana were commonly unemployed and afraid of being in public; therefore they spent their days at home (Schmalzbauer 2009, 2014). In this case women's networks were weak and dispersed, and depression was common. Yet, simultaneously, women found security in their isolation (see also Silvey 2004) because they felt it was less likely that, while at home, they would be deported and separated from their children.

As families negotiate new gendered experiences and expectations, immigrant women and men can sometimes find ways to transgress gendered ideals or reframe their expectations in ways that help families resist marginalization. For instance, some immigrant Latinas use their identities as mothers to seek opportunities for political socialization and organization (Coll 2004, 2010). They gain skills to navigate social institutions and to access organizations that may benefit their families, thus putting their knowledge in the service of resource mobilization toward creating a community (Cranford 2007; Hondagneu-Sotelo 1994). For instance, it is not uncommon for immigrant parents who are union members in Los Angeles to apply their union-organizing skills to access greater educational resources in their children's schools (Cranford 2007; Milkman and Terriquez 2012; Rogers, Saunders, Terriquez, and Velez 2008).

Gendered Expectations in Families across Borders

There are far-reaching gendered effects of migration within families that reach beyond US borders, as when the migration of a partner contributes to either strengthening gender inequalities or inspiring change in orthodox gender relations in the non-migrating family in the country of origin (Espiritu 2001; Hondagneu-Sotelo 1994; Menjívar 1999; Min 1998; Williams 2005; Zhou 2000). In the Philippines, for instance, the absence of migrant fathers results in a significant increase in power for their non-migrant wives (Parreñas 2005). Similarly, in a study of conjugal heterosexual relations between Ecuadorian transnational migrants in New York and their wives in the highlands of Ecuador, Pribilsky (2004) found that, contrary to the negative effects associated with male migration, Ecuadorian women's lives had improved because these women had assumed new roles and status. In turn, their conjugal relationships improved after migration through the negotiations involved in trying to maintain their relationships from afar. And in a study of Mexican families in California and Jalisco, Goodson-Lawes (1993) noted that, rather than simply waiting for their husbands to return or following them to the United States, women increased their personal authority in their families and communities after their husbands' migration (see also Andrews 2014).

However, men's migration does not *always* lead to increased emancipation or to gains in authority for non-migrant women. In many cases the absence of male partners (or fathers) can reaffirm their power and authority in the non-migrant household. This is particularly true when structural conditions do not allow women to enter the labor force and they must therefore remain economically dependent on remittances from migrating men. Women who are compelled into labor force (or economic activity) participation after their husbands' migration may acquire greater bargaining power as a result, but this transformation is likely to take place in urban areas, where employment opportunities for women are more plentiful than in the countryside (Aysa and Massey 2004). In a study of a Yucatec Maya community in Mexico, Bever (2002) observed that, despite obvious transformations in gender roles in the context of migration, both women and men continued to strongly defend gender ideology. And, in a comparative study of the effects of Armenian and Guatemalan men's migration, Menjívar and Agadjanian (2007) found that, although in contexts where women have limited access to employment gender inequalities in the home are reaffirmed when men migrate. In some cases the men's absence can facilitate socializing, which can strengthen women's networks. However, just as likely, women's activities are often closely watched and restricted when men are away, so as to preserve culturally appropriate images of how wives (and mothers) should behave in the absence of their male partners (see also Menjívar 2011a). In some instances, to tighten this control, male partners remit to wives through the men's parents, so that these parents may monitor the women's moves and only dispense the remittances if the latter are "well behaved."[5] Importantly, even if there is a transfer of power and authority to women as a result of men's migration, when this outcome occurs by default and not by choice, gender ideologies may remain unchanged (González de la Rocha 1989).

With respect to parenting, gendered expectations shape experiences across borders in multiple ways. Immigrant mothers are often held to high expectations of care even from afar, and even if they manage to send sufficient remittances (Abrego 2009; Abrego and Menjívar 2011; Parreñas 2005). Unable to fulfill the gendered expectations that require them to care for their non-migrating children intensively and on a daily basis, transnational mothers live with sadness, guilt, and deprivation, a pattern observed among various immigrant groups (Miranda et al. 2005; Parreñas 2001, 2005; Pratt 2012).[6] Such was the case for Esperanza. When Abrego (2014: 112–13) interviewed her, she recalled the hardships she underwent to ensure her family's economic well-being in El Salvador:

> I've always sent $300 [monthly] to my mother and I would get paid $100 weekly [working as a live-in nanny]. I would end up with $90 because I also had to pay the fee to wire the money ... It was horrible ... Each week I would buy a dozen ramen noodle soups that I don't even want to see anymore, really ... so my food was the ramen noodle soup. But I was the happiest woman in the world because my daughter had something to eat!

Given ideologies of motherhood and caring obligations, Salvadoran immigrant women tended to remit for longer periods of time than men and to send larger sums of money even if their US earnings were substantially lower than those of men (Abrego 2014). In contrast, migrant fathers, who are expected to be economic providers, can minimize family tensions when they send sufficient remittances (Dreby 2010). However, there are significant consequences for transnational fathers too, when they fail. Dreby (2010) found that, when fathers cut off communication with their families, it was typically *not* because they stopped caring about or missing them; it was because they had lost a job in the United States and could not afford to remit. The shame of being unable to live up to expectations of fatherhood prompted them to cut their ties. Additionally, constructions of masculinity sometimes prevent migrant men from expressing their melancholy and loneliness, and this makes it difficult for them to stay in touch with their families when they lose the ability to provide (Dreby 2010). Yet Dreby found that, perhaps due to the higher expectations of caring from mothers, transnational mothers continued to communicate and maintain ties with children and family at home even during times of economic duress, when they were sending few or no remittances (see also Abrego 2014).

Gender, Care Networks, and Those Who Stay

Immigrant parents who leave children behind depend on alternative care networks to help raise their children (Aranda 2003). Typically this help is supplied by female relatives and kin. Dreby (2010) calls these care workers "middle women." In Caribbean migration circuits there is a long history of "child shifting" (Gordon 1987; Plaza 2000) from biological mothers to middle women. Child shifting most commonly occurs when mothers migrate and place their children in the care of their own mother, the child's grandmother. This practice has become common in Mexican (Dreby 2010), Honduran (Sánchez Molina 2015; Schmalzbauer 2004, 2005), and Salvadoran (Abrego 2014; Menjívar 2000) families.

Grandmothers are often at the core of transnational care networks, sometimes providing care for three generations of children. Doña Rosa was 75 when Schmalzbauer interviewed her in 2003, in a barrio on the outskirts of San Pedro Sula, Honduras. At the time, three of her children were living in the United States, and she was raising five grandchildren. She explained how she came to care for so many:

> When Maria and Fidel got separated, Maria went to the United States and left me with her three children … I also raised Jenifer, Ignacia's daughter, as well as the daughter of my daughter Leticia. I had eleven children of my own and then I raised five of my grandchildren. But there was no other way. (Schmalzbauer 2005: 56)

In some cases, unwanted, uncertain separations between parents and their non-migrant children last for so long and are so uncertain that grandmothers become mothers to the children, particularly when the children are left as babies or toddlers. Children grow up calling their grandmothers "mothers," and sometimes even calling their own mothers by the first name, since they hear others in their immediate family refer to their mothers in this way. This was the case with a Salvadoran woman who grew up in the care of her grandmother. When she arrived in San Francisco to join her biological mother, she had spent so long referring to her by her first name that she could no longer call her "mother" (Menjívar 2000). In some cases grandmothers grow so accustomed to living with their grandchildren that, even when parents in the United States can send for their children, the grandmothers oppose it. A Guatemalan woman in Phoenix, Arizona explained to Menjívar that, even though she wanted to bring her son and daughter to the United States to live with her, her 75-year-old mother "would not be able to survive without them because they are her only company there. She would die if the *patojos* [kids] leave her" (Menjívar 2011b: 388).

While grandmothers may be the most common female relatives to step into a caretaking role in the absence of biological parents, aunts, cousins, and older female siblings also take on this responsibility. Carla, who was living on the Honduran Coast when Schmalzbauer interviewed her in 2003, raised her own two children plus a niece, a nephew, and the son of her cousin. Like many middle women, she provided the direct care for the children while the migrant parent provided financial support through remittances. Carla's care work extended beyond the basic tasks of feeding and clothing her nieces and nephews. She also guided them in their homework and school decisions, and demanded that they study English. Beyond this, she explained to them why their own mothers had to leave, reminding them always of their mothers' sacrifices (Schmalzbauer 2005).

The gendered nature of care for non-migrant family members extends to the differentiation of expectations that transnational parents place on their non-migrating sons and daughters. Parreñas (2005) found that, even in Filipino families in which fathers remained at home with their children, the eldest daughters typically took on the household duties of adult women and became surrogate mothers to their younger siblings. In poorer families they took on the household chores of cooking and cleaning. In middle-class families that could afford to hire domestic help, the eldest daughters made sure the domestic labor and all other household expenses were organized and paid.

In addition to ensuring the health and physical well-being of children, middle women play a key role in harmonizing family relations and in easing the anxiety and emotional burdens carried by children who are separated from their parents. This role is vital in transnational families in which the separations between parents and children are long and uncertain (Artico 2003), which creates emotional challenges for everyone (Carling, Menjívar, and Schmalzbauer 2012).[7] If middle women are consistent in presenting the absent parent as dedicated and sacrificing, as someone who migrated with only her or his children's best interest in mind, the children are more likely to retain or create a positive image of their biological parent and to find more peace in their transnational family life. Furthermore, middle women often live in precarious conditions and in extreme vulnerability and, instead of directing the parents' remittances to the children, they sometimes distribute them to other needy family members. These situations can lead to tensions between the family in the United States and the family in the country of origin that can eventually encourage children, particularly those from Central America and Mexico, to migrate on their own and reunite with their parents (Chavez and Menjívar 2010). When this happens, children may experience another traumatic rupture, as they have to separate from their grandmothers (or other caretakers), who have become their "maternal reference point" (Sánchez Molina 2015: 68). Along these lines, Parreñas (2005) found that Filipino children in mother-away households were more likely to idealize the nuclear family, and daughters in mother-away households were more likely than sons to be "traditionalists"—that is, to consider geographic proximity and omnipresence to be central to mothering.

Conclusion

We end this chapter by emphasizing the centrality of gender in shaping family dynamics, norms, and expectations. Gender is fluid, impacted by the economic, cultural, and policy contexts of immigrant family life. And it shapes how individuals respond to structural conditions. Gender relations are often transformed across generations, especially as individual family members come of age in different transnational contexts. Migration alters gender relations in the receiving and in the sending contexts. Yet, despite gender's fluidity, heteronormative gender expectations that charge women with care and domestic work and men with provision tend to influence most immigrant families' dynamics. In many cases this influence is oppressive. This is not to suggest essentialism. Importantly, even though heteronormative gender expectations are hegemonic, they are not biologically based, nor are they unchangeable. Rather, we note that structural forces and institutions—the economy, law, social services, and education—often interact with social norms to reproduce gender expectations in immigrants' lives. As family members resist the reproduction of gendered expectations, new possibilities emerge.

Familial gender arrangements and performances sometimes allow families to establish a sense of continuity through what can be a tumultuous migration process. Indeed, immigrant families may continue to produce and perform gender in ways that seem recognizable to them in a host society that otherwise feels foreign and exclusionist. At the same time, there are examples of immigrants who are challenging long-held gender ideals. For example, Korean immigrant men have attended boot camps in order to change their fathering practices to approaches that involve affective co-parenting (Kim 2014), and Latino gay men negotiate masculinity in different spaces (Ocampo 2012).

Expanding the notion of "family" beyond biological definitions is another way in which families can serve as sites of gendered resistance. Cantú (2009) found that gay Mexican immigrant men often formed households with other gay immigrant men and women. These "chosen families" were critical to their well-being, as these men were marginalized in other aspects of their lives. Cantú's participants, despite having experienced struggle and even trauma in their own biological families, especially in response to their sexuality, still sought to be a part of a stable partnership and to be geographically and emotionally close to family in both its orthodox and its expanded definitions. Family, despite its common gender trappings and inequalities, is still associated with the promise of love, security, and well-being.

5

Generations and Immigrant Families

At a press conference in support of the DREAM Act in 2010,[1] undocumented high school and college students shared details about their lives as they waited for the event to begin. Off to the side, an older woman carried a stack of banners and smiled shyly. Abrego walked over to introduce herself and, after some chitchat, Adela cautiously shared her story.

Adela is the mother of one of the students who helped organize the press conference. This was the first time she had participated in a protest, and she was nervous about her visibility. She and her family arrived in the United States from Mexico during the 1990s, but she had just recently started participating in a local immigrant rights organization, and only after prodding from her children. Among the dozens of people at the event, Adela was the only parent. Although she had invited several other immigrant women to attend, all had declined. Undocumented, they were afraid of becoming targets for deportation. Meanwhile the students proudly and without fear held up banners and chanted (Abrego 2011). This event illustrates one of the many differences of perspective and behavior between young and adult immigrants.

The concept of generations is useful in understanding differences in behavior, attitudes, and expectations across groups of immigrants that are linked through the factors of age at arrival, place in the life cycle, and generational location (Kasinitz, Mollenkopf, Waters, and Holdaway 2008; Portes and Rumbaut 2001; Rumbaut 2004; Waters 1999). Drawing on Mannheim's

(1952)[2] classic conceptualization of generations, we associate generation with the historical moment in which one is born and comes of age and with the ways in which this broader historical context shapes the cohort's collective understandings of the world as well as of its own behaviors within it. We also note the diversity that may exist within a generation, which depends on individuals' pre-migration experiences (Eckstein and Berg 2009) and on their intersections with other social categories. Since family members of different ages migrate at various historical moments and thus enter the United States facing different contexts of reception, a life-course perspective (see Giele and Elder 1998) is particularly informative in examining the experiences of immigrant families.

Formally defined, "immigrant generation" refers to age at the time of immigration and to how much time has passed since then. "First-generation immigrants" are those who migrated as adults; "1.5-generation immigrants" are those who were born elsewhere but were raised in the country of destination; "second-generation immigrants" are the first in their families to be born in the new country and have at least one immigrant parent (Portes and Rumbaut 2001). There are also immigrants who do not fit neatly into any of these categories, for example those who were born in the United States, returned to their parents' home country and spent their formative years there, then migrated back to the United States as teenagers or young adults. Officially, these are members of the second generation, yet they share the transnational experience of the 1.5 generation and, depending on the age at which they returned to the United States, the first generation's independence in decision-making.

This chapter explores how immigrant generation informs the identities, aspirations, expectations, and daily life routines of immigrant family members, as well as the ways in which it shapes relations within families. Even though there are cultural imperatives that determine a family's generational dynamics, here we understand "culture" as something that develops and is experienced within a broader structural context (Bean and Tienda 1987). These experiences, in turn, mold relations among family members from different generations. Therefore, in our exploration, we pay attention to the historical moment in which each generation's migration occurred, the context of reception at the time of arrival (Stepick and Stepick 2009), and the generation's intersections with age, legal status, and family configuration. (For an excellent review of generational relations within immigrant families, see Foner and Dreby 2011).

Locating Agency and Constraint within Immigrant Generations

Immigrant generations can be distinguished from one another by members' age at the time of migration and by the level of agency that characterizes the process of migration. First-generation immigrants are more likely to feel that they had a say in the decision to migrate. For the children of immigrants who are born outside the United States and who are also immigrants themselves, the category of 1.5-generation immigrant is meant to capture their "dual frame of reference" (Gu 2012; Rumbaut 2004; Menjívar and Bejarano 2004). Furthermore, those in the 1.5 generation typically do not migrate by their own choosing but instead follow the lead of their parents (Gonzales and Chavez 2012). Finally, immigrants of the second generation are born in the United States and are automatically granted US citizenship by virtue of their birth (Haller, Portes, and Lynch 2011).

Each generation experiences the host society on the basis of its lived knowledge of migration and its distance from the family's migration history, such that immigrants in the first generation develop a dual frame of reference as well. In the example of Adela, her immigrant generation frames her worldview in a way that precludes any desire to take risks (Abrego 2011). When she immigrated she was old enough to understand that she would likely be marginalized in the United States, and thus she is less inclined to demand greater inclusion. Instead, because she remembers the hardships in her native country, she prefers to live in the margins where she is at least earning more money and has some semblance of security by comparison with what she had in Mexico. Adela's children, however, were too young to remember the hardships in Mexico. They grew up in the United States, where their feelings of "home" developed enough to inspire them to fight for full inclusion.

Drawing on their dual frame of reference, those who were poor in their home country are likely to feel optimistic and grateful even for limited opportunities in the United States, and also apprehensive about returning to their home country (where they know for sure that their opportunities are limited). Their dual frame of reference may heighten their appreciation of the opportunities for relatively expansive mobility in the United States, creating what researchers have identified as an "immigrant optimism" (Kao and Tienda 1998).

Second-generation immigrants have a less developed dual frame of reference. They get a bit of a transnational perspective from growing up hearing their immigrant parents' explanations of why they migrated and stories about their initial adaptation to the United States. However, the second generation's members did not live the migration themselves and, by having been born in the United States, have rights that members of the first or 1.5 generations do not have.

The 1.5 generation straddles the first and the second generation. Because members of this middle generation often live their formative years in transition to the host society, they typically remember the initial challenges of adjustment. Some of them may remember when they did not speak or understand English. Moreover, they grow up understanding, in a more visceral way than do children of the second generation, the link between their parents' sacrifices and their aspirations for the children's educational achievement (Louie 2012; Suárez-Orozco and Suárez-Orozco 2001). Its connection to the migration process makes the 1.5 generation able to experience, at least partially, the dual frame of reference that guides the first generation—a lens that is mostly missing in the second generation.

Even though this chapter is devoted to relations across generations, we would like to note other key relationships in immigrant families, such as relations among siblings. These have not attracted much attention in immigration scholarship; but they are fundamental in several respects. Often it is siblings who are in charge of taking care of younger children, of taking them home from school, of preparing meals for them, and, importantly, of modeling their behavior. For instance, among Mexican immigrant children, older siblings are vital for molding participation in after-school activities for younger siblings (Price, Simpkins, and Menjívar forthcoming). Siblings represent a unique source of peer socialization (Furman and Buhrmester 1985; McHale, Updegraff, Tucker, and Crouter 2000), as they not only model behavior and attitudes but also provide information and advice about a range of issues and serve as a key source of emotional support (Hurtado-Ortiz and Gauvain 2007). Interactions between siblings are thus critical indicators of how immigrant families relate to others and shape interactions with institutions such as schools.

In illuminating the importance of sibling relations, we do not claim that these are always smooth or conducive to fruitful development. There are tensions that come with interdependence among siblings, even when they live in different contexts across borders (Aguilar 2013). There is also sibling competition, perhaps no different from competition among non-immigrant families. But among immigrants this competition may occur in immigrant-specific ways, as when siblings have different legal statuses and thus, because of where they were born, do not have access to the same goods in society (see Menjívar and Abrego 2009).

Intergenerational Relations

A focus on immigrant generations allows us to examine relations between parents and children, parents and grandparents, and grandparents and children. These relations are constitutive of immigrant families, as the very definition of a family changes with the addition of a grandparent or a stepparent. However, as we indicated at the beginning of this book, these are not the only possible family relations that define and redefine immigrant families. Often several forms of fictive kin[3] (or what Carsten 2000 has called "relatedness") become part of families and define their contour. Thus, while there is a core of relationships on which we focus when examining relations across generations, we remain cognizant that family dynamics are flexible and fluid and that immigrant families include types of relation not usually contained in the standard North American family (SNAF) (Smith 1993), with its narrowly heteronormative optic and tendential focus on immediate relations.

Intergenerational Obligations

Family relations supposedly provide various forms of support in the context of immigration (Massey, Alarcon, Durand, and González 1987). Building on Coleman's concept of social capital, Grace Kao (2004) identifies three types of resources that are generated through relations among people: obligations and expectations, information channels, and social norms. According to Kao, exchanges of resources are more likely to occur among immigrants because they rarely know people beyond their own social group. Thus, relatives and co-ethnics are expected to provide resources and information that are fundamental for life in the new context (Hagan 1994; Massey et al. 1987; Menjívar 2000).

Immigrants turn to those closest to them to obtain jobs and information about myriad activities, make decisions about renting or buying homes, and the like. Immigrants also obtain assistance from close family in the form of monetary loans designated to support travel to the United States and housing upon arrival (Menjívar 2000). Such familial assistance has been assumed to be effective and reliable (Tung 2000). However, when material conditions in the context of reception undermine immigrants' efforts to generate material resources, immigrants are unable to assist close relatives in need, even if they feel obligated and would like to do so (Menjívar 2000; Roschelle 1997).

Intergenerational relations, particularly among Asian immigrants, have been studied through the prism of culture (see Berry, Phinney, Sam, and Vedder 2006; Kwak 2003)—that is, from the angle of how distance between the culture of origin and the culture of destination affects relations within families. This framework focuses on how parents reference the values that supposedly shape intrafamily dynamics, how this distance can create tension, and how well immigrants manage such tensions (see Suárez-Orozco, Todorova, and Louie 2002). It also examines how collaboration and close relations within the family are influenced by cultural values. Particular attention has been given to the Confucian concept of filial piety, which accounts for the familial respect that purportedly drives Chinese immigrants to help their parents and older relatives. This concept has been used to explain close-knit intergenerational relations among Chinese immigrants (and sometimes among Asians in general). However, obligations to older family members on account of cultural values have also been referenced in Latino families (see Gelfand 1989).

Even though we acknowledge the importance of such practices, we recognize that scholars' depictions of family life as "overdetermined by cultural values" can be problematic when such depictions obscure the structural variations that exist across and within immigrant families, and when they erase the individual agency of immigrants, presenting them as passive enactors of cultural ideals (Ishii-Kuntz 2000; Shih and Pyke 2010). In this vein, whereas research has found that older Asian and Latino/a immigrants are more likely to live with their adult children, thus lending support to the cultural explanations of family obligations, respect, and obligations to the elderly, other research has indicated that what places them in a better position to fulfill family obligations is not so much a culture of obligation as improved socioeconomic conditions (Fukui and Menjívar 2015; Glick and van Hook 2002).

Along these lines, we highlight family members' resistance to cultural expectations and the forms of agency and creative strategies they develop to navigate intergenerational relations that culture-based examinations often miss. In the following example, Stella, a Chinese American immigrant, describes how she steers her relationship with her mother-in-law:

> She talked and I listened and nodded, which is, I think, typical of most intergenerational interaction with your elder.... There's supposed to

be a way around that, which is you thank them for their advice and say, "I'll think about it." Just don't say no to their face! (Shih and Pyke 2010: 350–1)

In this example the younger generation respectfully traverses the cultural expectations of the older generation. Yet it is too simplistic to assume that only the younger generations are flexible. The older generations too respond to cultural and structural change and thus adjust their expectations accordingly. Below Ms. Chen talks about her realization that, in the American context, children treat their parents differently:

As immigrants, we have to learn and adjust to US society ... Children who grow up in the United States will not prioritize your needs over theirs. We need to take care of ourselves rather than bothering our kids. We know that we have to be independent. We need to take care of our own business. If we don't set up our expectations right, we will put a lot of pressure on our children and end up having lots of inter-generational conflicts. (Sun 2014: 882)

Indeed, in a new structural context, elderly parents may come to understand that they cannot expect their own children to care for them (Sun 2014).

Narratives of obligation and tension also *coexist* across generations in Asian families, presenting challenges for the adult children especially when the parents face retirement and illness (see Yoo and Kim 2014). Karen Pyke (2000) reports that, while her Vietnamese and Korean study participants described their own families as strict and emotionally distant, they also couched their own attitudes and plans for caring for their parents in the language of filial obligations. This suggests the importance of interpreting changing expectations and obligations as linked to shifts in social structural contexts (see Menjívar 2000). Mrs. Fong, who is a member of a Taiwanese trans-national family, would like to have been able to be of more help to her parents. But the context of her life made it impossible:

When I learned that my father got cancer, I knew that he would not live much longer. And back then, I could not fly back to Taiwan regularly.

My kids were little. I had to work. And my financial situation was not stable yet. Making one trip home is not that easy. Yet I did try my best to send checks home as much as I could. Yet I still felt really bad about not being there with my father. You know it's exhausting to take care of sick old people ... You need to be constantly on call ... I could not do much because I was so far away ... So you asked me whether I expected my children to look after me. I didn't even take care of my own father. What can I say to my children? (Sun 2014: 879–80)

In Latino families, too, adult immigrants feel guilt about being unable to fulfill their family obligations in culturally expected ways. Like Mrs. Fong, many undocumented Latino/a immigrants are unable to return to their home country to care for a sick parent or grandparent (Schmalzbauer 2014). Indeed it is rather common across groups for legal, financial, and material constraints to limit immigrants' ability to assist their loved ones in need (Menjívar 2000), whether the parents reside in the United States or in the countries of origin. On the basis of her research on Latinos/as and aging, Flippen (2015) observes that connections between adult children and their parents powerfully affect aging both in Latin America and in the United States.

Intergenerational Tensions

While instances of adult children's family contributions and self-lessness are many, it is noteworthy that families are complex and rarely characterized by solidarity alone. Tensions and conflicts across and within generations, especially between parents and children, are common in all family forms (see Foner and Dreby 2011; Lee and Zhou 2004). Thus, clinical psychologists have noted that "Chinese family emphasis can be a source of support, an anchor and a haven, but it can also be suffocating and paralyzing" (Tung 2000: 8).

Nazli Kibria (1993) notes that, among the Vietnamese families in her study, members of different generations agreed that migration had increased family tensions, mostly due to cultural divisions between older and younger members and to demands in the new context. Role reversals between children and adults that are common in immigrant families made it difficult, if not impossible, for the older immigrants to exercise control over the young, as was the tradition in Vietnam. This situation bred tension, as parents (and sometimes grandparents) felt powerless in the face of the new forces (e.g., peers, schools, media, and lifestyles) that now shaped their children's lives. In one case, a father of three exclaimed: "I have children and I can't educate them. The films and TV show bad things, things which are not suited for an Asian culture. On TV, they show love couples doing things, and I think that way it directly teaches the children bad behavior" (Kibria 1993: 146).

Furthermore, Kibria came across cases of children who turned to the police or other authorities to seek protection from corporal punishment (or physical assault) from their parents. In one case a Vietnamese youth who skipped school and apparently had befriended members of a Vietnamese gang called the police after his father hit him for coming home late. This incident saddened the father, who could not understand why the authorities thought he had done something wrong. Different social norms surrounding children's discipline in the United States can cause confusion about what constitutes good parenting.

Similarly, Menjívar (2000) spoke with a Salvadoran teenage girl in San Francisco who had threatened to call the police on her mother if her family ever commented on her comings and goings. This (mis)use of power was even more striking given the context of her family's migration. Her mother had fled the civil war in El Salvador, was apprehensive of authorities in general, and was undocumented, which made her especially anxious. Mary Waters (1999) presents similar cases among West Indian immigrants.

Thus, like all families, immigrant families must navigate generational social norms that are in a process of constant change. However, for immigrant families, there are added challenges based on changes in social norms in the transition from the country of origin to the new society. This shifting social terrain makes parenting tricky, especially as immigrant parents must simultaneously learn a new language, work in a new industry, and adapt to a new society.

Adding another layer of complexity to immigrant families' intergenerational relations, the children's developmental stage upon arrival means that children are likely to learn the language of the host society more quickly than parents, setting up in this way an unequal power dynamic. For example, while parents may be strict and may desire to control their children, they are also likely to develop a certain amount of reliance on them, insofar as children become more adept at navigating social institutions. Dependence on children in central aspects of family life may, in some way, subvert the parent–child roles, offering an example of what Portes and Rumbaut (2001) term *dissonant acculturation*; and this phenomenon can have a negative impact on child development and on overall family well-being (Schmalzbauer 2014).

Interpretation and translation are regular forms of help from young to adult immigrants, and they are common among a variety of immigrant groups, such as Jews (Gold 1992), Mexicans (Schmalzbauer 2014), Vietnamese, Chinese (Buriel and De Ment 1997) and Salvadorans (Menjívar 2000). In this respect, children serve as "cultural brokers" (Buriel and De Ment 1997), interpreting and translating not only the language, but also cultural practices in the host society (in this case, the United States). Menjívar (2000, 2002a) came across Guatemalan and Salvadoran youngsters doing interpretation for their parents in school settings, in physicians' clinics, and in supermarkets (among other locations). Sometimes translations went smoothly and the youth did their best, while other times they used these occasions to assert their newfound authority, and translations did not go well. This reversed parent–child dependence is intensified in new immigrant destinations, where few social-service workers speak a foreign language and translation services are rare (Schmalzbauer 2014).

These examples of English-speaking and culturally savvy children of immigrants exploiting their newfound power over their parents are not new; nor are the tensions these inequalities generate new. Elizabeth Ewen (1985), for example, noted that mothers in the European migrations of the turn of last century were also conflicted about the influences of the new context on their children. They were especially ambivalent about how US institutions such as schools, while serving as a platform for mobility, also created rifts between themselves and their children. Among recent immigrants there are new contextual forces that place *additional* demands and challenges on relations between and across generations, such as the effects of legal status and the consequent risk of lengthy and uncertain parent–child separations (Menjívar and Abrego 2009; Reynolds and Orellana 2009).

Social class matters here too, as generational role reversals are less likely to happen in families from higher socioeconomic backgrounds. Immigrant families with college-educated parents and financial resources are more likely to include parents who already have a basic knowledge of English and familiarity with US institutions and lifestyles. Given the prevalence of English as a language of power throughout the world, immigrants coming from advantaged backgrounds are more likely to have learned some English prior to migration. Poor and working-class immigrants likely have few years of schooling, often have limited skills in their first language, and will therefore be more likely to rely on their children for translation.

Immigrant youth from less advantaged backgrounds may also have income-earning responsibilities within their families. This often happens in agricultural families, where it is expected that all members contribute their labor (Holmes 2013; Schmalzbauer 2014). Children work alongside their parents in urban areas as well, as Menjívar (2000) observed in San Francisco, where young children of Salvadoran immigrants helped their parents clean houses and work in gardening. Children in families that endure the deportation of an income-earning parent may take it upon themselves to find jobs to help cover lost wages. And children contribute labor when parents own small businesses (Hamilton and Chinchilla 2001).

Immigrant children also typically have responsibilities for work within the home (Orellana 2001). Labor within families has varying implications for children's education and for their future. In some cases, children may grow resentful that they are not allowed to experience the carefree childhood constructed as the norm in the contemporary United States (see Zelizer 1985). They may have to drop their activities in order to learn the details of the official family business, and much of this work, given its central-ity to overall family well-being, can become burdensome. On the other hand, children who grow up in areas where child labor is normalized may experience these added responsibilities as oppor-tunities to contribute to family well-being (Schmalzbauer 2014) and to develop skills that they continue to draw on as young adults (Katz 2014; Orellana 2009).

Caring for younger siblings is a common way for immigrant children to contribute labor within their families. When parents work long hours to make ends meet (Vasquez 2011), it often falls to older children, especially daughters, to step into a parenting role. In families with siblings of different immigrant generations, youth may also play an important bridging role. Schmalzbauer (2014) observes that sometimes children of the 1.5 generation can serve as language connectors between their Spanish-speaking parents and their English-preferring second-generation siblings. At the same time, Fernández-Kelly (2014) notes that 1.5- and second-generation children's increased use of English effectively connects them to peers while distancing them from their parents.

Even though there is an extensive scholarship on the potentially detrimental effects that caring activities may have on children, as these activities can sidetrack them from school activities and similar endeavors (see Katz 2014 for a review), researchers have also noted the benefits that can accrue from performing caring tasks. On the basis of a study of Mexican immigrants in Chicago, Dorner, Orellana, and Li-Grinning (2007) observe that language brokering has positive effects on academic achievement, particu-larly on standardized tests. And on the basis of an ethnographic study of various immigrant groups, Vikki Katz (2014) argues that the different tasks that children perform for their parents, often focused as they are on connecting the family with institutions in society, are ultimately beneficial for the children.

Life Cycle and Age at Migration

We focus on the intersection between immigration and the life course, as immigrants have widely different experiences, depending on when they arrive in the United States. Rooted in Karl Mannheim's conceptualization of generations, as we stated in the introduction, the life-course approach is defined as a "sequence of socially defined events and roles that the individual enacts over time" (Giele and Elder 1998: 22). This perspective is useful for our examination because we place immigrant families' relations within the socioeconomic and historic context in which they live today.

Age at the time of migration matters because it determines how immigrants are integrated into the formative institutional contexts that shape paths of incorporation (Abrego 2011; Carling, Menjívar, and Schmalzbauer 2012; Gleeson and Gonzales 2012). Age also informs the responsibilities and roles assigned to individuals within families as well as the aspirations and expectations people have for the future (Schmalzbauer 2014). Importantly, the life cycle is not static, as age can have different meanings depending on social class, race and ethnicity, gender, migration experience, cultural practices, and legal status.

Contextual and structural forces that intersect with age at arrival also inform the experiences that immigrants of different generations may have. For instance, changes to the Immigration and Nationality Act of 1965 shifted upwards the age structure of recent arrivals through family chain migration (Carr and Tienda 2013). Family sponsorship has led to a recent increase in the admission of legal permanent residents aged 50 and over. Thus, immigrants are not simply "aging in place"; but recent immigrants are arriving at older ages and this has consequences for their families, labor market participation, communities, and the provision of social services.

Older Immigrants

Research on older immigrants is scant as more attention has been given to immigrants who arrive either as adults and are expected to enter the workforce or as younger immigrants who enter educational institutions and will be the workforce of the future. And there is enormous variation in the experiences of older immigrants, some arriving at young ages and aging in place while others arrive as older adults. For these immigrants, as for those of any age, time of arrival has profound implications for their relationships with their families, communities, and institutions.

Research on the lives of older immigrants is consistent insofar as it reports the difficulties that they have in adjusting to life in the United States, particularly with regard to their relationships with their adult children and grandchildren. For many, their social worlds are turned upside down because, with migration, they lose the connections they have established over a lifetime. Their children and grandchildren, who are busy working to sustain their own families, often do not have the time and energy to lend them adequate support during this difficult transition (Menjívar 2000).

Older adults typically migrate to the United States to be closer to their children and grandchildren and often to provide child care for the latter while the parent generation works (Gilbertson 2009; Treas and Mazumdar 2004). If the older immigrants have legal permanent resident status or are naturalized US citizens, they have access to elder care facilities and to centers that provide activities and entertainment that help them build community. However, older immigrants are typically not able to acquire "labor force experience or English language fluency, [so] they remain dependent on their families for economic support and housing" (Treas and Batalova 2009: 390). In these cases they experience social isolation, as they are unable to expand their social networks, often have difficulty learning English, and, because their extended family may not be in the United States, many feel lonely (Menjívar 2000). A sense of loneliness can affect their overall well-being (Kim 1999).

Despite these challenges, research points to the significant contributions of grandparents and older adults to immigrant families: these contributions often go beyond child care and help with household chores, to include lending children emotional support and fomenting cultural traditions and practices from the home country. In some cases, the latter may prove challenging when the grandparents, seeking to fulfill their role as transmitters of culture and values, try to instill them in grandchildren who are uninterested and unappreciative (Menjívar 2000).

Often, as members of the older generation find it hard to fit in with the rest of the family, they venture into the community to find opportunities to talk and socialize. This was the case of an older Salvadoran woman whom Menjívar (2000) interviewed in San Francisco. Although her children and grandchildren had little time to spend with her, she discovered that the nurses and physicians at the clinic she attended would take the time to talk. Thus, she would stop by the clinic even when she did not have an appointment or was not ill. In her words: "I am enchanted with them. Oh, the doctors are beautiful. I don't mean physically because they're young, but because of the way they treat me ... [My doctor] is so kind. He asks, "Let's see, Señora Hilda, how you are feeling?" and he talks to me and sits with me and doesn't rush ... I feel happy when I leave" (Menjívar 2000: 203).

Although many immigrants initially plan to return to their home countries after retirement, their transnational ties often fade as they age, in large part because their family and kin have grown deeper roots in the United States. As their children and grandchildren become more rooted in the United States, it is difficult for elderly immigrants to leave. Simultaneously, their relationships to place change with time (Bedorf 2014).

Elderly immigrants develop a sense of belonging in the host society through participation in organized activities. They turn to senior centers, as the experiences of Latinos/as and Asians of various national origins in Phoenix show (Fukui and Menjívar 2015). In the cases studied, the visits to these centers, which for the seniors serve as alternatives to the isolation they experience in their families, had the benefit of generating social capital. Through the people they met at these centers, often other seniors, older immigrants would obtain information about good physicians in town, about applications for various services, and about other useful tips for navigating life in the city.

Social class offers an important angle from which to examine these experiences. The resettlement experience may be easier for older immigrants from higher class backgrounds who are sponsored by their adult children, arrive with immigrant visas, speak English already, and join their families in middle-class neighborhoods. Such was the case of Mrs. K—a retired immigrant from India who came to the United States to help her adult daughter care for her children. Given her family's social class standing and her English fluency, she quickly integrated into a local community center.

> I prefer to mix with non-Indians in the senior center. Indians tend to stick together and not mix very much with others ... They are very interested in personal matters. First question they ask is if my daughter-in-law is good?!! But, Americans don't ask any such personal questions. I have many American friends but they don't ask things like that. I make it a point to be with American friends so they can learn more about India through me rather than television. (Kalavar and van Willigen 2005: 217)

Adult Immigrants

This middle generation oftentimes serves as a bridge and mediator between grandparents and grandchildren. Like grandparents, adults are transmitters of cultural practices, traditions, and beliefs. Also like grandparents, parents can be conduits for what has been called *transgenerational trauma*, which is found among descendants of holocaust survivors and recently was also identified among Latinos/as (Phipps and Degges-White 2014).

A central feature of adult immigrants' lives is their participation in the labor force as a defining aspect of who they are. Their work lives shape family dynamics in fundamental ways, both in the United States and in the sending countries. Adult immigrants' earnings translate into remittances that are critical for the survival of non-migrant family members in the origin countries (Menjívar, DaVanzo, Greenwell, and Valdez 1998), and also shape the structure of households in the United States and the relations between parents and children as well as those within couples (Menjívar 1999).

For instance, Min Zhou (2009) observes that, in most Chinese immigrant families, both parents work full time and it is not unusual for them to hold several jobs at once. In these circumstances the children become "latch-key children," spending hours alone at home after school. This can create challenges for parental supervision in families with low educational levels and who live in low-income neighborhoods, given the risks that exist in low-income areas.

Low-skilled and undocumented migrants who come to the United States as adults face significant barriers to incorporation. Their migration was most likely precipitated by lack of opportunity in their home country, and they bring lower levels of human capital that result from their lack of access to education in the sending country. They may also have left close family members behind (Dreby 2010; Schmalzbauer 2004). Besides, even if first-generation adult immigrants are bold, brave, and ambitious, an undocumented status can thwart their initial optimism, as they learn that access to opportunity and thus to paths to mobility is severely limited (Menjívar 2008).

Given the centrality of work for adult immigrants, they tend to begin their socialization through experiences in the workplace. But the labor market is highly segregated by gender, class, race and ethnicity, and immigration status and thus it is likely that adult immigrants will be surrounded by others with similar experiences. While this may help adult immigrants feel comfortable around others, who speak their language and share an immigration history, it may also serve to isolate them from other sectors of society and prevent them from integrating more fluidly, as is more typical of immigrants who arrived as children. These experiences can have various consequences for their families.

The 1.5 Generation and the Second Generation

The age at which immigrant youth arrive in the host society shapes their perspectives and feelings of belonging (Carling et al. 2012). For example, young immigrants spend most of their time in a school context that permits them to experience the full socialization process along with classmates who likely have different backgrounds. Via their participation in school, they learn English and become incorporated into their communities. Depending on their and their parents' race, social class, and legal position, this incorporation may or may not lead to a path of upward mobility (Portes and Rumbaut 2001; Zhou and Bankston 1998). Race, discrimination, and racism are also consequential for children of immigrants of non-European origins, as authorities have the power to open doors for them or block them from opportunities. In too many cases, educators and service providers use racial and gender stereotypes as criteria that guide their work with children of immigrants and immigrant children of different ethnic and racial backgrounds (Ochoa 2013; Rios 2011).

Furthermore, depending on social class, adolescence may be prolonged in advantaged families as youth delay marriage and child-bearing, extending their dependence on their parents while they attend university and transition into the workforce. Or adulthood can be rushed, as is the case for poor and working-class youth, who often enter into parenthood and the workforce while still in their teens or early twenties because they lack the human, economic, and social capital to attend college or to maintain a state of dependence (Bettie 2003). Similarly, immigrant youth experience the life cycle differently depending on their social position. Most striking are the negative impacts that parental poverty and undocumented status have on child development and well-being, even for the US-born second-generation immigrant children (Yoshikawa 2011) or those in the third generation (Bean, Brown, and Bachmeier 2015).

Due to the 1982 ruling in *Plyler v. Doe*, in the United States all children, even undocumented children, have the constitutional right to K-12 education. However, once undocumented children turn 18, the incorporative shelter that school provides collapses and they must, as Roberto Gonzales (2011) suggests, "learn to be illegal." Undocumented youth face barriers to higher education and confront social challenges prompted by not having access to driver's licenses or formal identification documents that allow them entry into adult establishments.[4] Hence illegality limits undocumented youth's socialization into adulthood (Abrego 2006; Gonzales and Chavez 2012).

Second-generation children, though US citizens, come of age in the context of recent immigration. While they do not carry the burden of illegality, they may still face racism, discrimination, and blocked mobility (Portes and Rumbaut 2001; Portes and Zhou 1993). Racialized stereotypes, which are based on the conflation of culture and social class as well as on race and legal status, shape the life chances of children in the second generation too (see Chapter 3).

A significant body of research examines the trajectories of the second generation, noting the direct implications for the future of immigrant families. Some works articulate a generally optimistic outlook for the future of children of immigrants, while others portray an array of nuanced trajectories (Alba, Kasinitz, and Waters 2011; Haller et al. 2011; Portes and Fernández-Kelly 2008; Portes and Rumbaut 2001; Smith 2008). Some researchers conclude that second-generation immigrants are doing much better than their parents, particularly with regard to education and occupational concentration measures (Alba et al. 2011; Kasinitz et al. 2008). Others detect wide variation in the adaptation of the second generation, observing that, while there are many in it who are doing well on account of specific family-level factors and school contexts, many are not faring well as they follow downward paths of incorporation (Haller et al. 2011), a situation that can persist beyond the second generation (Telles and Ortiz 2008). Indeed, Bean et al. (2015) find that the negative effects of an undocumented status on educational levels persist into the third generation.

Unaccompanied Children

Recently, there has been significant attention to the flows of Central American unaccompanied children entering the United States through the southern Mexico–US border. However, Central American children have been migrating for years (Chavez and Menjívar 2010) and, more generally, children have been migrating alone since the times of migration through Ellis Island.[5] Historically, unaccompanied children sometimes had parents or relatives to receive them, but just as often they did not. Many were held in detention on Ellis Island, and volunteers, mostly women, would care for them there.[6]

Whereas the children arriving at Ellis Island came for a variety of reasons and seemed to initiate the migration process all on their own, contemporary flows of "unaccompanied" children differ in terms of the actors involved in organizing their migration. Historically, the migration of some of these children was highly organized by state agencies, community organizations, or the children's families, while that of others seemed to be more "spontaneous." One example comes from Operation Peter Pan,[7] which made possible the migration of approximately 14,000 unaccompanied Cuban children sent by their parents between 1960 and 1962, after the Cuban Revolution. Coordinated by the Catholic Welfare Bureau in Miami and aided by the US State Department, the program relied on a well-resourced network that received the children and placed them in foster care or with relatives. Parents sent their children in order to keep them from communist indoctrination under the new regime. This program was a highly coordinated effort by the US government in conjunction with the community organizations that received the children.

In other cases, the children's families at the sending and receiving ends coordinate the migration of seemingly unaccompanied children. Asian immigrant communities, particularly in southern California, may be familiar with so-called "parachute children." Children between eight and 17 years of age are sent by their parents to enroll in US schools, so that they have an advantage in admissions to prestigious US colleges and universities (Zhou 1998). They arrive from South Korea, the Philippines, and India, but mostly from Hong Kong and Taiwan, and overwhelmingly come from wealthy families to join relatives or paid caretakers in the United States. Although these Asian minors and the recent Central Americans could all be classified as "unaccompanied minors," there are striking differences between the two. Whereas the "parachute children" come from homes with substantial levels of financial and social capital, the Central American and Mexican youth do not. Not entirely coincidentally, the Central American children have attracted considerable attention from politicians, from the media, and from some members of the communities into which they have come to live: all of these debate whether the children should be sent back. In contrast, little attention was paid to the estimated 40,000 "parachute children" who arrived in the 1980s and 1990s (Zhou 2009) to live in affluent neighborhoods.

The recent increase in the migration of unaccompanied children from Central America and Mexico has direct implications for immigrant families. Although the media and the politicians discuss this flow in terms of Central American migration, it should be noted that minors from Guatemala, El Salvador, and Honduras make up 75 percent of those 68,541 apprehended in fiscal year 2014; but there is also a significant proportion coming from Mexico, the country that sent the overwhelming majority of minors to the United States up until 2014 (Stinchcomb and Hershberg 2014).[8] According to a United Nations High Commissioner on Refugees report based on a study of 404 children (UNHCR 2014), these children seek to arrive in the United States or other countries in the region for the purpose of reaching safety from structural violence—poverty, inequality, gangs, and domestic violence—in their countries of origin. The UNHCR report indicates that most are boys, but the number of girls is increasing; and 36 percent of these children have at least one parent in the United States and thus reunification may be an important reason for their migration. A study by Donato and Sisk (2015) that draws on large-scale data on child migrants from Nicaragua, El Salvador, Guatemala, and Mexico finds that the migration of children is often tied to the migration of their unauthorized parents, who cannot organize family reunification by legal means. Gender and age matter here too, as boys are more likely to migrate than girls and older children are more likely to migrate than younger ones. And there is important variation in family and migration experiences by nationality: while 49 percent of Salvadorans and 42 percent of Hondurans have at least one parent in the United States, only 27 percent of Guatemalans and 22 percent of Mexicans do.

The Special Place of the Generation within Mixed-Status and Undocumented Families

Many immigrant families in the United States are "mixed-status families." That is, they include various combinations of US citizens, permanent legal residents, undocumented immigrants, and individuals who live in "liminal legality" (Menjívar 2006a, 2006b). Furthermore, a family's legal composition is typically not static, as members may transition from being undocumented to being temporary workers, from being permanent legal residents to becoming citizens, or from holding some temporary status to being undocumented immigrants (Fix and Zimmerman 2001). These legal differences and this state of flux position family members differently with respect to accessing social services and institutions such as schools or hospitals.

The complexity and fluidity of legal status affect intergenerational relations and individuals' perceptions of their place within their families. In general, family members who are US citizens and legal permanent residents have relatively greater access to resources than liminally legal or undocumented members of the same family. This can create tensions across and within generations. Menjívar and Abrego (2009) describe the case of Mario, a 16-year-old undocumented Guatemalan immigrant who lives in Los Angeles. His younger brother was born in the United States, which made him the only member of the family with US citizenship. In the following excerpt, Mario describes the resentments that have arisen owing to the mixture of statuses in his family:

> I don't have medical insurance. My younger brother, whenever he's sick, they always take him to the hospital, and stuff like that, because the government pays for him ... My mom takes him to the dentist yearly, to the doctor, you know, but if I feel really sick, like I have to be dying to go to the hospital. But then, you know, my brother, he feels a stomach ache, "let's go to the hospital." (*laughs*) (Menjívar and Abrego 2009: 178–79)

As Mario's comments indicate, stratified access to health care may lead to differentiated treatment of some children on the basis of their legal status.[9] Although he understood that his brother had legal access to more resources, Mario harbored resentment toward his mother for what he perceived to be limited concern for his own well-being.

Yet in other situations, mixed legal statuses can create enhanced family solidarity and appreciation. Alisa, a 19-year-old Guatemalan undocumented college student in Los Angeles, is grateful that her entire family can benefit from her twin sisters' US citizenship. Because her sisters are US-born, they are eligible for government assistance, including public housing that is more spacious than what the other members of the family—all of whom are undocumented—could otherwise access:

> We moved over here because of the twins. I have two smaller twin sisters, they were born here, but when they were 5 months old, they got epilepsy, both of them, so it damaged their brain ... We used to live in a smaller apartment so they gave us a larger apartment for them ... so they could have more room to walk around and stuff ... This is not in a nice neighborhood, but from the inside, it's nicer than a lot of my friends' apartments. (Menjívar and Abrego 2009: 179)

Documented members of mixed-status families may also be appreciated for their ability to travel outside of the country and thus maintain transnational family ties. Specifically, US-born children can help maintain relations with grandparents back home (Menjívar 2002a). At the same time, undocumented members of the same family who cannot travel (lest they should not return) may feel transnationally detached from their extended family.

Analyzing the intersection of generation, life cycle, and legal status also helps us to better understand the divergent behaviors and expectations of individuals in mixed-status families. In particular, the youthfulness of certain undocumented youth may be the main factor that encourages them to take risks and be active in a social movement (see McAdam 1988). As exemplified in the chapter's introduction, since 2010 undocumented youth have spearheaded a vibrant immigrant rights movement that, with the chant "Undocumented and Unafraid!" calls for an end to mass deportations and legalization for all (Nicholls 2013). Undocumented adults, on the other hand, often have shied from political activity; yet small but now increasing numbers participate in collective actions (Letiecq and Schmalzbauer 2012; Pallares 2014), sometimes encouraged by their children (Bloemraad and Trost 2008; Terriquez and Kwon 2014).

Historical context helps to explain this generational divergence in political activity. In the past 30 years laws have criminalized undocumented immigrants while at the same time providing undocumented children with legal access to key social institutions. The surveillance of undocumented labor, coupled with legal access to public schooling for undocumented children, is paradoxical and confusing. Undocumented children, via their participation in primary and secondary education, are socialized to be members of society, with the expectation that they will remain in the country. Yet once they reach 18 they become legally prohibited from fulfilling their goals. These historically specific, discriminatory conditions have given rise to the current movement of undocumented youth, who are making public demands for their own as well as for their parents' social and legal inclusion (Abrego 2008, 2011; Bloemraad and Trost 2008; Nicholls 2013; Pallares 2014; Seif 2004).

While mixed-status families have rightfully been given attention in immigration scholarship and in policy discussions, we would like to draw attention to families in which all members are undocumented. Given the current climate of enforcement practices, the barriers to socioeconomic mobility and general well-being for undocumented families are enormous. In these families tensions can arise from the different meanings that children and parents attach to their undocumented status. Undocumented parents may feel less stigmatized by their status than youth raised in the United States, the latter having a stronger desire to fit in but facing harassment and marginalization at school. The parents may not understand their children's discomfort, while the children may be annoyed by what they view as their parents' acquiescent attitude (Abrego forthcoming).

Often, undocumented children who are socialized in the United

States develop different aspirations from those of their parents, but their legal status limits them to what they regard as (un)desirable jobs (Abrego 2006). Given the context in which they were raised, undocumented children are resentful of the low-level jobs available to them by virtue of their legal status and are therefore more reluctant to accept them than their parents' generation is. For Mexican and Central American women who migrate as adults, domestic jobs are common and even desirable (Hondagneu-Sotelo 2009). Yet young women who were largely raised and educated in the United States do not share this view and often reject such positions (Abrego 2006).

Compounding these difficulties, children sometimes do not make an effort in school or may even drop out because they are aware that, with a tenuous legal status, more schooling will not translate into the kinds of rewards they desire (Menjívar and Abrego 2012). Parents, in turn, are frustrated that their children do not want to reap the benefits of access to US education—benefits that they sacrificed so much for their children to attain. In this situation clashes may ensue (Menjívar 2000, 2002a, 2006a). The mother of Jovani, a 16-year-old undocumented Guatemalan high school student in Los Angeles, is a part-time nanny and active volunteer at his school. She expects Jovani to be a focused, successful student; but Jovani has been influenced by his older, also undocumented, cousin's inability to attend college despite academic effort. Jovani's mother requested advice from school staff to help her son pursue higher education, but Jovani, who feels the stigma associated with an unauthorized status, prefers to avoid authorities and is inclined to give up. Instead of working hard, he has enrolled in the 10th grade for the second year in a row, after failing all of his classes (Menjívar and Abrego 2009: 180–1).

Transnational Intergenerational Ties and Family Separations

Many immigrants, especially those who are poor and working class, must travel undocumented, by land or sea. The journey across one or more national borders is dangerous and costly and parents often prefer not to expose their children to such hardships, choosing to leave them home. Over time, some parents send for their children; but it becomes difficult, dangerous, and expensive to care for them in the United States, particularly when these children arrive to live in inner cities. Thus, some parents send children back, to be cared for by (usually female) relatives in the home country (see also Ho 1993; Levitt 2001; Menjívar 2002a; Miller Matthei and Smith 1998). Whether parents leave the children back home or send them back, the result is an often lengthy and uncertain separation with multiple consequences.

During times of separation, remittances represent tangible forms of care for the children back home (Dreby 2010; McKenzie and Menjívar 2011; Parreñas 2001; Schmalzbauer 2004, 2005). When parents and children remain separated, parents are more likely to remit and, when they do, to send more than if their children were with them (Menjívar, DaVanzo, Greenwell, and Burciaga Valdez 1998). Structural conditions, including legal status and labor market opportunities, determine the sums and frequency of the remittances that immigrants are able to remit (Abrego 2014; Schmalzbauer 2008). Several immigrant parents in our studies lost their jobs during the Great Recession, and the jobs they obtained after recession are more precarious and less well remunerated (Menjívar and Enchautegui 2015). Also, parents in this category injure themselves while performing dangerous jobs, which can force them to suspend remittances, at least temporarily (see also Walter, Bourgois, and Loinaz 2004). Therefore, all these conditions bear on parents' ability to remit.

In the home countries, children rely on remittances for their daily survival during long-term parental absences, and thus they come to associate remittances with love (McKenzie and Menjívar 2011). As Viviana Zelizer (2007) observes, remittances not only provide vital resources for survival but also serve to mitigate the trials of long-term separations. When parents are able to remit consistently, their children experience improved living conditions, greater access to education, and sometimes a notable upward boost of their socioeconomic status (Schmalzbauer 2005, 2008).

Despite the pain of separation, they are likely to appreciate their parents' sacrifices and they maintain strong, positive contact with their parents.

Those who receive regular sums of money, whose life improvements are visible and tangible—through luxury items in the home or greater access to education—have *proof* that their parents continue to be committed to the family. This became apparent during fieldwork in Guatemala and Honduras, where locals would gauge the risk of abandonment that a woman and her children faced by paying attention to expenditures on the children's clothing, toys, and even vitamins, all supposedly purchased with remittances from the children's fathers or the women's partners in the United States (McKenzie and Menjívar 2011; Menjívar 2011a; Menjívar and Agadjanian 2007).

Children who receive few or no remittances can feel abandoned and may come to resent their parents (Abrego 2014; Dreby 2010). When immigrants are unable to send money, the non-migrating children have nothing to show for their parents' absence. The prolonged separation, in these cases, seems unjustified and the impoverished conditions of the family in the home country can become evidence of the parents' failed commitment to their kin. This impression is due, in part, to the unrealistic expectations that many non-migrants have about migrants' living conditions and opportunities for success in the United States (Schmalzbauer 2005, 2008). It is also based on the real possibility that some parents, particularly fathers, form other unions and new families in the United States and thus discontinue regular remittances to their children (Menjívar 1999).

Family separation is also experienced differently depending on the gender of the migrant parent. Children in transnational families express sorrow about their family's separation, but narratives reveal more emotional language and greater suffering for children whose mother, as opposed to father, migrated (Abrego 2014; Parreñas 2001). Importantly, children's age when they were separated from parents is critical for parent–children relations across borders, as it influences their connection and the memories they have of each other (Carling et al. 2012). Children left as babies do not have memories of the parents. In contrast, children left at older ages retain a vivid sense of the separation, which creates feelings of resentment toward the parents.

Although many parents and children look forward to being reunited, reunification does not always go smoothly (Artico 2003; Suárez-Orozco et al. 2002). It usually involves a process of reacquaintance, accommodation, and learning to fit into a reconstituted family that may be significantly different from the one imagined. Economic readjustment adds complications when the gifts previously remitted must stop because life becomes more expensive when the children arrive to join their parents in the United States (Menjívar and Abrego 2009). Leigh Leslie (1993) notes that family reunification for Central Americans can be prob- lematic on account of unrealistic expectations that parents and children have of each other. Children come to the United States in search of their idealized parent, only to find that that parent is away from home most of the day, working to provide for them and living in a space that is often less than ideal; and they also find new step- and half-siblings from a parent's new union. Lengthy separations can also lead to estrangement between parents and children because both are exposed to different environments and experiences during their separation, and reunifications can even be traumatic (Menjívar and Abrego 2009; Suárez-Orozco, Bang, and Kim 2010). Reunifications can thus be bittersweet, with moments of happiness as well as of tension and disappointment.

Conclusion

Immigrant generation provides a critical lens for understanding the divergent experiences of immigrant family members. In this chapter we highlight how social context shapes generational expe- riences within immigrant families. Specifically, we show how a particular historical moment and structural context, legal status, social class, race, gender, age at arrival, and family configuration strongly impact family relations within and between generations. Resources and the stability that comes with legal status can ease tensions among members of different generations. This is not to say that cultural differences and social norms do not require negotiation; it suggests instead that culture is constructed and interpreted within a larger social context and can be resisted and transformed according to that context and historical moment. Thus, immigrants who arrive in the United States with high levels of social and economic capital and with a documented legal status are more likely to experience a smoother incorporation; but their experiences are further molded by age of arrival, gender, and generation. Finally, relations that immigrant families maintain across borders are similarly impacted by social position, broader context, and structural forces.

6

Institutions, Policy, and
Immigrant Families

In a recent Rasmussen Report (2014) designed to gauge public opinions about immigration among likely voters, 71 percent of respondents said that newly arrived undocumented immigrants should not have access to government services or benefits and 63 percent believed that government money and services are magnets that draw undocumented immigrants to the United States. Beyond the percentages, what is interesting about these results is that they are based on long-held misconceptions about what benefits and services immigrants—documented and undocumented—can access. As this chapter will underscore, contrary to popular opinion, undocumented and many of the documented immigrants lack access to a wide range of US government benefits. Except for emergency assistance and other forms of limited aid that vary by state of residence, a significant number of immigrants in the United States cannot avail themselves of government benefits or public goods.

Whereas Chapter 2 focused on immigration law and policies and on how these shape the contours of immigrant families, in this chapter we examine how family-related policies, such as the Personal Responsibility and Work Opportunity Reconciliation Act (PRWORA) and the Affordable Care Act (ACA), intersect with "immigrant policies" to shape the experiences of families. To bring into relief the impact of government policies and institutions on immigrant families' well-being, we will also cover the basics of how refugee law extends benefits to families, as refugees constitute the only group with a right to benefits that facilitate resettlement. Our focus on the links between families, institutions, and policies closely parallels a general interest among sociologists of the family in the relationship between the family and the state (see Aulette 2007; Cherlin 2008).

Immigration policies (the subject of Chapter 2), through control of the numbers of people who enter the country, create legal statuses that position individuals differently with respect to opportunities and barriers (Menjívar and Abrego 2012). *Immigrant policies* (the subject of this chapter), on the other hand, are policies that dictate how immigrants will be treated once they are in the country. Such policies can facilitate—or their absence can impede—immigrants' adjustment. Thus, immigrant policies intersect with *family policy*, which Cherlin (2008: 472) defines as the "political beliefs about how the government should assist families in caring for dependants." In this chapter we examine the link between immigrant family members and the institutions and policies that control their access to education and schools, to the healthcare system, and to housing (among other benefits). We bring to light how immigrant families are affected not only by policies of admission but also by other general laws and policies that impinge on their well-being.

The legal statuses of family members influence whether, when, where, and how immigrants and their families can access social benefits. The experiences of mixed-status families, discussed in Chapters 2 and 5, are particularly revealing in this respect, as they display varying levels of access—determined by legal status—to social benefits (Menjívar 2006a, 2012). There are approximately 2.3 million families that can be classified as of "mixed status" today (Passel 2011) and, given the system of immigration laws that is in place, their numbers will likely increase. For this reason mixed-status families provide an important opportunity to examine the link between government agencies and families (Castañeda and Melo 2014), particularly when access bifurcates the experiences of siblings, positioning them differently vis-à-vis resources (Abrego and Menjívar 2011).

These matters can be quite complex, because policies created with one objective in mind end up linking different institutions and agencies to various sets of policies. For instance, the removal of parents through deportation—an immigration enforcement-related issue—leads to the involvement of other government agencies, such as child welfare and child protective services, and creates the need for new policies, geared toward safeguarding parental rights. The detention and deportation of undocumented immigrant parents has sent at least 5,100 US-born children to the foster care system and, upon the termination of their parents' custodial rights,[1] these children can be (and have been) put up for adoption (Wessler 2011).[2] These enforcement actions, in turn, trigger the involvement of various other government agencies that aim to protect these children and meet their needs.

Geography and the location of one's residence also play an important role in the well-being of immigrant families. While the federal government passes laws and creates policies that dictate access to a range of federal assistance, there are significant variations by state, county, and municipality. Although the federal government still has preemptive powers to determine admission into the country and access to federally funded assistance, states and lower-level governments also have power to affect families. States can and do pass a wide range of immigrant laws and policies that determine access to state-level funds and benefits. Some states have taken legislative action in line with federal law, thus reinforcing what the federal government stipulates. Other states, however, have diverged and passed laws that have made it easier, or in certain cases more difficult, for immigrants to access social services and benefits. We examine these differences and their effects through the lens of geographical location.[3]

Next we summarize federal and state laws that determine families' access to goods and benefits. More than ever, eligibility for benefits hinges on the immigrants' legal and citizenship status, as certain basic benefits are extended to US citizens but not to immigrants, even if the latter have been formally (lawfully) admitted and are permanent legal residents. We will then discuss the difference that access (and lack of it) makes in terms of immigrant families' well-being and integration in the areas of education, health care, housing, and general aid. We end the chapter with a

Institutieeg

section on NGOs and community organizations that attempt to fill the vacuum of assistance when federal or state laws prevent immigrant families from accessing goods and services.

Federal and State Immigrant Policies

In the past two decades the federal government has passed several pieces of legislation that affect families in general and have particular effects on immigrant families. The effects of legislation span a wide range of issues that concern families in general, such as children's insurance, domestic violence, family leave, and same-sex marriage, among others (Cherlin 2008). In this brief overview we highlight only a few but important federal legislative actions passed in 1996 and still in effect today that have had particular influence on immigrant families: the PRWORA and the Illegal Immigration Reform and Immigrant Responsibility Act (IIRIRA). We also cover the ACA of 2010 along with some long-standing pieces of legislation, such as refugee policies and the *Plyer v. Doe* (1982) US Supreme Court decision, which gave undocumented immigrant children the right to K-12 education. All these federal-level policies have directly impacted immigrant families, and those passed in recent years have sought to limit immigrants' access to public benefits.

PRWORA was designed to move welfare recipients into the labor force more quickly, but in effect it rolled back policies that had been in place since 1935 and were designed to address the needs of poor families (Cherlin 2008). Among other provisions, it ended entitlement to welfare benefits, so that the government no longer guarantees aid to poor families. It set a five-year limit on cash assistance, reduced the federal government's role in the provision of aid, and transferred administrative authority to the states through a new funding strategy: the Temporary Assistance for Needy Families (TANF) program. These changes were significant. Yet, because they were implemented during a time of economic prosperity, their immediate effects were harder to discern. During an economic downturn, when jobs are harder to obtain, the devastating consequences of such policies for families became more clear (Collins and Mayer 2010).

With regard to immigrant families, there was an important shift after PRWORA became law. Whereas before 1996 undocumented immigrants were already ineligible for a range of public assistance programs such as non-emergency Medicaid or Supplemental Social Security Income and for cash assistance for low-income individuals, after PRWORA these restrictions were extended to a wider group of immigrants, not only the undocumented. PRWORA also reduced food stamp allotments for mixed-status households, thus increasing food insecurity for US citizen children living in mixed-status families (van Hook and Balistreri 2006). Additionally, permanent legal residents became ineligible for certain benefits or had to wait to become naturalized citizens to gain eligibility. For instance, after the 1996 law, permanent legal residents had to wait a period of five years for Medicaid coverage. Even though with time some of these benefits were restored,[4] several aspects of the law remain and many adult immigrants continue to be ineligible for federal assistance programs, such as food stamps.

In conjunction with PRWORA, IIRIRA was specifically directed at limiting lawfully admitted immigrants' access to public assistance, with direct effects on families. Among other provisions, this law sought to ensure that lawfully admitted immigrants (as well as undocumented immigrants) would not become a public charge—a long-standing concern in US immigration law (Fox 2012). IIRIRA would accomplish this through two mechanisms. First, this law requires that a sponsor who petitions for a close family member through family-based visas agree to support the petitioned immigrant until the latter becomes a US citizen or accumulates 40 quarters of work (approximately 10 years). This is ensured through a legally enforced affidavit of support provided by the sponsor that is included in the application for a family-based visa and in which the petitioner shows an income of at least 125 percent of the federal poverty level.

A second mechanism contained in IIRIRA that guarantees that immigrants will not need public assistance is the expansion of restrictions to welfare eligibility for documented (lawfully admitted) immigrants. No longer are undocumented immigrants the only ones barred from such benefits. Since IIRIRA went into effect in 1997, all lawfully admitted immigrants arrived after 1996 and those waiting for permanent residency or holding a temporary status are barred from federal public benefits during their first five years in the country.[5] This five-year bar does not apply to refugees or asylees and to a few other categories of lawfully admitted immigrants, such as Cuban and Haitian entrants (Fragomen 1997). Furthermore, with the exception of refugees and asylees, lawfully admitted (and certainly the undocumented) immigrants entering the country after 1996 are ineligible for supplemental social security income and food stamps even beyond the five-year bar, namely until they accumulate 40 quarters of work or become US citizens.[6]

To further complicate matters, immigrants who became permanent legal residents after 1996, though barred from receiving federal public benefits, can receive benefits that are not categorized as federal including some that accrue to work-authorized immigrants admitted to the United States under special treaties (Fragomen 1997). The 1996 law does not require non-profit charitable organizations that provide assistance to immigrants to "verify the eligibility of any applicant for such benefits" (Fragomen 1997: 448). However, because through PRWORA states were made responsible for administering their own welfare programs with block grants from the federal government, several states have passed laws that require the verification of the legal status of someone who applies for certain benefits. Each state decides whether immigrants (and which ones) can access various forms of aid such as TANF, social services, and Medicaid. Importantly, under federal law, "no prohibitions, limitations, or restrictions may be more restrictive than those imposed under comparable federal programs" (Fragomen 1997: 449). As we will see later, though, once states acquired increased responsibility for distributing federal funds, significant variation was created across them in the allocation of funds for immigrants in need, and some states have sought to institute stricter policies for eligibility.[7]

Another piece of legislation that affects whether and how immigrant families access public benefits is the ACA of 2010 (that is, the Affordable Care Act—as explained above). This law also highlights the key role that legal and citizenship statuses play in accentuating differences in access to benefits (see Chavez 2012). As initially publicized, the law sought to expand health insurance coverage for everyone; however, it specifically excluded undocumented immigrants. Undocumented immigrants have long been ineligible for Medicaid; but they can receive emergency medical care. The ACA further specifies that undocumented immigrants are ineligible for health-care exchanges, for tax credits, or for Medicaid benefits. On the other hand, all "lawfully present" immigrants (e.g., legal permanent residents and other categories of lawfully admitted immigrants) are eligible for the benefits that this law extends to US citizens—including access to private insurance coverage—without having to wait five years to apply (Ku 2013). The population (mostly Latinos/as) excluded from ACA benefits is significant, a situation that reverberates through families and communities (see González Block, Vargas Bustamante, de la Sierra, and Martínez Cardoso 2014).

Whereas in recent years federal law has sought to curtail immigrants' access to public benefits, there are long-standing provisions in it that extend key benefits to some immigrants. One of these is the right to public K-12 education for undocumented children. This was the result of a 1982 US Supreme Court decision that struck down a Texas statute that denied funding for the education of undocumented children and that the Court found in violation of the Fourteenth Amendment. Thus the children of immigrants, regardless of their legal status, have a constitutionally guaranteed right to K-12 education even when their other social rights (e.g., to vote or to access benefits) are significantly constrained and they are still at risk of deportation (Gonzales, Suárez-Orozco, and Dedios-Sanguineti 2013). Undocumented students and those with a non-permanent status have limited access to higher education because several states restrict the benefit of in-state tuition to lawful residents.

One recent federal program that extends some benefits to undocumented immigrants is President Obama's Deferred Action for Childhood Arrivals (DACA) program. Signed in 2012 and reapproved in 2014, DACA provides temporary relief from deportation, access to a temporary social security number, a renewable work permit, and a driver's license for immigrants who arrived as children and fulfill some additional requirements. Since this program was created through executive action, it confers documents, but not lawful status and all its accompanying benefits (Gonzales, Terriquez, and Ruszcyk 2014). For example, DACA recipients are not eligible for healthcare benefits through ACA. However, DACA recipients who already have ties to networks and educational resources are better able to access internships and jobs through their new benefits.

Other groups designated to receive certain public benefits are refugees and asylees, who constitute a small percentage of the total number of admissions (about 10 percent—usually around 70,000 of the approximately 750,000 annual admissions). They are authorized by the US Congress on an annual basis, and only a few selected countries are designated for this form of protection. For the fiscal year 2015, the US Congress authorized a total of 70,000 slots for refugee admissions, half of them going to countries in the Middle East.[8] The history of refugee admissions in the United States is closely tied to foreign policy; since the years of the Cold War, the United States' refugee legislation has reserved slots for individuals fleeing from communism or communist-dominated lands. This practice continued even after the United States adjusted its refugee policies in 1980 to align more closely with the United Nations' Protocol relating to the Status of Refugees.[9] Even though the IIRIRA of 1996 revamped the asylum process to create new categories of admission and new procedures to evaluate claims for asylum (see Fragomen 1997), the basic ideology that guided refugee and asylum protection during the Cold War is still in practice today, and thus the Department of State is involved in these admissions. Importantly, refugee admissions also mean that the government becomes responsible for the refugees' initial adjustment and settlement. Thus, instead of requiring that a petitioning family member be responsible for the petitioned person, refugee admissions require that a US-based resettlement agency with experience in refugee resettlement provide such assurance.

Furthermore, refugees approved for admission receive assistance through the Department of State's Reception and Placement Program, which supplies money for rent, food, and clothing as well as contacts with organizations that help these refugees settle and obtain employment and language skills. Assistance beyond the first few months is coordinated between the federal government and the states where the refugees resettle so as to provide long-term cash and medical assistance, employment (for which authorization is received upon arrival), and social services.

State-Level Laws

Federal immigration law controls who enters the country and when, but IIRIRA gives states the responsibility to create their own policies for distributing assistance that comes to immigrants from federal block grants, not from the Supplemental Security Income (SSI) or from the Food Stamps Program (FSP), and for determining eligibility (see Hessick and Chin 2014).[10] Thus, states and municipalities have created policies that affect access to social benefits and a host of other issues that shape quality of life for immigrant families. Since 2001 many states have been quite active in designing these policies.[11] Whereas in 2006 state legislators introduced 570 immigration-related bills, enacted 84 laws, and adopted 12 resolutions, in 2007 they introduced 1,562 immigration-related bills, passed 240 laws, and approved 50 resolutions, and by 2009, more than 1,500 immigration bills were introduced, 222 laws were enacted, and 131 resolutions were adopted (NCSL 2010).

Some of these policies have sought to integrate immigrants and to facilitate their adaptation (Mitnik and Halpern-Finnerty 2010); however, just as often there have been numerous legislative acts at the state and municipal levels that are restrictive and exclusionary (see Stewart 2012). What both integrative and punitive policies have in common is that they elucidate how policies directed at individual immigrants significantly impact the immediate well-being of entire families, even members who are US citizens. This legislative activity has created substantial variation in the climate that receives immigrants in different destinations (Pham and Van 2014) and in whether and how they access social services (Capps, Castañeda, Chaudry, and Santos 2007).

A significant number of states and cities have passed either pro-immigrant laws and ordinances *or* an array of negative laws and ordinances—such as penalizing employers for hiring undocumented immigrants, fining landlords who rent to individuals who lack proof of legal residence, and blocking access to a variety of social and public services. Across states, the trend seems to be to lean toward these restrictive policies, which affect immigrants negatively (Wides-Muñoz 2008). However, the enforcement of such laws varies considerably from one location to another (Decker, Lewis, Provine, and Varsanyi 2009; Steil and Ridgley 2012; Stewart 2012). And, importantly, the presence of organizations that assist immigrants seems to help immigrants confront restrictive laws in certain states.

The geography of legislative activity at the state, county, and municipal levels points to interesting patterns (see Walker and Leitner 2011). The dispersion of the immigrant population to new destinations within the past two decades permits an examination of the wide variety of responses to immigrants (see Lichter 2012); such responses do not correspond to the actual number of immigrants received, or even to their proximity to the southern border of the United States. For instance, localities that have experienced a rapid growth in their foreign-born population (not in absolute terms, but in relation to the total size of their populations) seem more likely to introduce exclusionary policies (Walker and Leitner 2011). Hence exclusionary laws have tended to be passed in new destinations, particularly in the South (Leerkes, Leach, and Bachmeier 2012). Concomitantly, inclusionary measures have been introduced in areas with long-established and large immigrant populations (Møller 2014; Walker and Leitner 2011). Thus, geography and the specificity of the context of arrival matter a great deal in deciding what resources the immigrants and their families may count on and whether and how they are able to access them (Dreby and Schmalzbauer 2013; Lichter 2012).

According to an analysis of state laws and ordinances passed in

2010—an analysis conducted by the National Conference of State Legislatures—of the 72 laws enacted in 24 states, 14 covered a variety of issues, 13 dealt with licenses and IDs, 11 with budgets, 8 with education-related matters, and 8 with employment (NCSL 2010). A concern in many states was to restrict undocumented immigrants' access to public benefits, because these public goods supposedly attracted undocumented immigration to their communities. Thus, 39 states passed legislation to institute requirements that would curtail access to benefits. These state- and municipal-level laws affect immigrant families directly.

Examples of these laws include Oklahoma's HB 1804, passed in 2007, which sought to hinder the state from providing education, health care, and other services to undocumented immigrants, including some services to infants. Passed in 2011, Alabama's HB 56 barred undocumented immigrants from receiving any state or local public benefits and from attending public colleges or universities. While it did not forbid undocumented immigrant children in K-12 to attend school, it required school officials to determine these children's legal status. Also in 2011, Georgia passed HB 87, which, in addition to authorizing the police to check the immigration status of suspects, made it far more difficult for undocumented immigrants to access public benefits. Arizona passed a battery of laws between 2004 and 2010, including one that required proof of eligibility to receive social services such as retirement, welfare, health, disability, public or assisted housing, post-secondary education, food assistance, unemployment, or similar benefits that are granted with the help of appropriated funds of state or local governments. Other Arizona laws deny in-state college tuition to immigrants who cannot produce proof of permanent legal residence or citizenship and bar undocumented immigrants from accessing subsidized childcare and adult education programs. At the municipal level, Hazelton, Pennsylvania passed an ordinance with the provision to impose a $1,000 fine on landlords who rented to undocumented immigrants. Indeed, housing became a key issue in a few of the state laws and municipal ordinances. And, considering that there are approximately 2.3 million mixed-status families in the country today (Passel 2011), efforts to curtail access to housing for undocumented immigrants also affect US-born citizens.

Several states have sought to pass policies that facilitate immigrant integration through the provision of key benefits. For instance, seventeen states, including Colorado, Indiana, Michigan, Minnesota, New Jersey, and Oregon passed laws expanding undocumented immigrants' access to higher education through tuition benefits. As of this writing, nineteen states, including California, Colorado, Connecticut, Illinois, Maryland, Nevada, New Mexico, Oregon, and Vermont, have passed bills extending undocumented immigrants' access to driver's licenses. California's AB 540 expanded the access of undocumented students to post-secondary education by allowing them to pay in-state tuition. And in late 2014 a California senator introduced a bill named "Health Care for All" that would extend health insurance benefits to undocumented immigrants left out of the ACA.

Importantly, depending on the political climate, the same state can shift policies dramatically. For instance, in 1999 Utah passed HB 36, which gave undocumented immigrants a state-issued card that allowed them to drive and to obtain car insurance and certain benefits, and thus was conducive to immigrant integration. In 2008 the state reversed its position and passed HB 81, one of the toughest anti-immigrant bills in the country (Stewart 2012). By 2013 it had reversed its policy once again.

Immigrant families' well-being is shaped by laws that determine access to public benefits, but also by many state-level policies that are not directly aimed at curtailing immigrants' access to public services. Some policies are so egregiously anti-immigrant that they end up curtailing immigrants' access to social services, even when this is not the stated objective. For instance, Arizona's SB 1070—the toughest omnibus bill in the country, signed into law in 2010—included, among other provisions, a requirement for individuals to be questioned about their legal status during a lawful stop. The law had manifold direct and indirect effects on families' access to services even when it did not formally mandate such restrictions. For example, young mothers in the Phoenix metro area—even those born in the United States—reported a decline in the utilization of public assistance and were less likely to take their babies to the doctor after SB 1070 passed (Toomey, Umaña-Taylor, Williams, Updegraff, and Jahromi 2014). The risk of detention and deportation (for oneself or a family member) in a context of heightened enforcement is detrimental to the generation of social capital and networking among undocumented immigrants, especially to mothers' connections to mainstream insitutions they have to interact with for their children (Valdez, Padilla, and Valentine 2013).

In another case, a school-based survey conducted in the Phoenix metro area among middle-school students (Santos and Menjívar 2013; Santos, Menjívar, and Godfrey 2013) indicated that just *awareness* of SB 1070 had a small but significant negative association with the youth's sense of being American; and this weakened sense of American identity resulted in a small but meaningful reduction in psychological well-being—namely in lower levels of self-esteem. A key finding was that this negative association was not moderated by race or ethnicity; the same negative associations between awareness of SB 1070, American identity, and self-esteem were detected in the entire sample of racially and ethnically diverse youth—including white youth who attend very diverse schools. Thus these laws reach beyond undocumented immigrants to affect their immediate families, but also the communities in which they live and their US-born members.

The complicated and ever-changing context of laws at the federal and state levels plays an important role in disrupting care patterns in immigrant families. Social-service workers often act as "street-level bureaucrats" who get to decide whether to abide by or bend the rules, either in favor of or to the detriment of immigrant clients (Deeb-Sossa 2013; Marrow 2009). In response, immigrants try to avoid interactions with social services and public institutions when they have reason to feel fear and insecurity (Marrow 2009). This holds true even in cases where the children are US citizens and are thus entitled to social supports (Abrego and Menjívar 2011; Balistreri and van Hook 2004). Additionally, mothers, who are typically charged with their children's well-being, may stay away from parent–teacher conferences or shy away from asking their children's teachers for help. This may be especially poignant in new rural destinations where school systems are not equipped to deal with non-English-speaking parents (Schmalzbauer 2014).

In new destinations where formal social supports are weak (Deeb-Sossa and Bickham-Mendez 2008; Silver 2012), children may bear the burden of having to facilitate their family's relationship with the public sector. In these cases it is often the daughters of undocumented immigrants who take on this charge (Orellana 2009). For example, Elena (in Schmalzbauer 2014), a US citizen child of undocumented parents, has become the public face of her family since her young teenage years and their formal representative since turning 18. Her family's pick-up truck and trailer are registered in her name. She attends the parent–teacher conferences of her two younger siblings. She also applied for Women, Infants, and Children (WIC) help for her youngest sister, as well as for state-funded healthcare support for all of her siblings. When Elena was stricken with thyroid cancer at the age of 19, she had to negotiate the ill-equipped healthcare system of rural Montana on her own. The stress of the situation fell heavily on Elena's shoulders. But this also traumatized her mother, who felt that there was nothing she could do to support her daughter through her sickness. This case exemplifies the adjustments and new practices immigrant families must develop in order to negotiate their complex and shrinking access to public benefits.[12]

Limited and blocked access to public benefits, paired with a widespread anti-immigrant sentiment, adds stress to families and relationships. Marital relationships, in particular, are likely to suffer under the duress of policies and their consequences for immigrant families (Landale, Thomas, and van Hook 2011). As we discussed in Chapter 4, it is not unusual for immigrants to experience marital dissolution (López 2015), unable as they are to provide for families in the gendered ways that are expected (Abrego 2013); and faced with the significant challenge of indefinite family separations.

General Policies

As the federal government and the states use legal status to distribute social services, a bifurcation in quality of life and well-being has been observed along axes of legal status within and between immigrant families, with effects extending to US citizen children living in mixed-status families (Yoshikawa 2011). When approximately 80 percent of the 5.5 million children who live with at least one undocumented parent are US citizens themselves (91 percent of those under the age of 6) (Passel and Cohn 2009, 2012), the parents' legal status is likely to have direct consequences for these US citizen children. In some cases laws have specifically denied them access to public goods and benefits. In others, since officials in state agencies in charge of disbursing benefits have been required to notify law enforcement agencies about the status of an undocumented applicant, immigrants are apprehensive about contacting these agencies. In other cases still, application forms require personal information, such as social security numbers for each household member, even when the US citizen children are the only ones who apply for a benefit. And, finally, there are cases where the climate of fear and anxiety created by increased enforcement and the criminalization of immigrants inhibit the latter's contact with institutions that provide some social goods, such as education and health (Landale et al. 2011). When immigration laws and policies block access to services for the US-born children of undocumented immigrants, these youth experience multiple physical, emotional, and developmental problems (Yoshikawa 2011).

Perhaps not surprisingly, there is a general trend toward the underutilization of social services among immigrant families, regardless of legal status or national origin (Watson 2014; White, Yeager, Menachemi, and Scarinci 2014). Chinese immigrants, for example, underutilize social services, and social workers' assistance is needed in order to increase these immigrants' links to social-service agencies (Yep, Zhao, Wang, Pang, and Wang 2014). The same is true of Arab immigrants (Elsouhag et al. 2014): these immigrants' rates of health-care utilization are significantly lower than the national rates. However, utilization rates were substantially higher among refugees, who reported a greater need for such services, but who also enjoy extended access to these benefits by virtue of their refugee status.

There is an important gender angle to the discussion we present in this chapter. In their position as caretakers of their families, immigrant women are often in charge of seeking services for their children or others in their families (Abrego and Menjívar 2011). So it is immigrant women who contact institutions and agencies and apply for benefits—and not only for themselves, though laws and policies that restrict access to benefits have direct effects on women too (Menjívar 2002b). For instance, pregnant women and mothers of US-born children have demonstrated concerns about accessing care (Doering-White et al. 2014; White et al. 2014), even if they are themselves US citizens (Toomey et al. 2014). Furthermore, the lack of access to social benefits—such as child care, elderly care, or other forms of public assistance to families—prompts women in immigrant families to step in and expand their caregiving responsibilities, paralleling the "triple shift" that non-immigrant women increasingly shoulder in society today.

Children in immigrant families also experience the consequences of blocked access to public services and institutions, especially regarding their education. For instance, Latino/a parents (and their children) often face challenges in dealing with school administrators and teachers, even when parents are willing to help their children succeed in school (Hill and Torres 2010). Even when parents arrive with optimism about what their children can achieve (and they have indeed migrated in order to secure educational opportunities and a better future for their children), their initial aspirations and expectations diminish as they spend time in the United States and interact with the educational system (Hill and Torres 2010; Menjívar 2008). This, of course, varies on the basis of immigrant families' pre- and postmigration class positions (Ochoa 2013). (For more on education in immigrant families, see Chapters 3 and 5.)

Healthcare Access

Despite a popular misconception that undocumented immigrants come to the United States to utilize the country's health-care system, a study based on the California Health Interview Survey (Pourat, Wallace, Hadler, and Ponce 2014) found that undocumented immigrants in that state had fewer physician visits and less preventive care service than US citizens and other immigrant groups—or, at best, an equal number with theirs. Undocumented immigrants are not eligible for most forms of public health insurance and are excluded from the ACA insurance exchanges. And their own legal status often prevents them from accessing health benefits such as Medicaid for their children. Indeed, this pattern has held for decades; the uninsured are less likely than the insured to utilize any hospital services, including emergency rooms—especially among undocumented immigrants (Chavez, Flores, and Lopez-Garza 1992).

According to Watson (2014), as of 2013, 38 percent of non-citizens were uninsured, by comparison to 11 percent among the native-born. A study that examined data from the National Survey of America's Families (Huang, Yu, and Ledsky 2006) found that foreign-born non-citizen children were four times more likely than children from native families to lack health insurance coverage. They were 40 percent and 80 percent more likely to not have visited a physician or a dentist in the previous year and twice as likely to lack a usual source of care. This study found that US citizen children born to undocumented parents were also disadvantaged with respect to health care and, overall, that these children were in worse physical health but used healthcare services significantly less than children from non-immigrant families. Several studies have identified aggressive immigration enforcement, which keeps undocumented parents from contacting social-service agencies, as playing a central role in the lower rates of usage of health services and high incidence of lack of insurance in the immigrant population (Capps et al. 2007; Watson 2014).

Highlighting the spillover effects of legal status in a context of heightened enforcement, a study conducted in Massachusetts (Hacker, Chu, Leung, Marra, and Pirie 2011) found that documented *and* undocumented immigrants experienced fear of deportation and high levels of stress in ways that affected their emotional well-being and access to health-care services. In the Lower Rio Grande Valley of Texas, despite the passage of the ACA, healthcare providers, caseworkers, and public health officials note that fear and uncertainty limit immigrant families' access to health care (Castañeda and Melo 2014). Once again, parents' undocumented legal status was found to have ripple effects on other members of the family and unintended consequences for the well-being of US-born children.[13] Of course, these experiences vary by race and ethnicity. Even though undocumented immigrants come from all over the world, Latinos/as (both US-born and immigrants) have more negative experiences in the legality— health nexus, as they have been racialized as undocumented in popular discourse.

The Role of Community Organizations and NGOs

Given the complex and often contradictory political and legal context surrounding public benefits throughout the United States, community organizations often fill in to provide critical support for immigrant families. These non-governmental organizations help immigrants transition into the United States, negotiate the social-service and education institutions, and deal with legal challenges. The specific role that community organizations play in family life depends in large part on the local context of settlement as well as on the race, class, and legal characteristics of the particular group they serve (Gleeson 2012). There are numerous examples of community organizations and NGOs, some of which are faith-based or work in coordination with faith-based organizations (Hondagneu-Sotelo 2008), assisting immigrants with English language classes, work placement and job training, food distribution projects, and the like (Menjívar 2000). Some organizations have been created in order to distribute the assistance that the federal government makes available for refugee resettlement.

Perhaps the most critical role that community organizations play for non-refugee immigrant families at this moment is helping them navigate, understand, and access legal services. Survey research by Wong, Kerwin, Atkinson, and McCarthy (2014), conducted in the context of DACA implementation, suggests that many undocumented immigrants are eligible for some type of immigration relief but do not know it. Specifically, 14.3 percent of those the researchers surveyed who were eligible for DACA were also eligible for another form of relief, which would put them on the path to permanent residency. The authors thus explored the role of legal service organizations in bridging the knowledge gap between opportunities for relief and those who are entitled to it. They found that, in places with a strong history of immigrant rights organizing, and thus with strong immigrant-based community organizations, like Los Angeles, undocumented immigrants were more likely to learn about, and thus apply for, the benefits to which they were entitled. The most common form of relief for which DACA individuals were eligible were family-based petitions, followed by U visas and Special Immigrant Juvenile (SIJ) status.

Wong and colleagues (2014) conclude that the organizations most effective in providing good legal services are those that also have information about the other programs for which immigrants are eligible. This is critical to keep in mind as scholars, activists, and policymakers think about the implications of DAPA's (Deferred Action for Parents of US Citizens and Lawful Permanent Residents) implementation for immigrant families. Community organizations, and especially legal service organizations, will be important actors in making sure that all who are eligible for the program actually benefit. Wong and colleagues (2014) suggest that the ethnic media may be a good arena from which to educate parents and families about DACA, DAPA, and other programs and to warn them about fraud.

However, even in places like Los Angeles, where immigrant organizing is strong, there is risk of fraud. In fact, anecdotal evidence suggests that immigrants of various nationalities have lost thousands of dollars to immigration fraud. Notaries or unscrupulous lawyers can easily take advantage of the fact that immigration law is complex, and they make yearning families promises that they cannot keep. In her research, Abrego encountered a Filipino college student in Los Angeles whose family was defrauded. He told Abrego:

> my parents' immigration lawyer defrauded ... the person was a very popular immigration lawyer among Filipino immigrants. So when they saw on the news that he was convicted for a fraud, all these other Filipinos, their [legalization application] papers were like, they went into shambles. My mom was mentioning that before that happened everything was going so smoothly and then he got convicted for fraud then all of a sudden getting our paperwork fixed just became so much more difficult. (Abrego interview, 2013)

Whereas fraud can happen anywhere, new destinations confront the additional problem of not having enough immigration lawyers and legal service organizations to support their immigrant population. A dearth of immigration lawyers, combined with having to travel long distances to access those who do exist, and the lack of easily accessible translation services often mean that migrant families in new destinations are unable to access the benefits for which they are eligible. Even though community organizations are being created across the country to serve the specific needs of immigrant families, this is not an even process and many immigrant families find that they are on their own (Schmalzbauer 2014).

Community organizations thus play an important role in providing social support for immigrant families. Here again, geographical location can shape the prevalence, role, and goal of community organizations. Saskia Sassen (Sassen-Koob 1979), for example, found that social class and the rurality or urbanity of the sending community were critical to understanding why there was a proliferation of Dominican voluntary associations in New York City, but far fewer Colombian associations. She contrasted the rural origins of the Dominican immigrants with the urban origins of the Colombians and concluded that this factor influenced the kind of organizations both formed in New York. Dominicans created organizations that focused mainly on culture and recreation, replicating the traditions of their rural background in their new US urban lives. Colombians, on the other hand, did not need the same cultural support in their transition to New York. As the majority of Colombian migrants were highly educated, they tended to focus the associations they formed on "instrumental" tasks like strengthening political and professional networks.

As Sassen observed in the 1970s, community groups today continue to provide a comfortable, culturally familiar place for immigrant families to gather for recreation, education or support. In her study of the Indian community in Phoenix, Emily Skop (2012) found that community and family well-being were intimately connected to the establishment of "permanent spaces" designated for the immigrant population. When the predominantly middle-class Indian community she studied was able to establish a permanent community center, that center became the backbone of Indian culture and heritage in the Phoenix area.

In poor and working-class urban communities, community organizations serve as providers of social support and as liaisons between immigrants and social-service organizations. In her ethnographic work in Chelsea, Massachusetts, Schmalzbauer worked with Proyecto Hondureño, a grassroots immigrant rights group that provided Central American immigrants with English and basic computer classes. Proyecto Hondureño also organized regular cultural events and poetry readings, and they had a weekly "women's empowerment group." Because many of the Hondurans in Chelsea were undocumented, Proyecto helped them apply for temporary protected status (TPS) and connected them with community health clinics and educational supports that catered to immigrant populations. For the fairly young Honduran community in the Boston area, comprised of many transnational families traumatized by separation and by the recent devastation of Hurricane Mitch, having a physical space to gather and find support was critical to their well-being (Schmalzbauer 2005).

Community organizations have special meaning for immigrant

youth, who are often navigating language and cultural differences at home, at school, and in their ethnic community. When immigrant youth are unable to find the support they need in any of these three places, or when they must spend a lot of time alone because of their parents' demanding work schedules (Li 2003; Suárez-Orozco and Suárez-Orozco 2001), a community group may be their social lifeline. In her research with low-income Chinese immigrant youth in an urban east-coast community, Wong (2010) found that a community center gave youth a sense of support, solidarity with other youth in the same social position, and a strengthened sense of self and ethnic pride. At a pragmatic level, the youth community organization provided a sense of "home" to the teenagers whose parents were often working and had to leave them alone. Similarly, Terriquez and Kwon (2014) found that immigrant youth in California were politicized via civic organizations and that their politicization had an influence on the political views and engagement of their parents. Thus, community organizations can strengthen families across generations.

In new destinations where community groups may not exist, other community spaces may substitute for them, providing education about social services as well as a place for immigrants to gather. In Schmalzbauer's (2014) study of the emerging Mexican community in Montana, what Skop terms "transitory" spaces were important to the well-being of immigrant families. Specifically, the Catholic Church became the hub that brought immigrants together to worship, celebrate Mexican holidays, and share other cultural traditions. Indeed, religious organizations have been instrumental not only in providing a space for immigrants to worship, but also as providers of material and emotional support and as institutional and pragmatic organizing tools through which they can advocate for their rights (Hagan 2008; Hondagneu-Sotelo 2008; Menjívar 2003). Thus, whereas there is no designated center or organization for Mexican families in Montana, the church became the place where community organizing began to happen.

There is an important gender angle here, as women, in their position as caretakers, are the family members most often in contact with a variety of community organizations, clinics, and

NGOs. They seek out community organizations in order to find information or resources for themselves and their families (Hondagneu-Sotelo 1994), and in the process they become adept at interacting with organizations and institutions (Menjívar 2000). In the course of spending time in such spaces and dealing with individuals beyond their circles, women expand their networks considerably, generating important social capital for the benefit of their families and creating community (Hondagneu-Sotelo 1994). Spending time in public spaces also affords women the opportunity to share concerns and organize so as to advocate for their families, as happened in the aftermath of the signing of Arizona's SB 1070. Mothers organized marches and kept a vigil outside the state capitol, to protest the injustices that this and similar state laws inflict on their families.[14]

Conclusion

In the process of integration into the United States, immigrants and their families rely to different degrees on social institutions. Historically, social welfare programs, operating in coordination with community organizations and government agencies, opened doors for Southern, Central, and Eastern European immigrant families to settle and thrive (Steinberg 2001), while shutting doors to African American and Mexican immigrants (Fox 2012). The consequences of those bifurcated practices at the end of the last century are still evident in the continued inequalities across racial and ethnic groups in the United States today. Thus, we know that today's practices matter for the future of contemporary immigrants. As immigrant laws have increasingly blocked access to public benefits for documented and undocumented immigrants, immigrant families have had to navigate complex legal terrain at the federal, state, and local levels to patch together education, health, and other services. Community organizations, street-level bureaucrats, and pro-immigrant laws have helped strengthen families' ability to thrive, though these families are also influenced by factors that vary across space and time, factors that mostly respond to the political currents of the moment in destinations where immigrants settle. These families would benefit from more consistent pro-immigrant policies, but also from federal, state, and local-level general policies designed to address more ubiquitous inequalities that affect all families in society today.

7

Conclusion

I never thought of myself as a "child of immigrants" per se, as I feel the term comes loaded with undertones of immigrant struggles—the old clichés of coming to a new country with nothing and struggling to assimilate. The truth of the matter is my father came to the United States comfortably with an MD from Italy, fluent in English since his youth, and I'm the fourth child to my parents, so by the time I was born they were very well established.

Michael Shami, 21, Syrian and Hungarian American[1]

Growing up, we ate traditional Indian food for breakfast and dinner every day and I would have had it for lunch, too, but unfortunately I was too embarrassed to bring Indian food to school. But if I could go back, I would have changed that.

Sruti Swaminathan, 22, Indian American[2]

In September 2014, *The New York Times*'s Sunday Review section titled "Exposures" included a series of photos of "Children of Immigrants." In the piece, the photographer, Quetzal Maucci, describes herself as "the daughter of two immigrant mothers from Peru and Argentina." In the project she captures the voices and experiences of a small sample from the 20 million adult children of immigrants in the United States (Pew Research Center 2013). It is telling that the project presents a diversity of participants and experiences. The 11 adult children of immigrants featured in this piece describe a sense of belonging in the United States as well as in their parents' homeland; they express a desire to fit in despite occasional shame of being "different"; and they discuss a variety of socioeconomic backgrounds and reasons that brought their parents to the United States.

We open this concluding chapter with words from the children of immigrants featured in the *New York Times* article, in order to underscore the richness, complexity, and diversity that characterize contemporary immigrant families. As Michael Shami suggests in the first epigraph of this chapter, immigrant experiences take place in and are shaped by broader social, political, economic, and discursive contexts. At their core, immigrant families are merely groups of people, closely connected biologically or socially, who have moved from their country of origin to another country. Popular discourses, however, produce assumptions and expectations that erase the element of diversity among immigrant families. The notion of the struggling immigrant, for example, is so prevalent in the United States that sometimes immigrants who do not have that experience (or do not fit with the model) have difficulty identifying as immigrants at all. In the contemporary historical moment, when many immigrants are vilified and represented mostly as people of color, whiteness, too, may weaken an immigrant's identity. Our book underscores that the places of origin, the reasons for migration, the conditions under which migration occurs, the resources that immigrants and their families bring with them, and the US contexts that receive them vary along a number of axes that merit recognition and analysis.

We position this book in the robust body of literature that highlights the diverse and dynamic demographics and experiences of contemporary immigrant families. As the *New York Times* story suggests, immigrants and their families span the full spectrum, both in education and in economy. Portes and Zhou's (1993) concept of segmented assimilation, for example, characterizes the mobility paths for some immigrants, especially young black second-generation Caribbean men, who integrate into the American underclass, ultimately faring economically the same as—or worse than—their parents. Portes and Zhou's insights demand that we think about the persistent ways race shapes immigrant opportunity structures. And yet, simultaneously, many other immigrants demonstrate high levels of intermarriage, lower fertility, and economic mobility—all markers of integration and upward mobility (Glick 2010; Landale and Oropesa 2007). Indeed demographic research (Kasinitz, Mollenkopf, Waters, and Holdaway 2008; Waters, Tran, Kasinitz, and Mollenkopf 2010) finds that, while immigrants do struggle, those in the second generation are on the whole doing well by comparison to their white native-born non-Hispanic peers.

Once settled in their newly adopted country, immigrant families experience a wide range of opportunities and barriers to integration. Factors at the individual, family, and community levels—such as class, gender, race, legal status, religion, and immigrant generation—mediate the macro-structural contexts that determine the life chances and the well-being of immigrants. Additionally, sociologists, demographers, and geographers are increasingly emphasizing the critical ways in which the specifics of place shape the integration paths of immigrant families (Jensen 2006; Lichter 2012; Nelson and Hiemstra 2008; Singer 2008). Cultural practices and expectations matter too.

Classic research by Portes and Rumbaut (2001) suggests that immigrants do best when they adapt strategies of *selective acculturation*, in which they both integrate into the United States' mainstream and maintain strong connections with the culture and language of their parents' country and culture of origin. We find that immigrants practice different levels and versions of selective acculturation, and that they experience acculturation in various ways (Suárez-Orozco and Suárez-Orozco 2001). Thus, there is no simple recipe for successful integration. For example, in the second epigraph to this chapter, 22-year-old Sruti Swaminathan, an adult and the child of Indian immigrants, reveals that food— and, by extension, culture—are central to the way immigrant families integrate and make a home for themselves in the host country. Members of her family had the resources and ability to enjoy some of their cultural practices in the private space of the home. And indeed, maintaining traditions and culture can instill pride and a sense of continuity that can be valuable for immigrant families. Yet these families must negotiate different social practices and expectations outside of the home, too. Depending on each person's subjectivity—which is in turn dictated by social class background, gender presentation, racialized characteristics, and immigrant generation—cultural practices may be interpreted as positive or negative, and this may lead in some cases to shame or stigma that are amplified during youth. Swaminathan's reflection hints at the evolving relationship that immigrants and their children have to the immigrant experience at different points in their life cycles.

The photographer and curator of the *New York Times* piece, Quetzal Maucci, describes her own immigrant family. Raised by two mothers from two different countries, who moved around several times, Maucci suggests that one of the greatest challenges in her life is that others do not recognize her "pale" skin, or light complexion, as belonging to a Latina. Her story reminds us that not all immigrant families conform to race-specific, stereotypical, heteronormative, or nuclear conceptions of "family." Immigrant families include same-sex partners, can hail from various parts of the world, may reside together in the destination country or may be indefinitely separated across borders, and may aim to find their sense of belonging within immigrant-dense or racially segregated pockets of the United States. In all cases, the experience of being a child of immigrants—and a member of an immigrant family, more broadly—can mean different things and generate diverse emotions for a single person at various moments of her or his life.

This is precisely the kind of complexity we have aimed to capture throughout the book. Immigrant families come from different parts of the world, and they migrate for numerous reasons via multiple paths. Their experiences of integration are shaped by the resources they bring with them in the form of economic, human, and social capital, by the cultural norms they heed, and by the various macro-forces that receive them upon arrival. Just like families in general, immigrant families encompass a multiplicity of experiences, which have added layers of complexity associated with the crossing of international borders and adaptation to a new society. All of this is integral to what makes immigrant families notable and worth studying. Yet, while there is no quintessential immigrant experience, there are vital lenses that can help us under-stand the vast array of experiences of contemporary immigrant families in the United States.

Along with having a history of migration, individual immigrant family members are situated in multiple social locations that shape their lived experiences over the short and long term (Zavella 1991). As we have discussed throughout the book, immigrant family members' lives, like those of all individuals, are influenced by interlocking systems of oppression based on gender, race, class, legal status, sexual orientation, nation of origin, language ability, general abilities, culture, and ethnicity (Collins 1998; Crenshaw 1991). Because members of immigrant families have multiple and even diverging social locations, their individual experiences may at times put them at odds with each other socially, culturally, and politically while setting them on different paths of integration, mobility, and well-being in their adopted country.

On the basis of a thorough review of the scholarly literature on contemporary immigrant families in the United States, we find it useful to highlight the hierarchies and inequities created by a number of axes of inequality. Legal status, social class, gender, race, and generation are especially consequential in organizing and stratifying experiences between and within immigrant families. The inequities that these social positions create play out differently in various spaces and social realms—for example in institutional contexts, as we demonstrated in Chapter 6.

In the next section, for analytic purposes, we summarize key points from each of the substantive chapters of the book, each point focusing on a single axis of inequality. Importantly, in day-to-day life immigrants experience these characteristics and their consequences simultaneously and in cumulative fashion, as various factors come into play with different levels of intensity at different points in time.

First, legal context matters, and it matters a lot. In a histori-cal moment marked by record numbers of deportations and by ever-changing and increasingly complex laws at the local, state, and federal levels, immigration laws and the legal categories they impose shape immigrant families in fundamental ways. Immigration policies, for example, determine who can migrate and under what conditions. Although the United States has a federal immigration system based largely on family reunification, it has up until very recently prioritized family bonds that conform to the ideal of a heteronormative nuclear family, thereby excluding families that do not fit within these parameters. In many parts of the developing world, moreover, immigrant and travel visas to the United States are hard to come by—a situation that leads to emigration flows composed of high numbers of unauthorized migrants who leave loved ones behind. Even when immigrants eventually access legal channels for reunification, these separations tend to be lengthy either because reunification is not legally sanctioned or because the bureaucratic process is driven by annual numerical limits that stretch the process of approval over years, or even decades.

It would be difficult to overstate the role of legally produced hierarchies in determining the life chances of immigrants and their families today. Individuals who reside in the United States feel the consequences of immigration policies in areas that are central to their lives—including work, education, and access to social services. Legal status stratifies access to jobs and other social goods while criminalizing undocumented immigrants on the grounds that they break civil and administrative laws in their search for ways to survive. Unlike the inequalities involved in other forms of stratification such as class, gender, and race, those produced by immigration policies are legitimated through the law, making it legally and socially acceptable (and sometimes even required) to deny immigrant families goods and services on the basis of their legal status. Without access to the educational and social services that helped previous generations of immigrants thrive and integrate fully into the United States (see Fox 2012), contemporary immigrants in undocumented and liminal legal statuses face diminished chances of prospering (Menjívar and Abrego 2012). And, as we have highlighted in this book, these effects do not apply to all immigrants and their families equally; today Latinos/as are particularly affected.

As a result, in the contemporary moment, legal status can trump the effects of other social positions on life chances (Menjívar

2011b). This is an important point, because immigrants from Southern, Central, and Eastern Europe in the early 1900s—the previous large wave of immigration—did not face the same complex web of legislation as the one currently in place. Family members migrated in stages (MacDonald and MacDonald 1964) or as "birds of passage" (Piore 1979), working to earn enough to send to family members and ultimately returning to their country of origin. While geography, transportation, and finances often limited reunification, legal status was less significant because the legal context was not as complex as it is today. Comparisons with previous immigrants must therefore take the legal context into consideration. Even immigrants in the contemporary period may not experience immigration policies in the same way, because their gender, their social class, or their race positions them differently, so that the enforcement of the law is uneven. It is therefore necessary to use an intersectional lens (Crenshaw 1991) that brings into relief the simultaneous and cumulative effects of multiple social locations on the life paths of members of immigrant families.

As we detailed in Chapter 3, social class background also determines—and mightily—why immigrants leave their countries of birth, how they pursue family integration, and what resources they have to forge a home in US society. Immigrants from more advantaged social class positions, for example, may use their economic capital to access immigrant visas on the basis of entrepreneurial activities or professional qualifications, and this makes it easier for them to bring their families with them. On the other hand, working-class and poor immigrants are less likely to qualify for a visa. This funnels them toward dangerous and costly unauthorized journeys. Even when class-privileged individuals overstay their visas and become undocumented, they still have more options for legalization; importantly, their status will not trigger the 3- and 10-year ban that harms families with undocumented members who have entered the country without inspection. The latter are more likely to come from the lower rungs of the socioeconomic ladder, most often from Mexico and Central America—countries that are geographically close enough for their citizens to pursue unauthorized entry across the border. In these ways immigration policies make it likely that social class maps onto national origin so that families, coming into a context where legal status and race intertwine, are racialized according to their class-based resources and backgrounds.

Although the most familiar of the popular narratives about immigration is one of advancing through hard work across generations, in reality there is significant diversity among immigrants in this respect. As we detail in Chapter 3, social class shapes the experiences of immigrant families in myriad ways. It informs their reasons for migration as well as the processes by which migration happens. It influences their modes of incorporation into the United States—whether they are to remain in poverty or to move quickly up the class ladder; the ways in which transnationalism structures family life; whether members separate out of necessity or in pursuit of greater riches; the roles that individual members play within their families; and the relationships between family members—insofar as they are based on resources that parents and children have to dedicate to each other's care at different points in the life cycle. Social class is especially influential on immigrant parenting practices, as class standing provides both economic and social capital—including a class-informed habitus—that parents pass on to children.

Social class is also central to the trajectories of socioeconomic mobility of immigrant families, both within a single generation and across several generations. Since family is an institution in which advantage and disadvantage are transmitted generationally, the children of poor and working-class parents confront barriers to upward mobility early on in the life cycle. Working-class immigrant families struggling through limited job options and difficult working conditions have fewer resources, including less time to spend with children. On the other hand, immigrant families in advantaged social positions are likely to transmit those benefits to their children. Immigrant families' experiences of economic stratification, moreover, are further shaped by legal status, English language proficiency, racial profiling, and anti-immigrant policies. Despite the many barriers, however, researchers have found that people from outside the family such as teachers, counselors, and

Conclusion

community workers—what Portes and Fernández-Kelly (2008) call "special helpers"—can play important roles in supporting children from working-class families acquire upward mobility through education.

Family experiences are further stratified by gender—a central organizing principle of all social life. Reasons for migrating, the migration journey, access to jobs, stratified wages, the experiences associated with "illegality," and social networks are all significantly delimited along gender lines. Moreover, as research by Hirsch (2003) and González-López (2005) shows, pre- and post-migration gender ideals inform individual behavior in ways that require gendered negotiations as part of the integration process. To capture these multilayered gendered experiences, in Chapter 4 we deployed a gender analysis of immigrant families at the structural level, highlighting how gender ideals inform immigrant women's and men's individual and collective agency within families. In a patriarchal society and as part of its typical conceptions of family, for example, immigrant women from various countries participate in the paid labor force, among family or other co-ethnics, by occupying poorly remunerated positions. When their contributions are erased, immigrant women become economically vulnerable. Researchers have consistently found that, given these common inequities, undocumented immigrant women are especially at risk of intimate partner violence and other forms of domestic and state-sanctioned violence, which on the whole blocks their access to vital social services and consequently to mobility.

Immigrant men are also vulnerable in gendered and raced ways. As working-class jobs available to undocumented Latino immigrants often require that they be in public spaces and perform labor-intensive and dangerous work, they are especially susceptible both to serious work-related injuries and to deportation. In fact Mexican and Central American men are targeted for detention and deportation at higher rates than any other immigrants, as is evident in the significant overrepresentation of Mexican, Guatemalan, Honduran, and Salvadoran men among deportees.

Within the home, immigrant families also negotiate changing gendered ideals, as these intersect with new economic and social realities in their adopted country. Children of immigrants are uniquely situated in these gendered negotiations, since they represent, in the eyes of immigrant parents, both a continuation of cultural traditions and the family's mobility trajectory. In this context daughters' behaviors and sexualities are especially policed, in the name of the family's cultural and moral integrity. Thus, researchers find that sons have more freedom sexually and generally—except when they deviate from heterosexuality. LGBTQ members of immigrant families are likely to be subjected to close scrutiny and to experience the greatest surveillance for not conforming to gender and sexuality norms.

For reasons having to do with sexuality, mobility, and general transitions across the life course, immigrant families must also negotiate a variety of issues across generations. Relations between parents and teenage children are often fraught with tensions and misunderstandings, because each individual has been influenced by different historical moments, which determine what is considered acceptable behavior. These relations are even more complicated for immigrant families whose various members may be drawing on social norms developed in different sociocultural contexts and historical eras. In Chapter 5 we suggest that, as immigrants' social positions intersect in the place of arrival but also across borders, different family configurations give special meaning to the notion of generation in the lives of immigrants. Indeed, each generation experiences the host society on the basis of its lived knowledge of migration and of its distance from the family's history of migration.

For example, first-generation immigrants are likely to feel optimistic and grateful for limited opportunities while at the same time apprehensive about returning to their home country, where they acquired first-hand knowledge of hardship. This dual frame of reference molds their worldview and may heighten their appreciation of the relatively expansive mobility opportunities in the United States. Members of the second generation have a less developed dual frame of reference. They get only a partially trans-national perspective, from growing up hearing their immigrant parents' explanations of why they migrated and their stories of the challenges of initial adaptation in the United States. However, members of the second generation did not live the migration themselves; but they are likely to have witnessed and experienced the limitations of justice and the harsh realities of racism in the United States, thereby developing a different worldview. The 1.5 generation, by comparison, straddles these positions. Often living their formative years during the transition to the host society, members of the 1.5 generation typically remember the initial hardships of adjustment and grow up understanding the link between their parents' sacrifices and their parents' desires for the children's educational achievement. The connection to the migration process makes the 1.5 generation able to experience, at least partially, the dual frame of reference of the first generation—a lens mostly missing from the second generation. Each of these worldviews, in turn, mediates intergenerational relations.

Together, all these factors—legal status, class, gender, and generation—work concurrently and cumulatively, along with race and sexual orientation, to determine the experiences and well-being of immigrant families as they navigate their new society and all of its institutions. Not all immigrant families, however, are constituted in the same way, and this is another important point that we underscore throughout the book. As a result of immigration policies that prevent members from migrating together and of enforcement policies that separate families through detention and deportation, most contemporary immigrant families experience long-term separation at some point. Limited paths to legalization and the bureaucratic nature of the reunification process translate into multiyear, even indefinite separations that affect people's economic and emotional well-being in both the home and the host societies. In these cases, living across borders heightens inequalities and tensions in ways that are difficult to negotiate at a distance.

For immigrant families residing together in the United States, immigration policies, geographical contexts, the demographic make-up of communities, and social class (among a number of other factors) also determine their settlement and integration experiences. Mixed-status families must navigate stratified access to rights and social services. Parenting entails unique challenges when one child has access to free health care and better prospects for education, but the other does not because of his or her legal status. Childhood also involves different responsibilities when US citizenship grants children privileges not available to their parents and to their older siblings. In such cases the consequences of immigration policies are evident not only in the material well-being of mixed-status families, but also in the heavy burden they place on daily interactions and negotiations between loved ones. These relationships must withstand heavy and consequential legal burdens as part of daily life.

Given the ongoing changes in immigration policies, programs like Deferred Action for Childhood Arrivals (DACA) and Deferred Action for Parents of US Citizens and Lawful Permanent Residents (DAPA) are creating greater numbers of mixed-status immigrant families that must negotiate stratified rights and resources as part of their settlement and integration processes. These programs grant a subsector of undocumented immigrants temporary work permits and protection from deportation for two years, with the possibility of renewal for a yet undetermined length of time. At the time of this writing, DAPA has still to be implemented and DACA is in its second renewal. Beneficiaries appreciate even the short-lived peace of mind that these programs provide; but there is general nervousness about the long-term implications of a tempo-rary program that can end with the next administration. Indeed, during the first renewal phase, the federal government was unable to renew work authorization on time for thousands of previous DACA recipients who had submitted their paperwork early. The fragile nature of these benefits is likely to trickle down and inform relations between family members and between immigrant families and institutions, adding yet another layer of complexity to immigrant families' integration experiences.

Another recent development affecting immigrant families is the media coverage of unaccompanied children from Central America. While this has been an ongoing phenomenon for many years (see Chavez and Menjívar 2010), the 2008 Trafficking Victims Protection Reauthorization Act (TVPRA) included a section (235) aimed at "enhancing efforts to combat the trafficking of children."

This section stipulated that children from countries that do not share a border with the United States, when apprehended at the border, shall be properly screened before being deported and thus possibly placed in danger of being trafficked. This law, passed under the administration of President George W. Bush, now requires Border Patrol agents to maintain statistics while they detain children during their screening. Thus, although unaccompanied children were coming to the United States for many years before, it is only since 2009 that we have specific data about these flows.

However, given politicians' attention to these flows and the heightened media coverage they receive (which tends to highlight violence with this migration), political pressure has led to speedy deportations of children who might have qualified for asylum or other authorized forms of residency. On the other hand, in many of these cases, the severely backlogged immigration courts will take one or two years to process children. Even though they may ultimately be deported, many of these children now have an opportunity to live with parents who were already residing in the United States, or perhaps to earn incomes, as this is the reason why many of these youngsters migrate (Stinchcomb and Hershberg 2014). Many children experience emotional challenges associated with adjusting to a new culture and integrating into a family with members whom they do not know well or at all. Some youth also bear the trauma of the violence they experienced in their home countries or on their journey. Providing services to meet these needs has strained the budgets of some localities, generating resentment against the resettlement of these youngsters. In many cases, families must negotiate the public outcry against these minors while also being preoccupied with their legal cases and struggling to pay back their smuggling debts. Undoubtedly intergenerational relations are likely to be challenging in these cases, as parents and children may have been apart for several years and must now reconnect within a tense context of imminent deportation.

We hope we have made clear throughout this book that immigrant families, like all families, are complex and have multiple layers of identity and social position that merit close study. They are also resilient. Despite the struggles, complications, long waiting periods, and separations that are part of the experience of immigration today, immigrant families survive and often thrive. We intend this book to be a testament to their strength, malleability, and dynamism.

Notes

Notes to Chapter I

1. In a summary essay on the evolution of American families, Stephanie Coontz (2010) makes a similar observation for families in general, noting that almost all cultural groups and historical periods have recognized certain relations as families.
2. Gamson (2015) discusses the many forms that contemporary families can take, as laws that govern family formation intersect with specific social, economic and political contexts.
3. Even though family admissions have been the bedrock of immigration policy historically, there has been a push in the past couple of decades to decrease these admissions in favor of expanding employment-based visas. But increases in employment-based admissions enacted with the Immigration and Nationality Act of 1990 have not altered the family-based system (see Duleep and Regets 2014; Lowell 1996).
4. Changes to immigration laws in the 1920s also excluded wives and children from the numerical limits of approximately 150,000 visas annually (Martin and Midgley 2003); the assumption was that men were the primary migrants and wives and children followed. And, although these family members were already exempted from numerical limits, various family preference categories were established with the 1965 Act, solidifying family as a fundamental organizing mechanism for migration.
5. In 1921 the US Congress implemented annual numerical limits for immigration; in 1924 it imposed the national quota system, which limited the number of immigrants on the basis of a ratio of admissions to the number of individuals from a particular country. The result was a shift in the ethnic make-up of the immigrant population through increases in the number of visa allotments for Northern and Western Europeans, reductions in the number for

Southern and Eastern Europeans, and restrictions on the number for those from outside the western hemisphere, particularly Asia.

6. Massey and Pren (2012) argue that the post-1965 changes in the demographic profile of migratory flows were not the result of the 1965 Act but were instead the unintended consequences of a series of ill-informed policies, coupled with the maturing of webs of social connections that linked sending and receiving communities.

7. For a discussion of how non-immigrant families are defined in US family law, how such definitions have changed historically, and the effects of these definitions on family members, see Struening (2010).

8. For a useful discussion of the rise of the "domestic family ideal," see Coontz (2010).

9. Duleep and Regets (2014) note the belief that exists about family admissions—that they are ultimately humanitarian, do not contribute economically, and can even be detrimental for national competitiveness. Summarizing evidence to the contrary, these authors show that family-based immigrants often come in with job skills that benefit the US economy.

10. Portes and Rumbaut (2006: 21) developed a typology to classify contemporary immigrants according to human capital and skill level (unskilled/semi-skilled laborers, skilled workers and professionals, and entrepreneurs) and legal status (unauthorized, legal/temporary, legal/permanent, and refugees/asylees). Human capital and legal status, together, shape immigrant incorporation, dictating the types of jobs immigrants obtain and how well they fare in US society.

11. Transnational families have existed throughout US history as well as throughout the world today (Foner 1997).

Notes to Chapter 2

1. Hallett (2014) examines the contradictions inherent in immigration policy, noting that they constrain and simultaneously include, creating opportunities for immigrants to respond to the power of the state.

2. Chang (2014) examines the experiences of Asian Indian women who migrate with H-4 visas through their husbands' H-1B work visas. As derivatives of the main visa holders, these women were not granted work permits even when they were highly skilled and were therefore fully dependent on their husbands. However, this policy changed; as of March 2015, holders of H-4 visas are allowed to apply for work permits.

3. Antognini (2014) argues that scholars usually disregard the situations in which family unity takes precedent over disunity in the admissions process, as for instance in the case of K-1 (for fiancés and fiancées) and B-2 (visitor for business) visas, visa statuses that can promote unity.

4. See http://www.legalmatch.com/law-library/article/waiting-periods-and-quotas-for-family-based-visas.html (accessed April 20, 2015).

5. For examples of other visa categories, number of visas allocated to each category, and waiting times for each, see http://www.legalmatch.com/law-library/article/waiting-periods-and-quotas-for-family-based-visas.html (accessed August 8, 2015).

6. Hawthorne (2007: 816) notes the forms of exclusion that arise from legal definitions of relationships within families, such as the stipulation that children born out of wedlock can be petitioned only if "the father has or had a bona fide parent–child relationship with the person"—which is to make assumptions about the type of relationships that a parent can have with his or her out-of-wedlock child. Furthermore, a person who is not the biological child of a parent is not entitled to family preference claims, even when s/he has a close bond that in practice is as close as that of an "immediate family" member.

7. At the time of this writing, the Deferred Action for Parents of US citizens and Lawful Permanent Residents (DAPA) program, announced by President Obama in November 2014, has yet to be implemented, but it is likely to follow similar procedures as TPS and DACA.

8. It is also instructive to examine the effects of temporary legality on immigrant families, because the most recent proposals for comprehensive immigration reform—the Comprehensive Immigration Reform Act S. 1348 of the 100th Congress in 2007 and the Border Security, Economic Opportunity, and Immigration Modernization Act S. 744 of 2012—include granting temporary legality to undocumented immigrants, as a way of providing them with relief from deportation.

9. See the site of the United States Citizenship and Immigration Services (uscis.gov) at http://www.uscis.gov/humanitarian/temporary-protected-status-deferred-enforced-departure/temporary-protected-status (accessed December 20, 2014).

10. While TPS recipients are eligible for advance parole to exit the country and return legally, in practice few pursue this possibility. The bureaucratic process can be lengthy and difficult and TPS holders are generally advised against risking unforeseen problems that may block them from reentering the United States.

11. This state of continuous legal uncertainty is so pervasive and consequential for certain immigrant groups, such as Salvadorans, that Bailey et al. (2002) have referred to it as "permanent temporariness," and Menjívar (2006b) defines it as "liminal legality."

12. Arizona and Nebraska were the last states to issue driver's licenses to DACA recipients; the former in 2014 and the latter in 2015.

13. This policy might be changing. During the first months of fiscal year 2015 the detainee population declined to 26,374 and the director of ICE indicated that the 34,000 detention beds required by law would not be used this year. See http://www.kpbs.org/news/2015/apr/17/ice-under-fire-detaining-too-few-immigrants (accessed April 20, 2015).

14. According to a recent report, about 10 percent, or 300 immigrants, are held in solitary confinement on a daily basis (Urbina and Rentz 2013).
15. The bar is likely to hold for 10 years, because someone who entered without inspection and has been living in the country for 365 days or longer receives an automatic 10-year bar on reentry and, given current estimates of the length of time for which the undocumented population has resided in the United States, the 10-year bar would suit the majority.
16. Consequently, sending countries like Mexico are now receiving returning families that are akin to mixed-status families in the United States, as these families often contain US-born children and parents who are Mexican nationals (see Medina and Menjívar 2015).
17. By bringing attention to mixed-status families, Fix and Zimmermann (2001) shed light on the complexity and heterogeneity of American families, which are not neatly divided into families composed of citizens with rights to social benefits and families composed of non-citizens. And the prevalence of mixed-status families is only increasing, as immigration laws continue to limit the ability of immigrants to adjust to legal statuses.
18. Of course, inequalities among siblings in non-immigrant families have been documented (see Conley 2004). These inequalities are reproduced in immigrant families as well, with the added layer of complexity that legal status creates.

Notes to Chapter 3

1. For more information on Immigrant Investor Visas (EB-5), see http://www.uscis.gov/working-united-states/permanent-workers/employment-based-immigration-fifth-preference-eb-5/eb-5-immigrant-investor (accessed December 10, 2014).
2. Feliciano (2005) examined the data for 32 national origin groups and showed that the selectivity of Asian immigrants matters a great deal for their socioeconomic mobility, even into the second generation; it explains Asian immigrants' higher college attendance in the second generation as compared to that of other groups, for example Latinos/as, Caribbeans, and Europeans.
3. This was also the case in Menjívar's (2000) study of Salvadoran immigrant social networks.
4. The "model minority" construct associated with Asian students' educational achievements can have detrimental consequences for those who cannot meet its tenets (see Lee and Zhou 2014b).
5. Spaces where parents, particularly mothers, come together on behalf of their children are critical to the development of social capital, which they can then deploy for the benefit of the family. Mario Small's (2009) study of the expansion of the size and effectiveness of the social networks of mothers who take

their children to childcare centers where they connect with other parents is instructive here.

Notes to Chapter 4

1. Even though more women migrate in search of work than for family reunification, they are overwhelmingly admitted under family reunification categories (or they enter without inspection).
2. We use the noun "illegality" (and not the corresponding adjective: the pejorative "illegal"), to denote the legally produced uncertain and precarious legal status into which approximately 11 million immigrants have been categorized (see Menjívar and Kanstroom 2014).
3. Chang (2014) observed similar situations among Asian Indian women with H-4 visas who depended on their husbands for their status. These women had little recourse when they experienced violence in the home, and they were highly constrained in exercising their rights in family law matters.
4. Indeed, motherhood is continually negotiated across class and ethnic boundaries in the United States as well (see Dill 1998; Glenn 2002; Segura 1994).
5. Migrant men's authority is reaffirmed in multiple ways, including through control over communication (e.g., when they initiate telephone calls to their non-migrant wives), through remittances, and even through gift giving (Mahler 2001; Menjívar 2011a). In these cases, as Mahler and Pessar (2001: 610) noted, "geographic location translates into social location."
6. The emotional costs to family members have repeatedly surfaced as central components of transnational family experiences, particularly for families in which the mother has migrated (Dreby 2006, 2007; Hondagneu-Sotelo and Avila 1997; McGuire and Martin 2007; Parreñas 2005; Pratt 2012; Suárez-Orozco, Bang, and Kim 2010).
7. The age of the children when their parents migrate is crucial in how these separations are handled (Carling et al. 2012).

Notes to Chapter 5

1. The Development, Relief, and Education for Alien Minors (DREAM) Act (S. 2075, H.R. 5131) is a bipartisan piece of legislation that would provide undocumented students who have grown up in the United States with a pathway to legal permanent residency. As of this writing, the DREAM Act has been stalled in the US Congress for years.
2. Mannheim (1952) posited that individuals are heavily influenced by the sociohistoric environment at the time they grow up, and thus generations are groups of individuals who have been exposed to the same historical events—that is, the events of a sociocultural milieu in a particular historical period.

3. "Fictive kin" refers to relationships that are not consanguinal (blood ties) or affinal (ties formed through marriage). Although the etymology of the term may convey that these ties are "fictitious" or not "real" (in contrast to consanguinal or affinal ones), fictive kinship ties are equally important for those involved, and therefore just as important socially as the more conventional forms of family ties. One of the most recognized forms of fictive kinship is that based on godparenthood, but others may also exist, for example ties based on common descent in a group.

4. Few states extend driver's licenses to undocumented immigrants; see http://www.pewtrusts.org/en/research-and-analysis/reports/2015/08/deciding-who-drives?utm_campaign=2+4+New+Report+Released+States+that+Issue+Unauth&utm_medium=email&utm_source=Pew (accessed August 18, 2015).

5. Whether children migrate "alone" is not always clear. For instance, Central American minors who migrate "alone" travel with other minors as well as with adults (often smugglers) who are not their parents. Thus it is important to examine how migrations are depicted in the media and by politicians and public officials.

6. See http://www.motherjones.com/politics/2014/07/child-migrant-ellis-island-history (accessed August 14, 2015).

7. See http://www.pedropan.org (accessed August 14, 2015).

8. For a complete analysis of trends by nationality and additional background, see Stinchcomb and Hershberg (2014).

9. Many eligible US citizen children do not access social-service programs because their non-citizen parents are unaware of the children's eligibility or are afraid that receiving these benefits may hurt their chances for legalization (Hagan, Rodriguez, and Kabiri 2003; Menjívar 2014).

Notes to Chapter 6

1. Wessler (2011) notes that victims of domestic or other forms of gender violence are uniquely at risk of losing their children when they are detained through immigration enforcement.

2. Parents in immigration detention cannot attend hearings in family court, cannot meet court-ordered requirements regarding custodial rights, and often do not know that they can be reunited with their children upon deportation. This was the case of a Guatemalan woman who lost custody of her son when she was detained during a raid at the poultry plant where she worked (Valbrun 2012). She was jailed for two years and a court terminated her rights on the basis of parental abandonment, granting legal adoption of the boy to another couple. As of this writing, the courts have not overturned the decision to allow her to regain custody of her child.

3. Research has consistently demonstrated the importance of context for a variety of outcomes for immigrant families. Filindra, Blanding, and Garcia

Coll (2011) observe that the policy context and political receptivity of a state affect the educational outcomes of immigrant children. In San Francisco and Chicago, healthcare outcomes among undocumented immigrants can approach those of documented immigrants when the context is more welcoming (Iten, Jacobs, Lahiff, and Fernández 2014). And a study of the experiences of 1.5-generation immigrants underscores the importance of context with regard to social-service infrastructure in various locales in shaping their experiences (Gonzales and Ruiz 2014).

4. Some benefits for the elderly, youth, and persons with disabilities have been restored, but in the context of increased immigration enforcement family members in charge of these individuals, particularly Latinos/as, fear contacting government agencies in order to apply for these benefits.

5. A federal public benefit is defined as "any grant, contract, loan, professional license, or commercial license provided by a federal agency or by appropriated US funds; any retirement, welfare, health, or disability benefits; public or assisted housing; postsecondary education; food assistance; unemployment benefits; or any similar benefits for which payments or assistance are provided to an individual, household, or family eligibility unit by a US agency or appropriated US funds" (Fragomen 1997: 447).

6. Successful applicants for President Obama's DACA executive action signed on November 20, 2014 and with a pending date of implementation could become eligible for social security benefits and Medicare.

7. Changes in eligibility for public benefits on the basis of legal and nationality status seemed to prompt an increase in naturalization rates among groups of immigrants most affected, such as Mexicans. However, as Balistreri and van Hook (2004) observe, although this proportion increased, the social and economic conditions that explain naturalization remained the same (though there was an increase in naturalization among those with non-citizen spouses).

8. A White House memorandum regarding refugee admissions for 2015 specifies the following national groups as having priority for admission under this special form of protection: persons from Cuba, Eurasia and the Baltics, Iraq, Honduras, Guatemala or El Salvador, and only under exceptional circumstances from any other location; see http://www.whitehouse. gov/the-press-office/2014/09/30/presidential-memorandum-fy-2015-refugee-admissions (accessed December 3, 2014).

9. In practice, refugee policy has been a derivative of US foreign policy, as it has consistently extended protection to individuals fleeing countries that were in tension with the United States but has turned away people fleeing violence in countries that the United States supports, thus advancing US foreign policy more than protecting bona fide refugees (Menjívar 2000).

10. Historically, the US Congress gave states and localities the task of controlling their own immigration (Klebaner, 1958).

11. Legislative activity at the state and municipal levels increased significantly in response to the federal government's perceived inaction regarding immigration-related enforcement. Actions of the state and municipal governments, however, may have more to do with the increased responsibility to shape immigrant policy that the federal government gave them in 1996, as the federal government has been quite active in enforcing immigration laws for about two decades.
12. It is not unusual for immigrants who lack access to health care to return to their home countries to seek such care (Horton and Cole 2011).
13. Furthermore, not only does the ACA leave many immigrants excluded from the opportunity to obtain health insurance, but a large proportion of those who cannot participate in the ACA exchanges are Latinos/as (González Block et al. 2014).
14. Importantly, immigrant women have organized and protested on behalf of their families, but also to advocate for their own rights as workers and as immigrants (see Bao 2001).

Notes to Chapter 7

1. Quoted and photographed in "Children of Immigrants" by Quetzal Maucci, *New York Times*, Sunday Review, Exposures, September 21, 2014. See http://www.nytimes.com/interactive/2014/09/21/opinion/sunday/exposures-children-immigrant.html (accessed August 15, 2015).
2. Quoted and photographed in "Children of Immigrants" by Quetzal Maucci, *New York Times*, Sunday Review, Exposures, September 21, 2014. http://www.nytimes.com/interactive/2014/09/21/opinion/sunday/exposures-children-immigrant.html (accessed August 15, 2015).

References

Abraham, Margaret. 2000. *Speaking the Unspeakable: Marital Violence Among South Asian Immigrants in the United States.* New Brunswick, NJ: Rutgers University Press.

Abrego, Leisy J. 2006. "'I Can't Go to College Because I Don't Have Papers': Incorporation Patterns of Latino Undocumented Youth." *Latino Studies* 4(3): 212–31.

Abrego, Leisy J. 2008. "Legitimacy, Social Identity, and the Mobilization of Law: The Effects of Assembly Bill 540 on Undocumented Students in California." *Law & Social Inquiry* 33(3): 709–34.

Abrego, Leisy J. 2009. "Economic Well-Being in Salvadoran Transnational Families: How Gender Affects Remittance Practices." *Journal of Marriage and Family* 71(4): 1070–85.

Abrego, Leisy J. 2011. "Legal Consciousness of Undocumented Latinos: Fear and Stigma as Barriers to Claims Making for First and 1.5 Generation Immigrants." *Law & Society Review* 45(2): 337–70.

Abrego, Leisy J. 2013. "Latino Immigrants' Diverse Experiences of Illegality." In *Constructing Immigrant "Illegality": Critiques, Experiences, and Responses,* edited by Cecilia Menjívar and Daniel Kanstroom, 139–60. Cambridge: Cambridge University Press.

Abrego, Leisy J. 2014. *Sacrificing Families: Navigating Laws, Labor, and Love Across Borders.* Stanford, CA: Stanford University Press.

Abrego, Leisy J. Forthcoming. "Illegality as a Source of Solidarity and Tension in Latino Families." *Journal of Latino and Latin American Studies.*

Abrego, Leisy J. and Shannon Gleeson. 2014. "Workers, Families, and Immigration Policies." In *Undecided Nation: Political Gridlock and the Immigration Crisis,* edited by Tony Payan and Erika de la Garza, 209–28. New York: Springer.

Abrego, Leisy J. and Sarah Morando Lakhani. 2015. "Incomplete Inclusion: Legal Violence and Immigrants in Liminal Statuses." *Law & Policy* 37(4): 265–93.

References

Abrego, Leisy J. and Cecilia Menjívar. 2011. "Immigrant Latina Mothers as Targets of Legal Violence." *International Journal of Sociology of the Family* 37(1): 9–26.

Acosta, Katie L. 2013. *Amigas y Amantes: Sexually Nonconforming Latinas Negotiate Family.* New Brunswick, NJ: Rutgers University Press.

Adler, Rachel H. 2006. "'But they claimed to be police, not *la migra*!': The Interaction of Residency Status, Class, and Ethnicity in a (Post-PATRIOT Act) New Jersey Neighborhood." *American Behavioral Scientist* 50(1): 48–69.

Aguilar Jr., Filomeno V. 2013. "Brother's Keeper? Siblingship, Overseas Migration, and Centripetal Ethnography in a Philippine Village." *Ethnography* 14(3): 346–68.

Ahmad, Muneer I. 2011. "Developing Citizenship." *Issues in Legal Scholarship* 9(1). doi: 10.2202/1539–8323.1129.

Åkesson, Lisa, Jørgen Carling, and Heike Drotbohm. 2012. "Mobility, Moralities and Motherhood: Navigating the Contingencies of Cape Verdean Lives." *Journal of Ethnic and Migration Studies* 38(2): 237–60.

Alba, Richard. 2009. *Blurring the Color Line: The New Chance for an Integrated America.* Cambridge, MA: Harvard University Press.

Alba, Richard, Philip Kasinitz, and Mary C. Waters. 2011. "The Kids Are (Mostly) Alright: Second-Generation Assimilation: Comments on Haller, Portes and Lynch." *Social Forces* 89(3): 763–73.

Alcalde, M. Cristina. 2010. "Violence across Borders: Familism, Hegemonic Masculinity, and Self-Sacrificing Femininity in the Lives of Mexican and Peruvian Migrants." *Latino Studies* 8(1): 48–68.

American Community Survey. 2012. US Census Bureau. At https://www.census.gov/programs-surveys/acs/data.html (accessed September 3, 2015).

Andrews, Abigail. 2014. "Women's Political Engagement in a Mexican Sending Community: Migration as Crisis and the Struggle to Sustain an Alternative." *Gender & Society*, 28(4): 583–608.

Antognini, Albertina. 2014. "Family Unity Revisited: Divorce, Separation, and Death in Immigration Law." *South Carolina Law Review* 66(1): 1–60.

Aranda, Elizabeth M. 2003. "Global Care Work and Gendered Constraints: The Case of Puerto Rican Transmigrants." *Gender & Society* 17(4): 609–26.

Arriagada, Irma. 2002. "Cambios y desigualdad en las familias latinoamericanas." *Revista de CEPAL* 77: 143–61.

Artico, Ceres I. 2003. *Latino Families Broken by Immigration: The Adolescents' Perspectives.* New York: LFB Scholarly Publishing.

Aulette, Judy Root. 2007. *Changing American Families*, 2nd ed. Boston: Pearson.

Aysa, María and Douglas S. Massey. 2004. "Wives Left Behind: The Labor Market Behavior of Women in Migrant Communities." In *Crossing the Border: Research from the Mexican Migration Project*, edited by Jorge Durand and Douglas S. Massey, 172–90. New York: Russell Sage Foundation.

Bailey, Adrian J., Richard A. Wright, Alison Mountz, and Ines M. Miyares.

References

2002. "(Re)producing Salvadoran Transnational Geographies." *Annals of the Association of American Geographers* 92(1): 125–44.

Balistreri, Kelly Stamper and Jennifer van Hook. 2004. "The More Things Change the More They Stay the Same: Mexican Naturalization before and after Welfare Reform." *International Migration Review* 38(1): 113–30.

Baluja, Kaari Flagstad. 2003. *Gender Roles at Home and Abroad: The Adaptation of Bangladeshi Immigrants*. New York: LFB Scholarly Publishing.

Banerjee, Pallavi. 2013. "Paradoxes of Patriarchy: Contradicting Experiences of South Asian Women in Ethnic Labor Markets." In *Immigrant Women Workers in the Neoliberal Age*, edited by Nilda Flores-González, Anna Romina Guevarra, Maura Toro-Morn, and Grace Chang, 96–116. Urbana: University of Illinois Press.

Bao, Xiaolan. 2001. *Holding up more than Half the Sky: Chinese Women Garment Workers in New York City, 1948–1992*. Urbana: University of Illinois Press.

Bean, Frank D. and Marta Tienda. 1987. *The Hispanic Population in the United States*. New York: Russell Sage.

Bean, Frank D., Ruth R. Berg, and Jennifer V. W. van Hook. 1996. "Socioeconomic and Cultural Incorporation and Marital Disruption among Mexican Americans." *Social Forces* 75(2): 593–617.

Bean, Frank D., Susan K. Brown, and James D. Bachmeier. 2015. *Parents without Papers: The Progress and Pitfalls of Mexican American Integration*. New York: Russell Sage Foundation.

Bean, Frank D., Jennifer Lee, Jeanne Batalova, and Mark Leach. 2004. *Immigration and Fading Color Lines in America*. Washington, DC: Population Reference Bureau and New York: Russell Sage Foundation.

Bean, Frank D., James D. Bachmeier, Susan K. Brown, Jennifer van Hook, and Mark A. Leach. 2014. "Unauthorized Mexican Migration and the Socioeconomic Integration of Mexican Americans." In *Diversity and Disparities: America Enters a New Century*, edited by John R. Logan, 341–74. New York: Russell Sage Foundation Press.

Bean, Frank D., Mark A. Leach, Susan K. Brown, James D. Bachmeier, and John R. Hipp. 2011. "The Educational Legacy of Unauthorized Migration: Comparisons across U.S.-Immigrant Groups in How Parents' Status Affects Their Offspring." *International Migration Review* 45(2): 348–85.

Bedorf, Franziska. 2014. "Transnationalism Fading? Elderly Mexican Migrants in Chicago and Shifting Notions of Belonging." *EthnoScripts* 16(2): 55–70.

Benería, Lourdes. 2003. *Gender, Development, and Globalization: Economics as if All People Mattered*. New York and Abingdon, Oxon: Routledge.

Berger Cardoso, Jodi, Erin Randle Hamilton, Nestor Rodriguez, Karl Eschbach, and Jacqueline Hagan. 2014. "Deporting Fathers: Involuntary Transnational Families and Intent to Remigrate among Salvadoran Deportees." *International Migration Review*. doi: 10.1111/imre.12106.

References

Berry, John W., Jean S. Phinney, David L. Sam, and Paul Vedder. 2006. *Immigrant Youth in Cultural Transition: Acculturation, Identity, and Adaptation across Generations*. New York: Taylor & Francis.

Bettie, Julie. 2003. *Women without Class: Girls, Race and Identity*. Berkeley: University of California Press.

Bever, Sandra Weinstein. 2002. "Migration and the Transformation of Gender Roles and Hierarchies in Yucatan." *Urban Anthropology* 31(2): 199–230.

Bloemraad, Irene and Christine Trost. 2008. "It's a Family Affair: Intergenerational Mobilization in the Spring 2006 Protests." *American Behavioral Scientist* 52(4): 507–32.

Boehm, Deborah A. 2012. *Intimate Migrations: Gender, Family, and Illegality among Transnational Mexicans*. New York and London: NYU Press.

Bosniak, Linda S. 2007. "Being Here: Ethical Territoriality and the Rights of Immigrants." *Theoretical Inquiries into Law* 8(2): 389–410.

Bourdieu, Pierre. 1984. *Distinction: A Social Critique of the Judgement of Taste*. Cambridge, MA: Harvard University Press.

Boyd, Monica. 1989. "Family and Personal Networks in International Migration: Recent Development and New Agendas." *International Migration Review* 23(3): 638–70.

Brooks-Gunn, Jeanne and Greg J. Duncan. 1997. "The Effects of Poverty on Children." *The Future of Children: Children and Poverty* 7(2): 55–71.

Brown, Susan L., Jennifer van Hook, and Jennifer E. Glick. 2008. "Generational Differences in Cohabitation and Marriage in the US." *Population Research and Development Review* 27(5): 531–50.

Bui, Hoan N. 2003. "Help-Seeking Behavior among Abused Immigrant Women: A Case of Vietnamese American Women." *Violence against Women* 9(2): 207–39.

Buriel, Raymond and Terri De Ment. 1997. "Immigration and Sociocultural Change in Mexican, Chinese, and Vietnamese American Families." In *Immigration and the Family: Research and Policy on US Immigrants*, edited by Alan Booth, Ann C. Crouter, and Nancy Landale, 165–200. Mahwah, NJ: Lawrence Erlbaum Associates.

Cantú, Lionel. 2009. *The Sexuality of Migration: Border Crossings and Mexican American Men*. New York: NYU Press.

Capps, Randy and Karina Fortuny. 2006. *Immigration and Child and Family Policy*. Washington, DC: Urban Institute.

Capps, Randy, Rosa María Castañeda, Ajay Chaudry, and Robert Santos. 2007. *Paying the Price: The Impact of Immigrant Raids on America's Children*. Washington, DC: National Council of La Raza. Also at http://www.urban.org/UploadedPDF/411566_immigration_raids.pdf (accessed December 8, 2014).

Carling, Jørgen. 2008. "The Human Dynamics of Migrant Transnationalism." *Ethnic and Racial Studies* 31(8): 1452–77.

Carling, Jørgen, Cecilia Menjívar, and Leah Schmalzbauer. 2012. "Central

References

Themes in the Study of Transnational Parenthood." *Journal of Ethnic and Migration Studies* 38(2): 191–217.

Carlson, Marcia J. and Paula England, eds. 2011. *Social Class and Changing Families in an Unequal America*. Stanford, CA: Stanford University Press.

Carr, Stacie and Marta Tienda. 2013. "Family Sponsorship and Late-Age Immigration in Aging America: Revised and Expanded Estimates of Chained Migration." *Population Research and Policy Review* 32(6): 825–49.

Carsten, Janet, ed. 2000. *Cultures of Relatedness: New Approaches to the Study of Kinship*. Cambridge: Cambridge University Press.

Castañeda, Heide and Milena Andrea Melo. 2014. "Health Care Access for Latino Mixed-Status Families: Barriers, Strategies, and Implications for Reform." *American Behavioral Scientist* 58(14): 1891–1909.

Castro Martín, Teresa. 2002. "Consensual Unions in Latin America: Persistence of a Dual Nuptiality System." *Journal of Comparative Family Studies* 33(1): 35–55.

Catron, Peter. 2013. "Immigrant Unionization through the Great Recession." *American Sociological Review* 78(2): 315–32.

Cebulko, Kara. 2014. "Documented, Undocumented, and Liminally Legal: Legal Status During the Transition to Adulthood for 1.5 Generation Brazilian Immigrants." *The Sociological Quarterly* 55(1): 143–67.

Chang, Stewart. 2014. "Dreams of My Father, Prison for My Mother: The H-4 Nonimmigrant Visa Dilemma and the Need for an 'Immigration-Status Spousal Support." *Asian Pacific American Law Journal* 19(1): 1–28. At http://ssrn.com/abstract=2538625 (accessed July 22, 2015).

Chant, Sylvia, ed. 1992. *Gender and Migration in Developing Countries*. New York: Wiley.

Chant, Sylvia and Nikki Craske. 2003. *Gender in Latin America*. New Brunswick, NJ: Rutgers University Press.

Chao, Xia. 2013. "Class Habitus: Middle-Class Chinese Immigrant Parents' Investment in Their Newcomer Adolescents' L2 Acquisition and Social Integration." *Anthropology and Education Quarterly* 44(1): 58–74.

Chaudry, Ajay, Randy Capps, Juan Manuel Pedroza, Rosa Maria Castañeda, Robert Santos, and Molly M. Scott. 2010. *Facing Our Future: Children in the Aftermath of Immigration Enforcement*. Washington, DC: Urban Institute. At http://www.urban.org/UploadedPDF/412020_FacingOurFuture_final.pdf (accessed June 11, 2014).

Chavez, Leo R. 2012. "Undocumented Immigrants and Their Use of Medical Services in Orange County, California." *Social Science & Medicine* 74(6): 887–93.

Chavez, Leo R., Estevan T. Flores, and Marta Lopez-Garza. 1992. "Undocumented Latin American Immigrants and US Health Services: An Approach to a Political Economy of Utilization." *Medical Anthropology Quarterly* 6(1): 6–26.

Chavez, Lilian and Cecilia Menjívar. 2010. "Children without Borders: A

References

Mapping of the Literature on Unaccompanied Migrant Children to the United States." *Migraciones Internacionales* 5(3): 71–111.

Cherlin, Andrew. 2008. *Public and Private Families: An Introduction.* Boston: McGraw Hill.

Chin, Ko-lin. 1999. "Smuggled Chinese in the Mountain of Gold." In *Illegal Immigration in America: A Reference Handbook*, edited by David W. Haines and Karen Rosenblum, 293–322. Santa Barbara, CA: Greenwood.

Chin, Margaret M. 2013. "Changing Expectations: Economic Downturns and Immigrant Chinese Women in New York City." In *Immigrant Women Workers in the Neoliberal Age*, edited by Nilda Flores-González, Anna Romina Guevarra, Maura Toro-Morn, and Grace Chang, 117–30. Urbana: University of Illinois Press.

Coe, Cati. 2013. *The Scattered Family: Parenting, African Americans, and Global Inequality.* Chicago: University of Chicago Press.

Coll, Kathleen. 2004. "Necesidades y Problemas: Immigrant Latina Vernaculars of Belonging, Coalition, and Citizenship in San Francisco, California." *Latino Studies* 2(2): 186–209.

Coll, Kathleen. 2010. *Remaking Citizenship: Latina Immigrants and New American Politics.* Palo Alto, CA: Stanford University Press.

Collins, Jane L. and Victoria Mayer. 2010. *Both Hands Tied: Welfare Reform and the Race to the Bottom of the Low-Wage Labor Market.* Chicago and London: University of Chicago Press.

Collins, Patricia Hill. 1998. *Fighting Words: Black Women and the Search for Justice.* Minneapolis and London: University of Minnesota Press.

Conley, Dalton. 2004. *The Pecking Order: A Bold New Look at How Family and Society Determine Who We Become.* New York: Vintage Books/Random House.

Conley, Dalton and Rebecca Glauber. 2008. "All in the Family? Family Composition, Resources, and Sibling Similarity in Socioeconomic Status." *Research in Social Stratification and Mobility* 26(4): 297–306.

Contreras, Ricardo and David Griffith. 2012. "Managing Migration, Managing Motherhood: The Moral Economy of Gendered Migration." *International Migration* 50(4): 51–66.

Coontz, Stephanie. 2010. "The Evolution of American Families." In *Families as They Really Are*, edited by Barbara J. Risman, 30–47. New York: W. W. Norton.

Corchado, Alfredo. 2014. "The Fresa Effect: Why Some of Mexico's Elite are Starting Over in Dallas." *FD Magazine*, July 27. At http://www.fdluxe.com/2014/07/fresa-effect.html (accessed August 19, 2015).

Cranford, Cynthia. 2007. "Constructing Union Motherhood: Gender and Social Reproduction in the Los Angeles Justice for Janitors Movement." *Qualitative Sociology* 30(3): 361–81.

Crenshaw, Kimberlé. 1991. "Mapping the Margins: Intersectionality, Identity

Politics, and Violence against Women of Color." *Stanford Law Review* 43(6): 1241–99.

Cruz, Evelyn H. 2010. "Because You're Mine I Walk the Line: The Trials and Tribulations of the Family Visa Program." *Fordham Urban Law Journal* 38(1): 1–27.

Dallalfar, Arlene. 1994. "Iranian Women as Immigrant Entrepreneurs." *Gender & Society* 8(4): 541–61.

Das Gupta, Monisha. 2014. "'Don't Deport Our Daddies': Gendering State Deportation Practices and Immigrant Organizing." *Gender & Society* 28(1): 83–109.

Dasgupta, Shamita Das. 2005. "Women's Realities: Defining Violence against Women by Immigration, Race, and Class." In *Domestic Violence at the Margins: Readings on Race, Class, Gender, and Culture*, edited by Natalie J. Sokoloff, with Christina Pratt, 56–70. New Brunswick, NJ: Rutgers University Press.

Decker, Scott, Paul G. Lewis, Doris M. Provine, and Monica W. Varsanyi. 2009. "On the Frontier of Local Law Enforcement: Local Police and Federal Immigration Law." *Sociology of Crime, Law, and Deviance* 13: 261–76.

Deeb-Sossa, Natalia. 2013. *Doing Good: Racial Tensions and Workplace Inequalities at a Community Clinic in El Nuevo South*. Tucson: University of Arizona Press.

Deeb-Sossa, Natalia and Jennifer Bickham-Mendez. 2008. "Enforcing Borders in the Nuevo South: Shifting Identities and Imagined Communities." *Gender & Society* 22(5): 613–38.

Demleitner, Nora V. 2004. "How Much Do Western Democracies Value Family and Marriage? Immigration Law's Conflicted Answers." *Hofstra Law Review* 32(1): 273–311.

Dill, Bonnie Thornton. 1998. "A Better Life for Me and My Children: Low-Income Single Mothers' Struggle for Self-Sufficiency in the Rural South." *Journal of Comparative Family Studies* 29(2): 419–28.

Doering-White, John, Pilar Horner, Laura Sanders, Ramiro Martinez, William Lopez, and Jorge Delva. 2014. "Testimonial Engagement: Undocumented Latina Mothers Navigating a Gendered Deportation Regime." *International Migration and Integration*. doi: 10.1007/s12134–014–0408–7.

Donato, Katharine M. and Donna Gabaccia. 2015. *Gender and International Migration*. New York: Russell Sage Foundation.

Donato, Katherine M. and Blake Sisk. 2015. "Children's Migration to the United States from Mexico and Central America: Evidence from the Mexican and Latin American Migration Projects." *Journal on Migration and Human Security* 3(1): 58–79.

Dorner, Lisa M., Marjorie Faulstich Orellana, and Christine Li-Grinning. 2007. "'I Helped My Mom, and It Helped Me': Translating Skills of Language

References

Brokers into Improved Standardized Test Scores." *American Journal of Education* 113(3): 451–78.

Douglas-Harrison, Elaine. 2014. *When Wives Migrate and Leave Husbands Behind: A Jamaican Marriage Pattern*. PhD dissertation, Department of Sociology, CUNY.

Dreby, Joanna. 2006. "Honor and Virtue: Mexican Parenting in the Transnational Context." *Gender & Society* 20(1): 32–59.

Dreby, Joanna. 2007. "Children and Power in Mexican Transnational Families." *Journal of Marriage and Family* 69(4): 1050–64.

Dreby, Joanna. 2009. "Gender and Transnational Gossip." *Qualitative Sociology* 32(1): 33–52.

Dreby, Joanna. 2010. *Divided by Borders: Mexican Migrants and Their Children*. Berkeley: University of California Press.

Dreby, Joanna. 2012. "The Burden of Deportation on Children in Mexican Immigrant Families." *Journal of Marriage and Family* 74(4): 829–45.

Dreby, Joanna. 2014. "US Immigration Policy and Family Separation: The Consequences for Children's Well-Being." *Social Science & Medicine*. doi: 10.1016/j.socscimed.2014.08.041.

Dreby, Joanna. 2015. *Everyday Illegal: When Policies Undermine Immigrant Families*. Berkeley: University of California Press.

Dreby, Joanna and Timothy Adkins. 2010. "Inequalities in Transnational Families." *Sociology Compass* 4(8): 673–89.

Dreby, Joanna and Leah Schmalzbauer. 2013. "The Relational Contexts of Migration: Mexican Women in New Destination Sites." *Sociological Forum* 28(1): 1–26.

Duleep, Harriet and Mark Regets. 2014. "Should the US Continue Its Family-Friendly Immigration Policy?" Discussion Paper No. 8406, IZA, Bonn, Germany.

Eckstein, Susan and Mette Louise Berg. 2009. "Re-imagining Diasporas and Generations." *Diaspora* 18(1/2): 1–23.

Ehrenreich, Barbara and Arlie Russell Hochschild, eds. 2002. *Global Woman: Nannies, Maids, and Sex Workers in the New Economy*. New York: Metropolitan Books.

Elsouhag, Dalia, Bengt Arnetz, Hikmet Jamil, Mark A. Lumley, Carissa L. Broadbridge, and Judy Arnetz. 2014. "Factors Associated with Healthcare Utilization among Arab Immigrants and Iraqi Refugees." *Journal of Immigrant Minority Health* 10. doi: 10. 1007/s10903–014–0119–3.

Enchautegui, Maria E. 2012. *Hit Hard But Bouncing Back: The Employment of Immigrants During the Great Recession and Recovery*. Washington, DC: Urban Institute.

Enchautegui, Maria E. and Cecilia Menjívar. 2015. "Paradoxes of Immigration Policy: Family Separation and Reorganization under Current Immigration Laws." *Law & Policy* 37(1–2): 32–60.

References

Espiritu, Yen Le. 1999. "Gender and Labor in Asian Immigrant Families." *American Behavioral Scientist* 42(4): 628–47.

Espiritu, Yen Le. 2001. "'We Don't Sleep around like White Girls Do': Family, Culture, and Gender in Filipina American Lives." *Signs* 26(2): 415–40.

Espiritu, Yen Le. 2008. *Asian American Women and Men: Labor, Laws, and Love*, 2nd edn. Washington, DC: Rowman and Littlefield.

Ewen, Elizabeth. 1985. *Immigrant Women in the Land of Dollars: Life and Culture on the Lower East Side, 1890–1925*. New York: Monthly Review Press.

Feliciano, Cynthia. 2005. "Does Selective Migration Matter? Explaining Ethnic Disparities in Educational Attainment among Immigrants' Children." *International Migration Review* 39(4): 841–71.

Fernández-Kelly, Patricia. 2014. "Spanish as a Vehicle of Adaptation between First and Second Generation Immigrants in the United States." In *The Future of Spanish in the United States: The Language of Hispanic Migrant Communities*, edited by José Antonio Alonso, Jorge Durand, and Rodolfo Gutiérrez,153–212. Madrid: Fundación Telefónica.

Ferree, Myra Marx. 1990. "Beyond Separate Spheres: Feminism and Family Research." *Journal of Marriage and the Family* 52(4): 866–84.

Ferree, Myra Marx. 2010. "Filling the Glass: Gender Perspectives on Families." *Journal of Marriage and Family* 72(3): 420–39.

Filindra, Alexandra, David Blanding, and Cynthia Garcia Coll. 2011. "The Power of Context: State-Level Policies and Politics and the Educational Performance of the Children of Immigrants in the United States." *Harvard Educational Review* 81(3): 407–37.

Fix, Michael and Wendy Zimmermann. 2001. "All under One Roof: Mixed-Status Families in an Era of Reform." *International Migration Review* 35(2): 397–419.

Flippen, Chenoa. 2013. "Intersectionality at work: Determinants of Labor Supply among Immigrant Hispanic Women in Durham, NC." *Gender and Society* 20: 1–31.

Flippen, Chenoa. 2015. "Lifelines: The Implications of Migrant Remittances and Transnational Elder Care for the Financial Security of Low-Income Hispanic Immigrants in the United States." In *Challenges of Latino Aging in the Americas*, edited by William A. Vega, Kyriakos S. Markides, Jacqueline L. Angel, and Fernando M. Torres-Gill, 121–40. New York: Springer.

Flores-González, Nilda, Anna Romina Guevarra, Maura Toro-Morn, and Grace Chang, eds. 2013. *Immigrant Women Workers in the Neoliberal Age*. Urbana: University of Illinois Press.

Foner, Nancy. 1995. *The Caregiving Dilemma: Work in an American Nursing Home*. Berkeley: University of California Press.

Foner, Nancy. 1997. "What's New about Transnationalism? New York Immigrants Today and at the Turn of the Century." *Diaspora* 6: 355–76.

References

Foner, Nancy, ed. 2009. *Across Generations: Immigrant Families in America*. New York: New York University Press.

Foner, Nancy and Joanna Dreby. 2011. "Relations between the Generations in Immigrant Families." *Annual Review of Sociology* 37: 545–64.

Fortuny, Karina, Randolph Capps, Margaret Simms, and Ajay Chaudry. 2009. "Children of Immigrants: National and State Characteristics." Brief, August 9, Urban Institute. At http://www.urban.org/sites/default/files/alfresco/publication-pdfs/411939-Children-of-Immigrants-National-and-State-Characteristics. PDF (accessed August 20, 2015).

Fox, Cybelle. 2012. *Three Worlds of Relief: Race, Immigration, and the American Welfare State from the Progressive Era to the New Deal*. Princeton: Princeton University Press.

Fragomen, Austin T. 1997. "The Illegal Immigration Reform and Immigrant Responsibility Act of 1996: An Overview." *International Migration Review* 31(2): 438–60.

Frank, Dana. 2014. "Who's Responsible for the Flight of Honduran Children?" *The Huffington Post*, July 9. At http://www.huffingtonpost.com/dana-frank/whos-responsible-for-the-honduras_b_5530518.html (accessed August 20, 2015).

Fukui, Haruna and Cecilia Menjívar. 2015. "Bound by Inequality: The Social Capital of Older Asians and Latinos in Phoenix, Arizona." *Ethnography*. doi: 10.1177/1466138114565550.

Furman, Wyndol and Duane Buhrmester. 1985. "Children's Perceptions of the Qualities of Sibling Relationships." *Child Development* 56(2): 448–61.

Gamson, Joshua. 2015. *Modern Families: Stories of Extraordinary Journeys to Kinship*. New York: NYU Press.

Gee, Gilbert C. and Chandra L. Ford. 2011. "Structural Racism and Health Inequities: Old Issues, New Directions." *Du Bois Review: Social Science Research on Race* 8(1): 115–32.

Gelfand, Donald E. 1989. "Immigration, Aging, and Intergenerational Relationships." *The Gerontologist* 29(3): 366–72.

George, Sheba Mariam. 2005. *When Women Come First: Gender and Class in Transnational Migration*. Berkeley: University of California Press.

Giele, Janet Z. and Glen H. Elder Jr., eds. 1998. *Methods of Life Course Research: Qualitative and Quantitative Approaches*. Thousand Oaks, CA: Sage.

Gilbertson, Greta. 2009. "Caregiving across Generations: Aging, State Assistance, and Multigenerational Ties among Immigrants from the Dominican Republic." In *Across Generations: Immigrant Families in America*, edited by Nancy Foner, 135–59. New York: NYU Press.

Gleeson, Shannon. 2012. *Conflicting Commitments: The Politics of Enforcing Immigrant Worker Rights in San Jose and Houston*. Ithaca and London: Cornell University Press.

References

Gleeson, Shannon and Roberto Gonzales. 2012. "When Do Papers Matter? An Institutional Analysis of Undocumented Life in the United States." *International Migration* 50(4): 1–19.

Glenn, Evelyn Nakano. 2002. *Unequal Freedom: How Race and Gender Shaped American Citizenship and Labor.* Cambridge, MA: Harvard University Press.

Glick, Jennifer. 2010. "Connecting Complex Processes: A Decade of Research on Immigrant Families." *Journal of Marriage and Family* 72(3): 498–515.

Glick, Jennifer E. and Jennifer van Hook. 2002. "Parents' Coresidence with Adult Children: Can Immigration Explain Racial and Ethnic Variation?" *Journal of Marriage and Family* 64(1): 240–53.

Glick Schiller, Nina and Georges Fouron. 2001. *Georges Woke up Laughing: Long-Distance Nationalism and the Search for Home.* Durham, NC: Duke University Press.

Golash-Boza, Tanya. 2014. "From Legal to 'Illegal': The Deportation of Legal Permanent Residents from the United States." In *Constructing Immigrant "Illegality": Critiques, Experiences and Responses*, edited by Cecilia Menjívar and Daniel Kanstroom, 203–22. New York: Cambridge University Press.

Golash-Boza, Tanya and Pierrette Hondagneu-Sotelo. 2013. "Latino Migrant Men and the Deportation Crisis: A Gendered Racial Removal Program." *Latino Studies* 11(3): 271–92.

Gold, Steven J. 1992. *Refugee Communities: A Comparative Field Study.* Newbury Park, CA: Sage.

Gomberg-Muñoz, Ruth. 2015. "The Punishment/El Castigo: Undocumented Latinos and US Immigration Processing." *Ethnic and Racial Studies.* doi: http://dx.doi.org/10.1080/1369183X.2015.1056118.

Gonzales, Roberto G. 2011. "Learning to Be Illegal: Undocumented Youth and Shifting Legal Contexts in the Transition to Adulthood." *American Sociological Review* 76(4): 602–19.

Gonzales, Roberto G. and Leo Chavez. 2012. "Awakening to a Nightmare: Abjectivity and Illegality in the Lives of the Undocumented 1.5-Generation Latino Immigrants in the United States." *Current Anthropology* 55(3): 255–81.

Gonzales, Roberto G. and Ariel G. Ruiz. 2014. "Dreaming beyond the Fields: Undocumented Youth, Rural Realities and a Constellation of Disadvantage." *Latino Studies* 12(2): 194–216.

Gonzales, Roberto G., Carola Suárez-Orozco, and Maria Cecilia Dedios-Sanguineti. 2013. "No Place to Belong: Contextualizing Concepts of Mental Health among Undocumented Immigrant Youth in the United States." *American Behavioral Scientist* 57(8): 1173–98.

Gonzales, Roberto G., Veronica Terriquez, and Stephen P. Ruszczyk. 2014. "Becoming DACAmented: Assessing the Short-Term Benefits of Deferred Action for Childhood Arrivals." *American Behavioral Scientist* 58(14): 1852–72.

References

González Block, Miguel Angel, Arturo Vargas Bustamante, Luz Angélica de la Sierra, and Aresha Martínez Cardoso. 2014. "Redressing the Limitations of the Affordable Care Act for Mexican Immigrants through Bi-National Health Insurance: A Willingness to Pay in Los Angeles." *Journal of Immigrant & Minority Health* 16(2): 179–88.

González de la Rocha, Mercedes. 1989. "El poder de la ausencia: Mujeres y migración en una comunidad de los altos de Jalisco." In *Coloquio de Antropología e Historia Regionales: Las Realidades Regionales de la Crisis Nacional*, 317–42. Zamora, Michoacán: El Colegio de Michoacán.

González de la Rocha, Mercedes. 1994. *The Resources of Poverty: Women and Survival in a Mexican City*. Cambridge, MA: Blackwell.

Gonzalez-Barrera, Ana. 2014. "Record Number of Deportations in 2012." Washington, DC: Pew Research Center. At http://www.pewresearch.org/fact-tank/2014/01/24/record-number-of-deportations-in-2012 (accessed August 20, 2015).

González-López, Gloria. 2004. "Fathering Latina Sexualities: Mexican Men and the Virginity of their Daughters." *Journal of Marriage and Family* 66(5): 1118–30.

González-López, Gloria. 2005. *Erotic Journeys: Mexican Immigrants and Their Sex Lives*. Berkeley: University of California Press.

Goodson-Lawes, Julie. 1993. "Feminine Authority and Migration: The Case of One Family from Mexico." *Urban Anthropology* 22(3–4): 277–97.

Gordon, Milton. 1964. *Assimilation in American Life: The Role of Race, Religion, and National Origins*. New York: Oxford University Press.

Gordon, Sally. 1987. "I Go to Tanties: The Economic Significance of Child-Shifting in Antigua, West Indies." *Journal of Comparative Family Studies* 18(3): 427–43.

Gratton, Brian, Myron P. Gutmann, and Emily Skop. 2007. "Immigrants, Their Children, and Theories of Assimilation: Family Structure in the United States, 1880–1970." *The History of the Family* 12(3): 203–22.

Griffith, David. 2006. *American Guestworkers: Jamaicans and Mexicans in the US Labor Market*. University Park: Pennsylvania State University Press.

Gu, Chien-Ju. 2012. "Contextualizing Vocabularies of Motive in International Migration: The Case of Taiwanese in the United States." *International Migration* 52(2): 158–77.

Hacker, Karen, Jocelyn Chu, Carolyn Leung, Robert Marra, and Alex Pirie. 2011. "The Impact of Immigration and Customs Enforcement on Immigrant Health: Perceptions in Everett, Massachusetts, USA." *Social Science & Medicine* 73(4): 586–94.

Hagan, Jacqueline. 1994. *Deciding to Be Legal: A Maya Community in Houston*. Philadelphia: Temple University Press.

Hagan, Jacqueline. 1998. "Social Networks, Gender and Immigrant Settlement: Resource and Constraint." *American Sociological Review* 63(1): 55–67.

References

Hagan, Jacqueline. 2008. *Migration Miracle: Faith, Hope, and Meaning on the Undocumented Journey*. Cambridge, MA: Harvard University Press.

Hagan, Jacqueline, Brianna Castro, and Nestor Rodriguez. 2010. "The Effects of US Deportation Policy on Immigrant Families and Communities: Cross Border Perspectives." *North Carolina Law Review* 88: 1799–823.

Hagan, Jacqueline, Karl Eschbach, and Nestor Rodriguez. 2008. "US Deportation Policy, Family Separation, and Circular Migration." *International Migration Review* 42(2): 64–88.

Hagan, Jaqueline, Nestor Rodriguez, and Nika Kabiri. 2003. "The Effects of Recent Welfare and Immigration Reforms on Immigrants' Access to Health Care." *International Migration Review* 37(2): 444–63.

Hahamovitch, Cindy. 2011. *No Man's Land: Jamaican Guestworkers in America and the Global History of Deportable Labor*. Princeton: Princeton University Press.

Hall, Matthew, Emily Greenman, and George Farkas. 2010. "Legal Status and Wage Disparities for Mexican Immigrants." *Social Forces* 89: 491–513.

Haller, William, Alejandro Portes, and Scott M. Lynch. 2011. "Dreams Fulfilled, Dreams Shattered: Determinants of Segmented Assimilation in the Second Generation." *Social Forces* 89(3): 733–62.

Hallett, Miranda Cady. 2014. "Temporary Protection, Enduring Contradiction: The Contested and Contradictory Meanings of Temporary Immigration Status." *Law & Social Inquiry* 39(3): 621–42.

Hamal Gurung, Shobha and Bandana Purkayastha. 2013. "Gendered Labor: Experiences of Nepali Women within Pan-Ethnic Informal Labor Markets in Boston and New York." In *Immigrant Women Workers in the Neoliberal Age*, edited by Nilda Flores-González, Anna Romina Guevarra, Maura Toro-Morn, and Grace Chang, 81–95. Urbana: University of Illinois Press.

Hamilton, Nora and Norma Stoltz Chinchilla. 2001. *Seeking Community in a Global City: Guatemalans and Salvadorans in Los Angeles*. Philadelphia: Temple University Press.

Hao, Lingxin. 2010. *Color Lines, Country Lines: Race, Immigration, and Wealth Stratification in America*. New York: Russell Sage Foundation.

Hawthorne, Monique Lee. 2007. "Family Unity in Immigration Law: Broadening the Scope of 'Family.'" *Lewis & Clark Law Review* 11(3): 809–32.

Hays, Sharon. 1996. *The Cultural Contradictions of Motherhood*. New Haven, CT: Yale University Press.

Hessick, Carissa Byrne and Gabriel J. Chin, eds. 2014. *Strange Neighbors: The Role of States in Immigration Policy*. New York: NYU Press.

Hill, Nancy E. and Kathryn Torres. 2010. "Negotiating the American Dream: The Paradox of Aspirations and Achievement among Latino Students and Engagement between Their Families and Schools." *Journal of Social Issues* 66(1): 95–112.

References

Hirsch, Jennifer S. 2003. *A Courtship after Marriage: Sexuality and Love in Mexican Transnational Families*. Berkeley: University of California Press.

Ho, Christine. 1993. "The Internationalization of Kinship and the Feminization of Caribbean Migration: The Case of Afro-Trinidadian Immigrants in Los Angeles." *Human Organization* 25(1): 32–40.

Hochschild, Arlie Russell. 2001. *The Time Bind: When Work Becomes Home and Home Becomes Work*. New York: Henry Holt.

Holmes, Seth. 2013. *Fresh Fruit, Broken Bodies: Migrant Farmworkers in the United States*. Berkeley: University of California Press.

Hondagneu-Sotelo, Pierrette. 1994. *Gendered Transitions: Mexican Experiences of Immigration*. Berkeley: University of California Press.

Hondagneu-Sotelo, Pierrette, ed. 2003. *Gender and US Immigration: Contemporary Trends*. Berkeley: University of California Press.

Hondagneu-Sotelo, Pierrette. 2008. *God's Heart Has No Borders: How Religious Activists Are Working for Immigrant Rights*. Berkeley: University of California Press.

Hondagneu-Sotelo, Pierrette. 2009. *Doméstica: Immigrant Workers Cleaning and Caring in the Shadows of Affluence*, 2nd edn. Berkeley: University of California Press.

Hondagneu-Sotelo, Pierrette and Ernestine Avila. 1997. "I'm Here, but I'm There: The Meanings of Latina Transnational Motherhood." *Gender & Society* 11(5): 548–71.

Horton, Sarah and Stephanie Cole. 2011. "Medical Returns: Seeking Health Care in Mexico." *Social Science & Medicine* 72(11): 1846–52.

Hossfeld, Karen. 1994. "Hiring Immigrant Women: Silicon Valley's Simple Solution." In *Women of Color in US Society*, edited by Maxine Baca Zinn and Bonnie Dill, 65–93. Philadelphia: Temple University Press.

Hout, Michael, Asaf Levanon, and Erin Cumberworth. 2011. "Job Loss and Unemployment." In *The Great Recession*, edited by David B. Grusky, Bruce Western, and Christopher Wimer, 59–81. New York: Russell Sage Foundation.

Hsin Amy, Yu Xie. 2014. "Explaining Asian Americans' Academic Advantage over Whites." *Proceedings of the National Academy of Science* 111: 8416–21.

Huang, Zhihuan Jennifer, Stella M. Yu, and Rebeca Ledsky. 2006. "Health Status and Health Service Access and Use among Children in US Immigrant Families." *American Journal of Public Health* 96(4): 634–40.

Human Rights Watch. 2011. "A Costly Move: Far and Frequent Transfers Impede Hearings for Immigrant Detainees in the United States." June 14. At http://www.hrw.org/sites/default/files/reports/us0611webwcover_0.pdf (accessed August 19, 2015).

Hume, Mo. 2004. "'It's as if You Don't Know, Because You Don't Do Anything about It': Gender and Violence in El Salvador." *Environment and Urbanization* 16(2): 63–72.

References

Hurtado-Ortiz, Maria T. and Mary Gauvain. 2007. "Postsecondary Education Among Mexican–American Youth: Contributions of Parents, Siblings, Acculturation, and Generational Status." *Hispanic Journal of Behavioral Sciences* 29(2): 181–91.

Hwang, Maria Cecilia and Rhacel Parreñas. 2010. "Not Every Family: Selective Reunification in Contemporary US Immigration Laws." *International Labor and Working Class History* 78(1): 100–9.

Inda, Jonathan Xavier. 2013. "Subject to Deportation: IRCA, 'Criminal Aliens,' and the Policing of Immigration." *Migration Studies* 1(3): 253–7.

Ishii-Kuntz, Masako. 2000. "Diversity within Asian American Families." In *Handbook of Family Diversity*, edited by David H. Demo, Katherine R. Allen, and Mark A. Fine, 274–92. New York: Oxford University Press.

Iten, A. Elizabeth, Elizabeth A. Jacobs, Maureen Lahiff, and Alicia Fernández. 2014. "Undocumented Immigration Status and Diabetes Care among Mexican Immigrants in Two Immigration 'Sanctuary' Areas." *Journal of Immigrant & Minority Health* 16(2): 229–38.

Jasso, Guillermina. 2011. "Migration and Stratification." *Social Science Research* 40(5): 1292–336.

Jasso, Guillermina and Mark R. Rosenzweig. 1990. *The New Chosen People: Immigrants in the United States*. New York: Russell Sage Foundation.

Jensen, Leif. 2006. *New Immigrant Settlements in Rural America*. Durham, NH: Carsey Institute.

Jiménez, Tomás R. 2010. *Replenished Ethnicity: Mexican Americans, Immigration, and Identity*. Berkeley: University of California Press.

Johnson, Kevin R. 2007. *Opening the Floodgates: Why America Needs to Rethink Its Borders and Immigration Laws*. New York and London: NYU Press.

Kalavar, Jyotsna M. and John van Willigen. 2005. "Older Asian Indians Resettled in America: Narratives about Households, Culture, and Generation." *Journal of Cross-Cultural Gerontology* 20(3): 213–30.

Kang, Milian. 2010. *The Managed Hand: Race, Gender and the Body in Beauty Service Work*. Berkeley: University of California Press.

Kanstroom, Daniel. 2007. *Deportation Nation: Outsiders in American History*. Cambridge, MA: Harvard University Press.

Kao, Grace. 2004. "Social Capital and Its Relevance to Minority and Immigrant Populations." *Sociology of Education* 77(2): 172–83.

Kao, Grace and Marta Tienda. 1998. "Educational Aspirations of Minority Youth." *American Journal of Education* 106(3): 349–84.

Kasinitz, Philip, John H. Mollenkopf, Marcy C. Waters, and Jennifer Holdaway. 2008. *Inheriting the City: The Children of Immigrants Come of Age*. New York: Russell Sage Foundation.

Katz, Vikki S. 2014. *Kids in the Middle: How Children of Immigrants Negotiate Community*. New Brunswick, NJ: Rutgers University Press.

References

Kibria, Nazli. 1990. "Power, Patriarchy, and Gender Conflict in the Vietnamese Immigrant Community." *Gender & Society* 4(1): 9–24.

Kibria, Nazli. 1993. *Family Tightrope: The Changing Lives of Vietnamese Americans*. Princeton: Princeton University Press.

Kibria, Nazli, Cara Bowman, and Megan O'Leary. 2014. *Race and Immigration*. Cambridge: Polity.

Kim, Allen J. 2014. "Gender Boot Camp for Korean Immigrant Patriarchs: Father School and the New Father Conversion Process." *Sociological Perspectives* 57(3): 321–42.

Kim, Nadia Y. 2006. "'Patriarchy Is so Third World': Korean Immigrant Women and 'Migrating' White Western Masculinity." *Social Problems* 53(4): 519–36.

Kim, Nadia Y. 2008. *Imperial Citizens: Koreans and Race from Seoul to LA*. Stanford, CA: Stanford University Press.

Kim, Oksoo. 1999. "Predictors of Loneliness in Elderly Korean Immigrant Women Living in the United States of America." *Journal of Advanced Nursing* 29(5): 1082–8.

Klebaner, Benjamin J. 1958. "State and Local Immigration Regulation in the United States before 1882." *International Journal of Social History* 3(2): 269–95.

Kofman, Eleonore. 2004. "Family-Related Migration: A Critical Review of European Studies." *Journal of Ethnic and Migration Studies* 30(2): 243–62.

Ku, Leighton. 2013. "Strengthening Immigrants' Health Access: Current Opportunities." Issue Brief. At http://publichealth.gwu.edu/pdf/hp/current_opportunities_for_immigrants.pdf (accessed December 5, 2014).

Kwak, Kyunghwa. 2003. "Adolescents and Their Parents: A Review of Intergenerational Family Relations for Immigrant and Non-immigrant Families." *Human Development* 46(2–3): 115–36.

Landale, Nancy and Ralph Salvador Oropesa. 2007. "Hispanic Families: Stability and Change." *Annual Review of Sociology* 33: 381–405.

Landale, Nancy S., Kevin J. Thomas, and Jennifer van Hook. 2011. "The Living Arrangements of Children of Immigrants." *The Future of Children* 21(1): 43–70.

Landolt, Patricia and Wei Wei Da. 2005. "The Spatially Ruptured Practices of Migrant Families: A Comparison of Immigrants from El Salvador and the People's Republic of China." *Current Sociology* 53(4): 625–53.

Lareau, Annette. 2003. *Unequal Childhoods: Class, Race, and Family Life*. Berkeley: University of California Press.

Lareau, Annette and Dalton Conley, eds. 2010. *Social Class: How Does It Work?* New York: Russell Sage.

Lee, Catherine. 2013. *Fictive Kinship: Family Reunification and the Meaning of Race and Nation in American Immigration*. New York: Russell Sage Foundation.

References

Lee, Jennifer and Min Zhou. 2004. *Asian American Youth: Culture, Identity and Ethnicity*. New York: Routledge.

Lee, Jennifer and Min Zhou. 2014a. "From Unassimilable to Exceptional: The Rise of Asian Americans and 'Stereotype Promise.'" *New Diversities* 16(1): 7–22.

Lee, Jennifer and Min Zhou. 2014b. "The Success Frame and Achievement Paradox: The Costs and Consequences for Asian Americans." *Race and Social Problems* 6(1): 38–55.

Leerkes, Arjen, Mark Leach, and James Bachmeier. 2012. "Borders Behind the Borders: An Exploration of State Level Differences in Migration Control and Their Effects on US Migration Patterns." *Journal of Ethnic and Migration Studies* 38(1): 111–29.

Leslie, Leigh. 1993. "Families Fleeing War: The Case of Central Americans." *Marriage and Family Review* 19(1–2): 193–205.

Letiecq, Bethany and Leah Schmalzbauer. 2012. "Community-Based Participatory Research with Mexican Migrants in a New Rural Destination: A Good Fit?" *Action Research* 10(3): 244–59.

Levitt, Peggy. 2001. *The Transnational Villagers*. Berkeley: University of California Press.

Li, Guofang. 2003. "Literacy, Culture, and Politics of Schooling: Counternarratives of a Chinese Canadian Family." *Anthropology and Education Quarterly* 34(2): 182–204.

Lichter, Daniel T. 2012. "Immigration and the New Racial Diversity in Rural America." *Rural Sociology* 77(1): 1–34.

Lichter, Daniel T., Zhenchao Qian, and Dmitry Tumin. 2015. "Whom Do Immigrants Marry? Emerging Patterns of Intermarriage and Integration in the United States." *Annals of the American Academy of Political and Social Science*. doi: 10.1177/0002716215594614.

Lichter, Daniel T., J. Brian Brown, Zhenchao Qian, and Julie M. Carmalt. 2007. "Marital Assimilation among Hispanics? Evidence of Declining Cultural and Economic Incorporation?" *Social Science Quarterly* 88: 745–65.

Licona, Adela C. and Marta Maria Maldonado. 2013. "The Social Production of Latino/a Visibilities and Invisibilities: Geographies of Power in Small Town America." *Antipode* 46(2): 517–36.

Lieberson, Stanley. 1980. *A Piece of the Pie: Blacks and White Immigrants Since 1880*. Berkeley: University of California Press.

Light, Michael T., Mark Hugo Lopez, and Ana Gonzalez-Barrera. 2014. "The Rise of Federal Immigration Crimes: Unlawful Reentry Drives Growth." Washington, DC: Pew Research Center. At http://www.pewhispanic.org/files/2014/03/2014–03–18_federal-courts-immigration-final.pdf (accessed May 5, 2015).

López, Jane Lilly. 2015. "'Impossible Families': Mixed-Citizenship Status Couples and the Law." *Law and Policy* 37(1–2): 93–118.

References

Lorber, Judith. 1994. *Paradoxes of Gender*. New Haven, CT: Yale University Press.

Louie, Vivian S. 2004. *Compelled to Excel: Immigration, Education, and Opportunity among Chinese Americans*. Stanford, CA: Stanford University Press.

Louie, Vivian S. 2011. "Complicating the Story of Immigrant Integration." In *Writing Immigration: Scholars and Journalists in Dialogue*, edited by Marcelo Suárez-Orozco, Vivian Louie, and Roberto Suro, 218–235. Berkeley: University of California Press.

Louie, Vivian S. 2012. *Keeping the Immigrant Bargain: The Costs and Rewards of Success in America*. New York: Russell Sage.

Lowell, B. Lindsay. 1996. "Skilled and Family-Based Immigration: Principles and Labor Markets." In *Immigrants and Immigration Policy: Individual Skills, Family Ties, and Group Identities*, edited by Harriet Orcutt Duleep and Phanindra V. Wunnava, 353–72. Greenwich: JAI Press.

Lu, Wei-Ting. 2013. "Confucius or Mozart? Community Cultural Wealth and Upward Mobility among Children of Chinese Immigrants." *Qualitative Sociology* 36: 303–21.

Luibhéid, Eithne. 1998. "'Looking like a Lesbian': The Organization of Sexual Monitoring at the United States–Mexican Border." *Journal of the History of Sexuality* 8(3): 477–506.

Luibhéid, Eithne. 2002. *Entry Denied: Controlling Sexuality at the Border*. Minneapolis: University of Minnesota Press.

Luibhéid, Eithne. 2008. "Sexuality, Migration, and the Shifting Line between Legal and Illegal Status." *GLQ: A Journal of Lesbian and Gay Studies* 14(2–3): 289–315.

Luibhéid, Eithne. 2013. *Pregnant on Arrival: Making the Illegal Immigrant*. Minneapolis: University of Minnesota Press.

Lutz, Helma. 2010. "Gender in the Migratory Process." *Journal of Ethnic and Migration Studies* 36(10): 1647–63.

MacDonald, John S. and Leatrice D. MacDonald. 1964. "Chain Migration, Ethnic Neighborhood Formation, and Social Networks." *The Milibank Memorial Fund Quarterly*, 42 (1): 82–97.

Maddali, Anita. 2014. "The Immigrant 'Other': Racialized Identity and the Devaluation of Immigrant Family Relations." *Indiana Law Journal* 89(2): 643–702.

Madrigal, Larry and Walberto Tejeda. 2009. "Facing Gender-Based Violence in El Salvador: Contributions from the Social Psychology of Ignacio Martín-Baró." *Feminism & Psychology* 19(3): 368–74.

Mahler, Sarah J. 1998. "Theoretical and Empirical Contributions toward a Research Agenda for Transnationalism." In *Transnationalism from Below* (Comparative Urban and Community Research 6), edited by Michael Peter Smith and Luis Eduardo Guarnizo, 64–102. Transaction Publishers.

References

Mahler, Sarah J. 1999. "Engendering Transnational Migration: A Case Study of Salvadorans." *American Behavioral Scientist* 42(4): 690–719.

Mahler, Sarah J. 2001. "Transnational Relationships: The Struggle to Communicate across Borders." *Identities: Global Studies in Culture and Power* 7(4): 583–619.

Mahler, Sarah J. and Patricia R. Pessar. 2001. "Gendered Geographies of Power: Analyzing Gender Across Transnational Spaces." *Identities: Global Studies in Culture and Power* 7(4): 441–59.

Mahler, Sarah J. and Patricia R. Pessar. 2006. "Gender Matters: Ethnographers Bring Gender from the Periphery Toward the Core of Migration Studies." *International Migration Review* 40(1): 28–63.

Maldonado, Marta Maria. 2014. "Latino Incorporation and Racialized Border Politics in the Heartland: Interior Enforcement and Policeability in an English-Only State." *American Behavioral Scientist* 58(14): 1927–45.

Mannheim, Karl. 1952. *Essays on the Sociology of Knowledge*, edited by P. Kecskemeti. New York: Routledge and Kegan Paul.

Marrow, Helen. 2009. "Immigrant Bureaucratic Incorporation: The Dual Roles of Professional Missions and Government Policies." *American Sociological Review* 74(5): 756–76.

Marrow, Helen. 2011. *New Destination Dreaming: Immigration, Race, and Legal Status in the Rural American South*. Stanford, CA: Stanford University Press.

Martin, Philip and Elizabeth Midgley. 2003. "Immigration: Shaping and Reshaping America." *Population Bulletin* 58(2): 1–44.

Martínez, Oscar. 2013. *The Beast: Riding the Rails and Dodging the Narcos on the Migrant Trail*. London and New York: Verso.

Massey, Douglas S. 2007. *Categorically Unequal: The American Stratification System*. New York: Russell Sage Foundation.

Massey, Douglas S. 2013. "America's Immigration Policy Fiasco: Learning from Past Mistakes." *Daedalus* 142(3): 5–15.

Massey, Douglas S. 2014. "Manufacturing Marginality among Women and Latinos in Neo-Liberal America." *Ethnic and Racial Studies* 37(10): 1747–52.

Massey, Douglas S. n.d. "The New Latino Underclass: Immigration Enforcement as a Race-Making Institution." Stanford University: The Stanford Center on Poverty and Inequality. At http://web.stanford.edu/group/scspi/_media/working_papers/massey_new-latino-underclass.pdf (accessed August 14, 2015).

Massey, Douglas S. and Julia Gelatt. 2010. "What Happened to the Wages of Mexican Immigrants? Trends and Interpretations." *Latino Studies* 2(8): 328–54.

Massey, Douglas S. and Karen Pren. 2012. "Unintended Consequences of US Immigration Policy: Explaining the Post-1965 Surge from Latin America." *Population and Development Review* 38(1): 1–29.

References

Massey, Douglas S., Jorge Durand, and Nolan J. Malone. 2002. *Beyond Smoke and Mirrors: Mexican Immigration in an Era of Economic Integration.* New York: Russell Sage.

Massey, Douglas S., Mary J. Fischer, and Chiara Capoferro. 2006. "International Migration and Gender in Latin America: A Comparative Analysis." *International Migration* 44(5): 1–29.

Massey, Douglas S., Rafael Alarcon, Jorge Durand, and Humberto González. 1987. *Return to Aztlán: The Social Process of Migration from Western Mexico.* Berkeley: University of California Press.

Massey, Douglas S., Joaquín Arango, Graeme Hugo, Ali Kouaouci, Adela Pellegrino, and J. Edward Taylor. 1993. "Theories of International Migration: A Review and Appraisal." *Population and Development Review* 19(3): 431–66.

Maucci, Quetzal. 2014. "Children of Immigrants." *New York Times*, Sunday Review, Exposures. September 21. At http://www.nytimes.com/interactive/2014/09/21/opinion/sunday/exposures-children-immigrant.html (accessed July 18, 2015).

McAdam, Doug. 1988. *Freedom Summer.* Oxford: Oxford University Press.

McConnell, Eileen Diaz. 2013. "Who Has Housing Affordability Problems? Disparties in Housing Cost Burden by Race, Nativity and Legal Status in Los Angeles." *Race and Social Problems* 5(3): 173–97.

McGuire, Sharon and Kate Martin. 2007. "Fractured Migrant Families: Paradoxes of Hope and Devastation." *Family and Community Health* 30(3): 178–88.

McHale, Susan M., Kimberly A. Updegraff, Corinna J. Tucker, and Ann C. Crouter. 2000. "Step In or Stay Out? Parents' Roles in Adolescent Siblings' Relationships." *Journal of Marriage and Family* 62(3): 746–60.

McKay, Deirdre. 2007. "'Sending Dollars Shows Feeling': Emotions and Economies in Filipino Migration." *Mobilities* 2(2): 175–94.

McKenzie, Sean and Cecilia Menjívar. 2011. "The Meanings of Migration, Remittances, and Gifts: The Views of Honduran Women Who Stay." *Global Networks: A Journal of Transnational Affairs* 11(1): 63–81.

Medina, Dulce and Cecilia Menjívar. Forthcoming. "A Context of Return Migration: Mexico's Mixed-Status Families." *Ethnic and Racial Studies.*

Menjívar, Cecilia. 1999. "The Intersection of Work and Gender: Central American Immigrant Women and Employment in California." *American Behavioral Scientist* 42(4): 595–621.

Menjívar, Cecilia. 2000. *Fragmented Ties: Salvadoran Immigrant Networks in America.* Berkeley: University of California Press.

Menjívar, Cecilia. 2002a. "Living in Two Worlds? Guatemalan-Origin Children in the United States and Emerging Transnationalism." *Journal of Ethnic and Migration Studies* 28(3): 531–52.

References

Menjívar, Cecilia. 2002b. "The Ties that Heal: Guatemalan Immigrant Women's Networks and Medical Treatment." *International Migration Review* 36(2): 437–67.

Menjívar, Cecilia. 2003. "Religion and Immigration in Comparative Perspective: Salvadorans in Catholic and Evangelical Communities in San Francisco, Phoenix, and Washington DC." *Sociology of Religion* 64(1): 21–45.

Menjívar, Cecilia. 2006a. "Family Reorganization in a Context of Legal Uncertainty: Guatemalan and Salvadoran Immigrants in the United States." *International Journal of Sociology of the Family* 32(2): 223–45.

Menjívar, Cecilia. 2006b. "Liminal Legality: Salvadoran and Guatemalan Immigrants' Lives in the United States." *American Journal of Sociology* 111(4): 999–1037.

Menjívar, Cecilia. 2008. "Educational Hopes, Documented Dreams: Guatemalan and Salvadoran Immigrants' Legality and Educational Prospects." *Annals of the American Academy of Political and Social Science* 620(1): 177–93.

Menjívar, Cecilia. 2010. "Immigrants, Immigration, and Sociology: Reflecting on the State of the Discipline." Inaugural Sociological Inquiry Distinguished Essay, *Sociological Inquiry* 80(1): 3–26.

Menjívar, Cecilia. 2011a. *Enduring Violence: Ladina Women's Lives in Guatemala*. Berkeley: University of California Press.

Menjívar, Cecilia. 2011b. "The Power of the Law: Central Americans' Legality and Everyday Life in Phoenix, Arizona." *Latino Studies* 9(4): 377–95.

Menjívar, Cecilia. 2012. "Transnational Parenting and Immigration Law: The Case of Central Americans in the United States." *Journal of Ethnic and Migration Studies*, 38 (2): 301–22.

Menjívar, Cecilia. 2014. "Implementing a Multilayered Immigration System: The Case of Arizona." In *Hidden Lives and Human Rights in the United States: Understanding the Controversies and Tragedies of Undocumented Immigration*, edited by Lois A. Lorentzen, 179–204. Santa Barbara, CA: Praeger.

Menjívar, Cecilia and Leisy J. Abrego. 2009. "Parents and Children across Borders: Legal Instability and Intergenerational Relations in Guatemalan and Salvadoran Families." In *Across Generations: Immigrant Families in America*, edited by Nancy Foner, 160–89. New York: NYU Press.

Menjívar, Cecilia and Leisy J. Abrego. 2012. "Legal Violence: Immigration Law and the Lives of Central American Immigrants." *American Journal of Sociology* 117(5): 1380–1421.

Menjívar, Cecilia and Victor Agadjanian. 2007. "Men's Migration and Women's Lives: Views from Rural Armenia and Guatemala." *Social Science Quarterly* 88(5): 1243–62.

Menjívar, Cecilia and Cynthia Bejarano. 2004. "Latino Immigrants' Perceptions of Crime and Police Authorities: A Case Study from the Phoenix Metropolitan Area." *Ethnic and Racial Studies* 21(1): 120–48.

References

Menjívar, Cecilia and María Enchautegui. 2015. "Confluence of the Economic Recession and Immigration Laws in the Lives of Latino Immigrant Workers in the United States." In *Immigrant Vulnerability and Resilience: Comparative Perspectives on Latin American Immigrants During the Great Recession*, edited by María Aysa-Lastra and Lorenzo Cachón, 105–26. Netherlands: Springer.

Menjívar, Cecilia and Daniel Kanstroom, eds. 2014. *Constructing Immigrant "Illegality": Critiques, Experiences and Responses*. New York: Cambridge University Press.

Menjívar, Cecilia and Olivia Salcido. 2002. "Immigrant Women and Domestic Violence: Common Experiences in Different Countries." *Gender & Society* 16(6): 898–920.

Menjívar, Cecilia, Julie DaVanzo, Lisa Greenwell, and R. Burciaga Valdez. 1998. "Remittance Behavior among Salvadoran and Filipino Immigrants in Los Angeles." *International Migration Review* 32(1): 97–126.

Milkman, Ruth and Veronica Terriquez. 2012. "'We Are the Ones Who Are Out in Front': Women's Leadership in the Immigrant Rights Movement." *Feminist Studies* 38(3): 723–52.

Miller Matthei, Linda and David A. Smith. 1998. "'Belizean Boyz 'n the 'Hood'"? Garifuna Labor Migration and Transnational Identity." In *Transnationalism from Below*, edited by Michael P. Smith and Luis E. Guarnizo, 270–90. New Brunswick, NJ: Transaction Publishers.

Min, Pyong Gap. 1998. *Changes and Conflicts: Korean Immigrant Families in New York*. Boston: Allyn & Bacon.

Min, Pyong Gap and Mehdi Bozorgmehr. 2000. "Immigrant Entrepreneurship and Business Patterns: A Comparison of Koreans and Iranians in Los Angeles." *International Migration Review* 34(3): 707–38.

Miranda, Jeanne, Juned Siddique, Claudia Der-Martirosian, and Thomas R. Belin. 2005. "Depression among Latina Immigrant Mothers Separated From Their Children." *Psychiatric Services* 56(6): 717–20.

Mitnik, Pablo A. and Jessica Halpern-Finnerty. 2010. "Immigration and Local Governments: Inclusionary Local Policies in the Era of State Rescaling." In *Taking Local Control: Immigration Policy Activism in US Cities and States*, edited by Monica Varsanyi, 51–72. Palo Alto, CA: Stanford University Press.

Møller, Pia. 2014. "Restoring Law and (Racial) Order to the Old Dominion: White Dreams and New Federalism in Anti-immigrant Legislation." *Cultural Studies* 28(5–6): 869–910.

Moon, Seungsook. 2003. "Immigration and Mothering: Case Studies from Two Generations of Korean Immigrant Women." *Gender & Society* 17(6): 840–60.

Moran-Taylor, Michelle and Cecilia Menjívar. 2005. "Unpacking Longings to Return: Guatemalans and Salvadorans in Phoenix, Arizona." *International Migration* 43(4): 91–121.

Muir, Karen L. S. 1988. *The Strongest Part of the Family: A Study of Lao Refugee Women in Columbus, Ohio*. New York: AMS Press.

References

NCSL (National Conference of State Legislatures). 2010. "2010 Immigration-Related Bills and Resolutions in States (January–March 2010)." Immigrant Policy Project, April 27. At http://www.ncsl.org/portals/1/documents/immig/immigration_report_april2010.pdf (accessed August 12, 2015).

Nelson, Lise and Nancy Hiemstra. 2008. "Latino Immigrants and the Renegotiation of Place and Belonging in Rural America." *Social and Cultural Geography* 9(3): 319–42.

Nicholls, Walter J. 2013. *The DREAMers: How the Undocumented Youth Movement Transformed the Immigrant Rights Debate.* Palo Alto, CA: Stanford University Press.

Ocampo, Anthony C. 2012. "Making Masculinity: Negotiations of Gender Presentation among Latino Gay Men." *Latino Studies* 10(4): 448–72.

Ochoa, Gilda. 2013. *Academic Profiling: Latinos, Asian Americans, and the Achievement Gap.* Minneapolis: University of Minnesota Press.

Okamoto, Dina G. 2014. *Redefining Race: Asian American Panethnicity and Shifting Ethnic Boundaries.* New York: Russell Sage Foundation.

Orellana, Marjorie Faulstich. 2001. "The Work Kids Do: Mexican and Central American Immigrant Children's Contributions to Households and Schools in California." *Harvard Educational Review* 71(3): 366–90.

Orellana, Marjorie Faulstich. 2009. *Translating Childhoods: Immigrant Youth, Language, and Culture.* New Brunswick, NJ: Rutgers University Press.

Orozco, Manuel. 2012. "Future Trends in Remittances to Central America and the Caribbean." *Remittances and Development: Inter-American Dialogue.* Report, May. At https://www.monroecollege.edu/uploadedFiles/_Site_Assets/PDF/Remittances-to-the-Caribbean.pdf (accessed August 28, 2015).

Padilla, Yajaira M. 2012. *Changing Women, Changing Nation: Female Agency, Nationhood, and Identity in Trans-Salvadoran Narratives.* Albany: SUNY Press.

Pallares, Amalia. 2014. *Family Activism: Immigrant Struggles and the Politics of Noncitizenship.* New Brunswick: Rutgers University Press.

Parrado, Emilio A. and Chenoa Flippen. 2005. "Migration and Gender among Mexican Women." *American Sociological Review* 70(4): 606–32.

Parrado, Emilio A. and S. Philip Morgan. 2008. "Intergenerational Fertility Patterns among Hispanic Women: New Evidence of Immigrant Assimilation." *Demography* 45(3): 651–71.

Parreñas, Rhacel. 2001. *Servants of Globalization: Women, Migration, and Domestic Work.* Palo Alto, CA: Stanford University Press.

Parreñas, Rhacel. 2005. *Children of Global Migration: Transnational Families and Gendered Woes.* Palo Alto, CA: Stanford University Press.

Passel, Jeffrey. 2011. "Demography of Immigrant Youth: Past, Present, and Future." *The Future of Children* 21(1): 19–41.

Passel, Jeffrey S. and D'Vera Cohn. 2009. "A Portrait of Unauthorized Immigrants in the United States." Hispanic Trends Project. Washington, DC:

References

Pew Research Hispanic Center. At http://www.pewhispanic.org/2009/04/14/a-portrait-of-unauthorized-immigrants-in-the-united-states (accessed September 27, 2014).

Passel, Jeffrey S. and D'Vera Cohn. 2012. "Unauthorized Immigrants: 11.1 Million in 2011." Washington, DC: Pew Research Hispanic Center. At http://www.pewhispanic.org/2012/12/06/unauthorized-immigrants-11-1-million-in-2011 (accessed September 27, 2014).

Passel, Jeffrey S., D'Vera Cohn, and Ana Gonzalez-Barrera. 2013. "Population Decline of Unauthorized Immigrants Stalls, May Have Reversed." Washington, DC: Pew Research Center. At http://www.pewhispanic.org/files/2013/09/Unauthorized-Sept-2013-FINAL.pdf (accessed September 26, 2014).

Passel, Jeffrey S., D'Vera Cohn, Jens Manuel Krogstad, and Ana Gonzalez-Barrera. 2014. "As Growth Stalls, Unauthorized Population Becomes More Settled." Washington, DC: Pew Research Hispanic Trends Project. At http://www.pewhispanic.org/files/2014/09/2014-09-03_Unauthorized-Final.pdf (accessed September 26, 2014).

Pastor, Manuel and Susan Alva. 2004. "Guest Workers and the New Transnationalism: Possibilities and Realities in an Age of Repression." *Social Justice* 31(1–2): 92–112.

Pérez, Zenen Jaimes. 2014. "How DACA Has Improved the Lives of Undocumented Young People." Report published by the Center for American Progress. Washington, DC. At https://cdn.americanprogress.org/wp-content/uploads/2014/11/BenefitsOfDACABrief2.pdf (accessed December 10, 2014).

Perlmann, Joel and Mary C. Waters. 2007. "Intermarriage and Multiple Identities." In *The New Americans: A Guide to Immigration since 1965*, edited by Mary C. Waters and Reed Ueda, with Helen Marrow, 110–23. Cambridge, MA: Harvard University Press.

Pessar, Patricia R. 1999. "The Role of Gender, Households, and Social Networks in the Migration Process: A Review and Appraisal." In *The Handbook of International Migration: The American Experience*, edited by Charles Hirschman, Philip Kasinitz, and Josh DeWind, 53–70. New York: Russell Sage Foundation.

Pessar, Patricia R. 2005. *Women, Gender, and International Migration across and beyond the Americas: Inequalities and Limited Empowerment*. Report published by the Population Division, United Nations Secretariat, Mexico City, Mexico. At http://www.un.org/esa/population/migration/turin/Symposium_Turin_files/P08_Pessar.pdf (accessed January 9, 2015).

Pessar, Patricia and Sara Mahler. 2003. "Transnational Migration: Bringing Gender In." *International Migration Review* 23: 812–46.

Pew Research Center. 2012. *The Rise of Asian Americans*. Report published by the Pew Research Center, Washington, DC. At http://www.pewsocialtrends.org/files/2013/04/Asian-Americans-new-full-report-04-2013.pdf (accessed January 4, 2015).

References

Pew Research Center. 2013. *A Nation of Immigrants: A Portrait of the 40 Million, Including 11 Million Unauthorized.* Report published by the Pew Hispanic Center, Washington, DC. At http://www.pewhispanic.org/files/2013/01/statistical_portrait_final_jan_29.pdf (accessed January 4, 2015).

Pham, Huyen and Pham Hoang Van. 2014. "Measuring the Climate for Immigrants: A State-by-State Analysis." In *Strange Neighbors: The Role of States in Immigration Policy*, edited by Carissa Byrne Hessick and Gabriel J. Chin, 21–39. New York: NYU Press.

Phipps, Ricardo M. and Suzanne Degges-White. 2014. "A New Look at Transgenerational Trauma Transmission: Second-Generation Latino Immigrant Youth." *Journal of Multicultural Counseling and Development* 42(3): 174–87.

Physicians for Human Rights. 2011. *Punishment before Justice: Indefinite Detention in the US.* At https://s3.amazonaws.com/PHR_Reports/indefinite-detention-june2011.pdf (accessed August 19, 2015).

Piore, Michael. 1979. *Birds of Passage: Migrant Labor in Industrial Societies.* New York: Cambridge University Press.

Plaza, Dwaine. 2000. "Transnational Grannies: The Changing Family Responsibilities of Elderly African Caribbean-Born Women Residents in Britain." *Social Indicators Research* 51(1): 75–105.

Portes, Alejandro. 1995. "Children of Immigrants: Segmented Assimilation and its Determinants." In *The Economic Sociology of Immigration*, edited by Alejandro Portes, 248–80. New York: Russell Sage.

Portes, Alejandro and Patricia Fernández-Kelly. 2008. "No Margin for Error: Educational and Occupational Achievement among Disadvantaged Children of Immigrants." *Annals of the American Academy of Political and Social Science* 620(1): 12–36.

Portes, Alejandro and Leif Jensen. 1989. "The Enclave and the Entrants: Patterns of Ethnic Enterprise in Miami before and after Mariel." *American Sociological Review* 54(6): 929–49.

Portes, Alejandro and Rubén Rumbaut. 2001. *Legacies: The Story of the Second Immigrant Generation.* Berkeley: University of California Press.

Portes, Alejandro and Rubén Rumbaut. 2006. *Immigrant America: A Portrait.* Berkeley: University of California Press.

Portes, Alejandro and Min Zhou. 1993. "The New Second Generation: Segmented Assimilation and Its Variants among Post-1965 Immigrant Youth." *Annals of the American Academy of Political and Social Science* 530(1): 74–96.

Pourat, Nadereh, Steven P. Wallace, Max W. Hadler, and Ninez Ponce. 2014. "Assessing Health Care Services Used by California's Undocumented Immigrant Population in 2010." *Health Affairs* 33(9): 840–7.

Powell, Brian, Catherine Bolzendahl, Claudia Geist, and Lala Carr Steelman. 2010. *Counted Out: Same-Sex Relations and Americans' Definitions of Family.* New York: Russell Sage Foundation.

Pratt, Geraldine. 2012. *Families Apart: Migrant Mothers and the Conflicts of Labor and Love*. Minneapolis: University of Minnesota Press.

Pribilsky, Jason. 2004. "'Aprendemos a convivir': Conjugal Relations, Co-parenting, and Family Life among Ecuadorian Transnational Migrants in New York City and the Ecuadorian Andes." *Global Networks* 4(3): 313–34.

Pribilsky, Jason. 2007. *La Chulla Vida: Gender, Migration, and the Family in Andean Ecuador and New York City*. Syracuse, NY: Syracuse University Press.

Price, Chara, Sandra Simpkins, and Cecilia Menjívar. Forthcoming. "Sibling Behaviors and Mexican-Origin Adolescents' After-school Activities." *Journal of Adolescent Research*.

Pyke, Karen. 2000. "'The Normal American Family' as an Interpretive Structure of Family Life among Grown Children of Korean and Vietnamese Immigrants." *Journal of Marriage and Family* 62(1): 240–55.

Pyke, Karen and Denise L. Johnson. 2003. "Asian American Women and Racialized Femininities: 'Doing Gender' across Cultural Worlds." *Gender & Society* 17(1): 33–53.

Qian, Zhenchao. 2014. "Divergent Paths of American Families." In *Diversity and Disparities: America Enters a New Century*, edited by John Logan, 237–69. New York: Russell Sage Foundation.

Qian, Zhenchao and Daniel T. Lichter. 2001. "Measuring Marital Assimilation: Intermarriage among Natives and Immigrants." *Social Science Research* 30(2): 289–312.

Qian, Zhenchao, Sampson Lee Blair, and Stacey Ruf. 2001. "Asian American Interracial and Interethnic Marriages: Differences by Education and Nativity." *International Migration Review* 35: 557–86.

Raj, Anita and Jay Silverman. 2002. "Violence against Immigrant Women: The Roles of Culture, Context, and Legal Immigrant Status on Intimate Partner Violence." *Violence against Women* 8(3): 367–98.

Raj, Anita and Jay Silverman. 2003. "Immigrant South Asian Women at Greater Risk for Injury from Intimate Partner Violence." *American Journal of Public Health* 93(3): 435–7.

Rasmussen Report. 2014. "Voters Strongly Oppose Legal Rights, Government Benefits of Illegal Immigrants." October 10. At http://www.rasmussenreports.com/public_content/politics/current_events/immigration/september_2014/voters_strongly_oppose_legal_rights_government_benefits_for_illegal_immigrants (accessed July 22, 2015).

Repak, Terry A. 1995. *Waiting on Washington: Central American Workers in the Nation's Capital*. Philadelphia: Temple University Press.

Reynolds, Jennifer F. and Marjorie Faulstich Orellana. 2009. "New Immigrant Youth Interpreting in White Public Space." *American Anthropologist* 111(2): 211–23.

Rios, Victor. 2011. *Punished: Policing the Lives of Black and Latino Boys*. New York: NYU Press.

References

Rodriguez, Nestor and Jacqueline Maria Hagan. 2004. "Fractured Families and Communities: Effects of Immigration Reform in Texas, Mexico, and El Salvador." *Latino Studies* 2(3): 328–51.

Rogers, John, Marisa Saunders, Veronica Terriquez, and Veronica Velez. 2008. "Civic Lessons: Public Schools and the Civic Development of Undocumented Students and Parents." *Northwestern Journal of Law and Social Policy* 3(2): 201–18.

Roschelle, Anne R. 1997. *No More Kin: Exploring Race, Class, and Gender in Family Networks*. Thousand Oaks, CA: Sage.

Rumbaut, Rubén. 1997. "Ties that Bind: Immigration and Immigrant Families." In *Immigration and the Family: Research and Policy on US Immigrants*, edited by Alan Booth, Ann C. Crouter, and Nancy S. Landale, 3–46. Mahwah, NJ: Lawrence Erlbaum Associates.

Rumbaut, Rubén. 2004. "Ages, Life Stages, and Generational Cohorts: Decomposing the Immigrant First and Second Generations in the United States." *International Migration Review* 38(3): 1160–205.

Rumbaut, Rubén. 2005. "Turning Points in the Transition to Adulthood: Determinants of Educational Attainment, Incarceration, and Early Childbearing Among Children of Immigrants." *Ethnic and Racial Studies* 28(6): 1041–86.

Salcido, Olivia and Madelaine Adelman. 2004. "'He Has Me Tied with the Blessed and Damned Papers': Undocumented Immigrant Battered Women in Phoenix, Arizona." *Human Organization* 63(2): 162–72.

Salcido, Olivia and Cecilia Menjívar. 2012. "Gendered Paths to Legal Citizenship: The Case of Latin–American Immigrants in Phoenix." *Law & Society Review* 46(2): 335–68.

Sanchez, Teresa Figueroa. 2002. *Immigrant Family Farms in the California Strawberry Industry*. PhD Dissertation, University of California at Santa Barbara, California.

Sanchez, Teresa Figueroa. 2015. "Gendered Sharecropping: Waged and Unwaged Mexican Immigrant Labor in the California Strawberry Fields." *Signs* 40(4): 917–38.

Sánchez Molina, Raul. 2015. "Caring while Missing Children's Infancy: Transnational Mothering among Honduran Women Working in Greater Washington." *Human Organization* 74(1): 62–73. doi: 10.17730/humo.74.1.p456q732p644p601.

Santos, Carlos and Menjívar, Cecilia. 2013. "Youth's Perspective on Senate Bill 1070 in Arizona: The Socioeconomic Effects of Immigration Policy." *Association of Mexican American Educators Journal* 7(2): 7–17.

Santos, Carlos, Cecilia Menjívar, and Erin Godfrey. 2013. "The Effects of SB 1070 on Children." In *Latino Policies and Arizona's Immigration Law SB 1070*, edited by Lisa Magaña and Erik Lee, 79–92. New York: Springer.

Sassen, Saskia. 1988. *The Mobility of Labor and Capital: A Study in International Capital and Labor Flow*. Cambridge: Cambridge University Press.

References

Sassen, Saskia. 1990. *The Mobility of Capital and Labor: A Study of International Investment and Labor Flow*. New York: Cambridge University Press.

Sassen, Saskia. 1998. *Globalization and Its Discontents: Essays on the New Mobility of People and Money*. New York: New Press.

Sassen, Saskia. 2008. "Two Stops in Today's New Global Geographies: Shaping Novel Labor Supplies and Employment Regimes." *American Behavioral Scientist* 52: 457–96.

Sassen-Koob, Saskia. 1979. "Formal and Informal Associations: Dominicans and Colombians in New York." *International Migration Review* 13(2): 314–32.

Sassen-Koob, Saskia. 1984. "Notes on the Incorporation of Third World Women into Wage Labor through Immigration and Off-Shore Production." *International Migration Review* 18(4): 1144–67.

Schmalzbauer, Leah. 2004. "Searching for Wages and Mothering from Afar: The Case of Honduran Transnational Families." *Journal of Marriage and Family* 66(5): 1317–31.

Schmalzbauer, Leah. 2005. *Striving and Surviving: A Daily Life Analysis of Honduran Transnational Families*. New York: Routledge.

Schmalzbauer, Leah. 2008. "Family Divided: The Class Formation of Honduran Transnational Families." *Global Networks* 8(3): 329–46.

Schmalzbauer, Leah. 2009. "Gender on a New Frontier: Mexican Migration and Economic Crisis in the Rural Mountain West." *Gender & Society* 23(6): 747–67.

Schmalzbauer, Leah. 2011. "'Doing Gender,' Ensuring Survival: Mexican Migration and Economic Crisis in the Rural Mountain West." *Rural Sociology* 76(4): 441–60.

Schmalzbauer, Leah. 2013. "Motherhood and Transformation in the Field: Reflections on Access, Meaning and Trust." In *Family and Work in Everyday Ethnography*, edited by Tamara Brown and Joanna Dreby, 81–96. Philadelphia: Temple University Press.

Schmalzbauer, Leah. 2014. *The Last Best Place? Gender, Family and Migration in the New West*. Stanford, CA: Stanford University Press.

Schmalzbauer, Leah. 2015. "Temporary and Transnational: Gender and Emotion in the Lives of Mexican Guestworker Fathers." *Ethnic and Racial Studies* 38(2): 211–26.

Schrover, Marlou and Deidre M. Moloney, eds. 2013. *Gender, Migration and Categorization: Making Distinctions between Migrants in Western Countries, 1945–2010* (IMISCOE-AUP Series). Amsterdam, Netherlands: Amsterdam University Press.

Segura, Denise. 1994. "Working at Motherhood: Chicana and Mexican Immigrant Mothers and Employment." In *Mothering: Ideology, Experience, and Agency*, edited by Evelyn Nakano Glenn, Grace Chang, and Linda Rennie Forcey, 211–33. New York: Routledge.

Seif, Hinda. 2004. "'Wise Up!' Undocumented Latino Youth, Mexican–American

References

Legislators, and the Struggle for Higher Education Access." *Latino Studies* 2(2): 210–30.

Shih, Kristy Y. and Karen Pyke. 2010. "Power, Resistance, and Emotional Economies in Women's Relationships with Mothers-in-Law in Chinese Immigrant Families." *Journal of Family Issues* 31(3): 333–57.

Silver, Alexis. 2012. "Aging into Exclusion and Social Transparency: Undocumented Immigrant Youth and the Transition to Adulthood." *Latino Studies* 10(4): 499–522.

Silvey, Rachel. 2004. "Geographies of Gender and Migration: Spatializing Social Difference." *International Migration Review* 40(1): 64–81.

Simanski, John F. 2014. *Immigration Enforcement Actions: 2013*. Washington, DC: US Department of Homeland Security, Office of Statistics.

Simanski, John F. and Lesley M. Sapp. 2012. *Immigration Enforcement Actions: 2011*. Annual Report, DHS, Office of Immigration Statistics, September. At http://www.dhs.gov/sites/default/files/publications/immigration-statistics/enforcement_ar_2011.pdf (accessed October 1, 2014).

Singer, Audrey. 2008. "Twenty-First Century Gateways: An Introduction." In *Twenty-First Century Gateways: Immigrant Integration in Suburban America*, edited by Audrey Singer, Susan W. Hardwick, and Caroline B. Brettell, 3–30. Washington, DC: Brookings Institution.

Skop, Emily. 2012. *The Immigration and Settlement of Asian Indians in Phoenix, Arizona 1965–2011: Ethnic Pride vs. Racial Discrimination in the Suburbs.* Lampeter: Edwin Mellen Press.

Sladkova, Jana. 2010. *Journeys of Undocumented Honduran Migrants to the United States.* New York: LFB Scholarly Publishing.

Small, Mario Luis. 2009. *Unanticipated Gains: Origins of Network Inequality in Everyday Life.* New York: Oxford University Press.

Smith, Dorothy. 1993. "The Standard North American Family: SNAF as an Ideological Code." *Journal of Family Issues* 14(1): 50–65.

Smith, Robert C. 2006. *Mexican New York: Transnational Lives of New Immigrants.* Berkeley: University of California Press.

Smith, Robert C. 2008. "Horatio Alger Lives in Brooklyn: Extrafamily Support, Intrafamily Dynamics and Social Neutral Operating Identities in Exceptional Mobility among the Children of Mexican Immigrants." *Annals of the American Academy of Political and Social Science* 620(1): 270–90.

Sousa-Rodriguez, Isabel. Forthcoming. "Unauthorized Mothering: Legal Status, Legal Violence, and the Resilience of Undocumented Families." In *New Materialisms: Tales of Motherwork Dislodging the Unthinkable*, edited by Roksana Badruddoja and Maki Motapanyane. Ontario, Canada: Demeter Press.

SPLC (Southern Poverty Law Center). 2007. *Close to Slavery: Guestworker Programs in the United States.* Montgomery, AL: Southern Poverty Law Center.

References

Stark, Oded and J. Edward Taylor. 1989. "Relative Deprivation and International Migration." *Demography* 26(1): 1–14.

Steil, Justin and Jennifer Ridgley. 2012. "Small Town Defenders: The Production of Citizenship in Hazelton, Pennsylvania." *Environment & Planning D: Society and Space* 30: 1028–45.

Steinberg, Stephen. 2001. *The Ethnic Myth: Race, Ethnicity, and Class in America*. Boston: Beacon Press.

Stephen, Lynn. 2007. *Transborder Lives: Indigenous Oaxacans in Mexico, California, and Oregon*. Durham, NC and London: Duke University Press.

Stepick, Alex and Carol Dutton Stepick. 2009. "Diverse Contexts of Reception and Feelings of Belonging." *Forum: Qualitative Social Research* 10(3). At http://www.qualitative-research.net/index.php/fqs/article/view/1366/2863 (accessed August 20, 2015).

Stewart, Julie. 2012. "Fiction over Facts: Competing Narrative Forms Explain Policy in a New Immigrant Destination." *Sociological Forum* 27(3): 591–616.

Stinchcomb, Dennis and Eric Hershberg. 2014. *Unaccompanied Migrant Children from Central America: Context, Causes, and Reponses*. Washington, DC: Center for Latin American & Latino Studies, American University.

Stoll, David. 2013. *El Norte or Bust! How Migration Fever and Microcredit Produced a Financial Crush in a Latin American Town*. Lanham, MD: Rowman and Littlefield.

Stoney, Sierra and Jeanne Batalova. 2013. "Central American Immigrants in the United States." Washington, DC: Migration Policy Institute. At http://www.migrationpolicy.org/article/central-american-immigrants-united-states (accessed July 19, 2015).

Striffler, Steve. 2005. *Chicken: The Dangerous Transformation of America's Favorite Food*. New Haven, CT: Yale University Press.

Struening, Karen. 2010. "Families 'in Law' and Families 'in Practice': Does the Law Recognize Families as They Really Are?" In *Families as They Are*, edited by Barbara J. Risman, 75–90. New York: W. W. Norton.

Suárez-Orozco, Carola and Marcelo Suárez-Orozco. 2001. *Children of Immigration*. Cambridge, MA: Harvard University Press.

Suárez-Orozco, Carola, Hee Jin Bang, and Ha Yeon Kim. 2010. "I Felt like My Heart Was Staying Behind: Psychological Implications of Family Separations and Reunifications for Immigrant Youth." *Journal of Adolescent Research* 26(2): 222–57.

Suárez-Orozco, Carola, Irina Todorova, and Josephine Louie. 2002. "Making up for Lost Time: The Experience of Separation and Reunification among Immigrant Families." *Family Process* 41(4): 625–43.

Suárez-Orozco, Carola, Hirokazu Yoshikawa, Robert T. Teranishi, and Marcelo Suárez-Orozco. 2011. "Growing up in the Shadows: The Developmental Implications of Unauthorized Status." *Harvard Educational Review* 81(3): 438–72.

References

Sun, Ken Chih-Yan. 2014. "Reconfigured Reciprocity: How Aging Taiwanese Immigrants Transform Cultural Logics of Elder Care." *Journal of Marriage and Family* 76(4): 875–89.

Takaki, Ronald. 1989. *Strangers from a Different Shore: A History of Asian Americans*. Boston: Little, Brown.

Takei, Isao, Rogelio Sáenz, and Jing Li. 2009. "Cost of Being a Mexican Immigrant and Being a Mexican Non-citizen in California and Texas." *Hispanic Journal of Behavioral Sciences* 31(1): 73–95.

Telles, Edward and Vilma Ortiz. 2008. *Generations of Exclusion: Mexican Americans, Assimilation and Race*. New York: Russell Sage Foundation.

Teranishi, Robert T., Carola Suárez-Orozco, and Marcelo Suárez-Orozco. 2015. *In the Shadows of the Ivory Tower: Undocumented Undergrads and the Liminal State of Immigration Reform*. Report by the UndocuScholars Project, the Institute for Immigration, Globalization, & Education, and the University of California, Los Angeles. At http://undocuscholars.org/assets/undocuscholarsreport2015.pdf (accessed August 18, 2015).

Terriquez, Veronica and Hyeyoung Kwon. 2014. "Intergenerational Family Relations, Civic Organisations, and the Political Socialisation of Second-Generation Immigrant Youth." *Journal of Ethnic and Migration Studies* 41(3): 425–47.

Thai, Hung Cam. 2014. *Insufficient Funds: The Culture of Money in Low-Wage Transnational Families*. Stanford, CA: Stanford University Press.

Thomas, William I. and Florian Znaniecki. 1996. *The Polish Peasant in Europe and America*, edited and abridged by Eli Zaretsky. Urbana: University of Illinois Press.

Tienda, Marta and Karen Booth. 1991. "Gender, Migration, and Social Change." *International Sociology* 6(1): 51–72.

Toomey, Russell B., Adriana J. Umaña-Taylor, David R. Williams, Kimberly A. Updegraff, and Laudan B. Jahromi. 2014. "The Impact of Arizona's Immigration Law on Health and Service Utilization of Mexican-Origin Teen Mothers." *American Journal of Public Health* 104: S1, S28–S34.

Toro-Morn, Maura. 2013. "Elvira Arellano and the Struggles of Low-Wage Undocumented Latina Immigrant Women." In *Immigrant Women Workers in the Neoliberal Age*, edited by Nilda Flores-González, Anna Romina Guevarra, Maura Toro-Morn, and Grace Chang, 38–55. Urbana: University of Illinois Press.

TRAC (Transactional Records Access Clearinghouse) Immigration. 2013. "Legal Noncitizens Receive Longest ICE Detention." At http://trac.syr.edu/immigration/reports/321 (accessed October 1, 2014).

Treas, Judith and Jeanne Batalova. 2009. "Immigrants and Aging." In *International Handbook of Population Aging*, edited by Peter Uhlenberg, 365–94. Netherlands: Springer.

Treas, Judith and Shampa Mazumdar. 2004. "Kinkeeping and Caregiving:

References

Contributions of Older People in Immigrant Families." *Journal of Comparative Family Studies* 35(1): 105–22.

Tung, May Paomay. 2000. *Chinese Americans and Their Immigrant Parents: Conflict, Identity, and Values.* New York and London: Routledge.

UNHCR (United Nations' High Commissioner for Refugees). 2014. *Children on the Run: Unaccompanied Children Leaving Central America and Mexico and the Need for International Protection.* Report published by the United Nations' High Commissioner for Refugees. Washington, DC. At http://www.unhcrwashington.org/sites/default/files/UAC_UNHCR_Children%20on%20the%20Run_Full%20Report.pdf (accessed August 20, 2015).

Urbina, Ian and Catherine Rentz. 2013. "Immigrants Held in Solitary Cells, Often for Weeks." *New York Times*, March 23. At http://www.nytimes.com/2013/03/24/us/immigrants-held-in-solitary-cells-often-for-weeks.html?pagewanted=all (accessed October 1, 2014).

US Department of Homeland Security. 2011. *Yearbook of Immigration.* Washington, DC. At http://www.dhs.gov/sites/default/files/publications/immigration-statistics/yearbook/2011/ois_yb_2011.pdf (accessed May 17, 2014).

US Department of Homeland Security. 2012. *Yearbook of Immigration Statistics: 2012, Aliens Removed by Criminal Status and Region and Country of Nationality: Fiscal Years 2003 to 2012.* At https://www.dhs.gov/yearbook-immigration-statistics-2012-enforcement-actions (accessed October 1, 2014).

Valbrun, Marjorie. 2012. "Immigrant Children Face Uncertain Futures, Foster Care." *Huffington Post*, January 25. At http://www.huffingtonpost.com/2012/01/25/immigrant-children-face-u_n_1231668.html (accessed December 2, 2014).

Valdez, Carmen R., Brian Padilla, and Jessa Lewis Valentine. 2013. "Consequences of Arizona's Immigration Policy on Social Capital among Mexican Mothers with Unauthorized Immigration Status." *Hispanic Journal of Behavioral Sciences* 35(3): 303–22.

Valdez, Zulema. 2011. *The New Entrepreneurs: How Race, Class, and Gender Shape American Enterprise.* Stanford, CA: Stanford University Press.

Valenzuela, Abel, Jr. 2002. "Working on the Margins in Metropolitan Los Angeles: Immigrants in Day-Labor Work." *Migraciones Internacionales* 1(2): 6–28.

Vallejo, Jody Agius. 2012. *Barrios to Burbs: The Making of the Mexican American Middle Class.* Stanford, CA: Stanford University Press.

van Hook, Jennifer and Kelly Stamper Balistreri. 2006. "Ineligible Parents, Eligible Children: Food Stamps Receipt, Allotments, and Food Insecurity among Children of Immigrants." *Social Science Research* 35(1): 228–51.

van Hook, Jennifer and Jennifer Glick. 2007. "Immigration and Living Arrangements: Moving Beyond Instrumental Needs Versus Acculturation." *Demography* 44(2): 225–49.

Vaquera, Elizabeth, Elizabeth Aranda, and Roberto G. Gonzales. 2014. "Patterns

References

of Incorporation of Latinos in Old and New Destinations: From Invisible to Hypervisible." *American Behavioral Scientist* 58(4): 1823–33.

Vasquez, Jessica M. 2011. *Mexican Americans across Generations: Immigrant Families, Racial Realities*. New York: NYU Press.

Vasquez, Jessica M. 2015. "Disciplined Preferences: Explaining the (Re) Production of Latino Endogamy." *Social Problems* 62: 455–75.

Waldinger, Roger and Greta Gilbertson. 1994. "Immigrants' Progress: Ethnic and Gender Differences among US Immigrants in the 1980s." *Sociological Perspectives* 37(3): 431–44.

Walker, Kyle and Helga Leitner. 2011. "The Variegated Landscape of Local Immigration Policies in the United States." *Urban Geography* 32(2): 156–78.

Walter, Nicholas, Philippe Bourgois, and H. Margarita Loinaz. 2004. "Masculinity and Undocumented Labor Migration: Injured Latino Day Laborers in San Francisco." *Social Science & Medicine* 59(6): 1159–68.

Wang, Wendy. 2012. "The Rise of Intermarriage." Washington, DC: Pew Research Center. At http://www.pewsocialtrends.org/2012/02/16/the-rise-of-intermarriage (accessed August 20, 2015).

Waters, Mary C. 1999. *Black Identities: West Indian Immigrant Dreams and American Realities*. New York: Russell Sage Foundation.

Waters, Mary C., Van Tran, Philip Kasinitz, and John Mollenkopf. 2010. "Segmented Assimilation Revisited: Types of Acculturation and Socioeconomic Mobility in Young Adulthood." *Ethnic and Racial Studies* 33(7): 1168–93.

Watson, Tara. 2014. "Aggressive Immigration Enforcement Discourages Non-citizen Parents from Enrolling Their Citizen Children in Medicaid." The London School of Economics and Political Science. At http://blogs.lse.ac.uk/usappblog/2014/10/15/aggressive-immigration-enforcement-discourages-non-citizen-parents-from-enrolling-their-citizen-children-in-medicaid (accessed December 8, 2014).

Wessler, Seth Freed. 2011. *Shattered Families: The Perilous Intersection of Immigration Enforcement and the Child Welfare System*. The Applied Research Center. At http://www.atlanticphilanthropies.org/sites/default/files/uploads/ARC_Report_Shattered_Families_FULL_REPORT_Nov2011Release.pdf (accessed September 24, 2014).

West, Candace and Don H. Zimmerman. 1987. "Doing Gender." *Gender & Society* 1(2): 125–51.

White, Kari, Valerie A. Yeager, Nir Menachemi, and Isabel C. Scarinci. 2014. "Impact of Alabama's Immigration Law on Access to Health Care among Latina Immigrants and Children: Implications for National Reform." *American Journal of Public Health*, 104(3): 397–405.

Wides-Muñoz, Laura. 2008. "Immigration Proposals Abound." *Deseret News*, March 9. At http://www.deseretnews.com/article/695260077/Immigration-proposals-abound.html?pg=all (accessed July 19, 2015).

Williams, Catharina Purwani. 2005. "'Knowing One's Place': Gender, Mobility and Shifting Subjectivity in Eastern Indonesia." *Global Networks* 5(4): 401–17.

Wong, Nga-Wing Anjela. 2010. "'Cuz They Care about the People Who Goes There': The Multiple Roles of a Community-Based Youth Center in Providing 'Youth(Comm)Unity' for Low-Income Chinese American Youth." *Urban Education* 45(5): 708–39.

Wong, Tom, Donald Kerwin, Jeanne Atkinson, and Mary Meg McCarthy. 2014. "Paths to Lawful Immigration Status: Results and Implications from the PERSON Survey." *Journal on Migration and Human Security* (Center for Migration Studies of New York). Downloadable from http://jmhs.cmsny.org/index.php/jmhs/article/view/37 (accessed August 20, 2015).

Yep, Kathleen S., Tracy Zhao, Catherine Wang, Samuel Pang, and Pauline Wang. 2014. "The Revised Naturalization Exam and Chinese Immigrants in the United States: Key Issues for Social Workers." *Journal of Multicultural Social Work* 23(3–4): 271–88.

Yoo, Grace J. and Barbara Kim. 2014. *Caring across Generations: The Linked Lives of Korean American Families*. New York: NYU Press.

Yoshikawa, Hirokazu. 2011. *Immigrants Raising Citizens: Undocumented Parents and Their Young Children*. New York: Russell Sage Foundation.

Zavella, Patricia. 1991. "Reflections on Diversity among Chicanas." *Frontiers: A Journal of Women Studies* 12(2): 73–85.

Zavella, Patricia. 2011. *I'm Neither Here Nor There: Mexicans' Quotidian Struggles with Migration and Poverty*. Durham, NC and London: Duke University Press.

Zavella, Patricia. 2012. "Why Are Immigrant Families Different Now?" Policy Reports and Research Briefs, Center for Latino Policy Research, Institute for the Study of Societal Issues, University of California, Berkeley. At http://www.researchgate.net/publication/262973219_Why_Are_Immigrant_Families_Different_Now (accessed August 19, 2015).

Zelizer, Viviana. 1985. *Pricing the Priceless Child: The Changing Social Value of Children*. Princeton: Princeton University Press.

Zelizer, Viviana. 2007. "Culture and Uncertainty." Paper presented at the conference on the work of Robert K. Merton, Columbia University.

Zhou, Min. 1992. *Chinatown: The Socioeconomic Potential of an Urban Enclave*. Philadelphia: Temple University Press.

Zhou, Min. 1998. "'Parachute Kids' in Southern California: The Educational Experience of Chinese Children in Transnational Families." *Educational Policy* 12(6): 682–704.

Zhou, Min. 2009. "Conflict, Coping, and Reconciliation: Intergenerational Relations in Chinese Immigrant Families." In *Across Generations: Immigrant Families in America*, edited by Nancy Foner, 21–46. New York: NYU Press.

Zhou, Min and Carl L. Bankston. 1998. *Growing up American: How Vietnamese*

References

Children Adapt to Life in the United States. New York: Russell Sage Foundation.

Zhou, Min and Jennifer Lee. 2014. "Assessing What Is Cultural about Asian Americans' Academic Advantage." *Proceedings of the National Academy of Sciences* 111(23): 8321–2.

Zhou, Yu. 2000. "The Fall of 'the Other Half of the Sky'? Chinese Immigrant Women in the New York Area." *Women's Studies International Forum* 23(4): 445–59.

Index

Abraham, Margaret, 95
Abrego, Leisy J.
  on gender issues, 88, 89, 97
  on generational issues, 106, 128–9
  on lawyers' fraud, 155
  on mixed-status families, 51–2, 73
  on relative poverty, 54
  on transnational families, 43
activism and politicization, 106,
    129–30, 157, 158
Adela (Mexican immigrant), 106,
    108–9
adoption, 138
Affordable Care Act (ACA; 2010),
    136, 141–2, 181
African American immigrants, 84,
    158
Agadjanian, Victor, 35, 99
age, 15, 119–27
agriculture, 90, 91
AIDS, 6
Alabama, 146
Alba, Richard, 21
Alejandro (Mexican immigrant),
    42–3
Alisa (Guatemalan immigrant), 129
Antognini, Albertina, 175
Arab immigrants, 150–1
Arizona, 39, 45, 50–1, 146, 147–8,
    156, 158
Armenian immigrants, 35, 99
Arvin (Filipino immigrant), 43

Asian immigrants
  assimilation, 160, 162
  community organizations, 157
  demographic characteristics, 14–22
  and deportation/detention, 43, 45
  domestic violence, 94–5, 178
  educational performance, 71–2
  employment, 11, 12, 90, 92, 96,
    175
  ethnic enclaves, 13
  fraud against, 155
  gender and gender issues, 12, 62,
    80, 90, 95, 96, 98, 102, 103
  generational issues, 111–13,
    114–15, 116, 121
  immigration policy and legislation,
    3, 5, 7, 87
  migration costs, 58
  older immigrants, 122
  parenting, 65–6, 72, 92, 104
  qualifications and skills, 11, 12,
    60–1, 62
  sexuality as reason for migration,
    86
  social class/mobility, 58, 61–3, 65,
    71–2, 76
  social networks, 72, 96
  statistics, 6
  stereotyping, 71, 86
  in transnational families, 98, 102,
    103
  unaccompanied children, 126–7

Index

Asian immigrants (*cont.*)
  use of social services, 150
  visa backlogs, 33
assimilation and integration, 15,
    68–9, 123–4, 161–3
asylees *see* refugees and asylees
Atkinson, Jeanne, 154
Atlanta, 94

Bailey, Adrian J., 176
Balistreri, Kelly Stamper, 180
Bangladeshi immigrants, 90
Batalova, Jeanne, 120
Bean, Frank D., 17–18
benefits, government *see* immigrant
  policies
Berg, Ruth R., 17–18
Bever, Sandra Weinstein, 99
birds of passage, 4
births, 16–17
Blanding, David, 180
Border Security, Economic
    Opportunity, and Immigration
    Modernization Act (2012), 176
Boston, 90, 94–5, 156
Bowman, Cara, 24
Brazilian immigrants, 38–9

Calderon, Citlalli Valero, 63
California, 90, 91, 98, 147, 152, 157
  see also Los Angeles; San Francisco
Cantú, Lionel, 86, 104–5
Cape Verdean immigrants, 84
Capoferro, Chiara, 85–6
Cardoso, Berger, 41
care industry, 85–6
care networks, 101–3
Carla (Honduran child carer), 102
Carsten, Janet, 110
Castro, Brianna, 44
Cebulko, Kara, 38–9
chain migration, 3–4, 5, 59, 85, 119
Chang, Stewart, 175, 178
Chao, Xia, 65–6
Chaudry, Ajay, 49
Chelsea, Massachusetts, 156
Chen, Ms. (Chinese immigrant), 113

Cherlin, Andrew, 137
Chicago, 118, 180
child shifting, 101
children
  changed relationship with parents,
    114–18, 149
  child labor, 117–18
  community organizations, 156–7
  constitutional right to education,
    124, 142
  definition in immigration law, 31–4
  of deportees, 41, 49, 138
  educational performance, 71–2, 74,
    98, 148–9, 151
  English-speaking skills, 66–7, 116,
    118
  gender issues, 169
  health care, 152–3
  latch-key children, 123
  in mixed-status families, 51–2, 73,
    170–1
  numbers with undocumented
    parents, 47
  parachute children, 126–7
  and racialized stereotypes, 125
  in transnational families, 34–5, 43,
    131–4
  unaccompanied child migrants,
    125–7, 171–2
  undocumented, 124, 128–31
  of undocumented parents, 150
  younger immigrants' migration
    experience, 123–5
  see also parenting
Chinese Exclusion Act (1882), 5
Chinese immigrants
  community organizations, 157
  demographic characteristics, 14–22
  employment, 90, 96
  gender and gender issues, 12, 96
  generational issues, 112–13, 114,
    116
  immigration policy and legislation,
    5, 87
  parenting, 65–6, 72
  qualifications and skills, 11, 12,
    60–1

Index

employment and labor market (*cont.*)
 immigrant-owned businesses, 13, 69–70, 117–18
 immigrants' qualifications and skills, 11, 12, 60–1, 62, 175
 and legal status, 88–9
 and parenting, 92
 relationship between education and employment opportunity, 63
 reproductive labor, 21–2
 service sector's rise, 10–11
 and social class/mobility, 10, 21, 67
 and temporary statuses, 39–40
 undocumented youth, 131
 unpaid family labor, 90
entrepreneurship, 13, 69–70
Esperanza (Salvadoran immigrant), 100
Espiritu, Yen Le, 7, 86
ethnic enclaves, 13, 68, 96
ethnic replenishment, 15
European immigrants, 10, 116–17, 158, 166
Ewen, Elizabeth, 116–17
EWIs, 48–9
Expatriation Act (1907), 87

families
 definition in family law, 175
 domestic family ideal, 175
 immigrant families as insight to, 3
 see also immigrant families
family policy, 137
Feliciano, Cynthia, 177
Fernández-Kelly, Patricia, 118, 168
fertility, 16–17
fictive kin, 110–11
Filindra, Alexandra, 180
Filipina/o immigrants
 demographic characteristics, 14–22
 and deportation/detention, 43, 45
 fraud against, 155
 gender and gender issues, 12, 98, 102, 103
 qualifications and skills, 12
 sexuality as reason for migration, 86

social class/mobility, 76
state encouragement, 87
in transnational families, 98, 102, 103
unaccompanied children, 126
visa backlogs, 33
Fischer, Mary J., 85–6
Fix, Michael, 50
Flippen, Chenoa, 114
Flushing, New York, 72
Foner, Nancy, 108
Fong, Mrs. (Taiwanese immigrant), 113–14
food-processing industry, 91
food stamps, 140, 141, 144
foster care, 138
fraud, 154–5

Gabaccia, Donna, 84
Gamson, Joshua, 2
Garcia, Cynthia, 180
gender issues
 care of elderly, 83
 and community organizations, 157–8
 definition, 79
 and deportation/detention, 46–7
 division of labor, 64–5, 80–1
 domestic violence, 52, 94–5
 and employment, 85–6, 89–95
 and employment-based immigration, 7, 28
 gender of migrant and social class, 62
 and guest worker programs, 60
 immigrant gender statistics, 12
 and legal status, 87–8
 and marriage to foreign spouses, 87
 and migration process, 83–6
 overview, 79–105, 168–9
 parenting, 64–5, 83–4, 99–103
 sexual mores postmigration, 86, 169
 social networks, 95–8
 social surveillance, 94

220

Index

Index

Index

Index